AFTER THE CROSSING: IMMIGRANTS AND MINORITIES IN CARIBBEAN CREOLE SOCIETY

AFTER THE CROSSING
Immigrants and Minorities in Caribbean Creole Society

Edited by
HOWARD JOHNSON

FRANK CASS

First published 1988 in Great Britain by
FRANK CASS AND COMPANY LIMITED
Gainsborough House, 11 Gainsborough Road,
London E11 1RS, England

and in the United States of America by
FRANK CASS AND COMPANY LIMITED
c/o Biblio Distribution Centre,
81 Adams Drive, P.O. Box 327, Totowa, N.J. 07511

Copyright © 1988 Frank Cass & Co. Ltd.

British Library Cataloguing in Publication Data

After the crossing : immigrants and
  minorities in Caribbean Creole society.
  1. Caribbean region. Ethnic minorities,
  to 1988
  I. Johnson, Howards, *1945–*   II. Immigrants
  & minorities
  305.8'009182'1

  ISBN 0-7146-3357 7

Library of Congress Cataloging-in-Publication Data

After the crossing : immigrants and minorities in Caribbean Creole
  society / edited by Howard Johnson.
    p.   cm.
    "This groups of studies first appeared in ... Immigrants &
  minorities, vol. 7, no. 1" —Verso of t.p.
    Includes index.
    ISBN 0-7146-3357-7
    1. Immigrants—Caribbean Area—History. 2. Minorities—Caribbean
  Area—History. 3. Caribbean Area—History—1810–1945. 4. Social
  integration—Caribbean Area—History.   I. Johnson, Howard, 1945–

F2190.A38 1988
972.9'004—dc19   88-20420
                                               CIP

This group of studies first appeared in a Special Issue: After the
Crossing: Immigrants and Minorities in Caribbean Creole Society
of *Immigrants & Minorities*, Vol. 7, No. 1, published by Frank Cass
& Co. Ltd.

Printed in Great Britain by
Antony Rowe Ltd, Chippenham

Contents

Notes on Contributors

Hilary McD. Beckles is Senior Lecturer in History at the University of the West Indies, Cave Hill, Barbados. His article on the Barbados free coloured and the 1816 slave rebellion appears in an earlier issue of *Immigrants and Minorities*. His book, a general history of Barbados, is scheduled for publication by Cambridge University Press later this year.

Howard Johnson currently lectures at the College of the Bahamas, Nassau. His articles on the anti-Chinese riots of 1918 in Jamaica and the beginnings of immigration restrictions in the Bahamas were published in previous issues of *Immigrants and Minorities*.

Brian L. Moore is Lecturer in History at the University of the West Indies, Mona, Jamaica. He is the author of *Race, Power and Social Segmentation in Colonial Society* (New York, 1987).

Sr. M. Noel Menezes, RSM, Professor of History at the University of Guyana, is of Portuguese descent. Her recent publication, *Scenes from the History of the Portuguese in Guyana* (1986) was written to commemorate the 150th anniversary of the arrival of the Portuguese in British Guiana.

Peter D. Fraser lectures at Goldsmiths' College, University of London. This article is part of a larger project on West Indian migration.

Verene A. Shepherd is completing a Ph.D. at Lucy Cavendish College, University of Cambridge. Her article on East Indians in Kingston, Jamaica in the late nineteenth and early twentieth centuries appeared in an earlier issue of *Immigrants and Minorities*.

Kusha R. Haraksingh is Senior Lecturer in History and a former Chairman of the Institute of African and Asian Studies, University of the West Indies, St. Augustine, Trinidad. His publications have centred on the East Indian community in Trinidad during and after the period of indentureship.

Ravindra K. Jain is Professor of Social Anthropology at Jawaharlal Nehru University, New Delhi. Between 1984 and 1987, he was visiting Professor at the University of the West Indies, St. Augustine, Trinidad. He is the author of *South Indians on the Plantation Frontier in Malaya*.

Editor's Introduction

Immigration is a central theme of Caribbean history. The virtual extinction of the indigenous population after European contact and the development of Caribbean colonies as a locus for large-scale sugar production in the seventeenth century resulted in the voluntary and involuntary immigration of Europeans and Africans to the region. The subsequent immigration of other ethnic groups into the Caribbean area in the years after the abolition of slavery was also primarily a movement of labour in response to the demands of the dominant plantation economy.

This collection of essays examines the position of immigrants and minorities in Caribbean creole society which, as M.G. Smith and Edward Brathwaite have pointed out, originated from the interaction between Europeans and Africans in the New World context during the period of slavery. An important feature of slave creole society (with relevance for the discussions in this volume) was the development of attitudes on race and colour which persisted into freedom and informed creole responses to the newcomers.

The time-frame with which the articles deal extends from the pre-slavery era to the present day encompassing the three successive flows of immigrant labour. In their discussions, the contributions have generally concentrated on the process of economic, social and cultural adjustment to the new environment, in the case of immigrants, and on a delineation of the position of minorities in the social and economic structure of creole society. A central theme of the essays is the extent of the assimilation of the immigrant groups and minorities in the receiving society.

In the context of these discussions, it is possible to identify certain 'variables of assimilation' which the authors have examined. Among the issues raised are the extent to which the male-dominated nature of the immigrant inflows promoted or retarded assimilation; the 'structural location' of the immigrants in the labour force of creole society and its effects on race relations; the impact of the plantation experience on cultural patterns; the consequences of the activities of the Christian churches for cultural integration or persistence and the question of cross-cultural transmission.

Those contributors who have discussed the process of sociocultural integration of immigrants into creole society in the late nineteenth and early twentieth centuries have concluded that assimilation was most often incomplete. Kusha Haraksingh has argued, however, that for the Indian community in Trinidad the important process of adjustment has been one of inter-Indian syncretism rather than one of creolization.

Collectively, then, these essays offer a series of views about the historical processes involved in the development of Caribbean societies and provide a more analytical framework for further discussion.

HOWARD JOHNSON

Black over White: The 'Poor-White' Problem in Barbados Slave Society

By the end of slavery in 1838, a white proletariat, not infrequently lower in the social scale than free non-whites, had developed in Barbados slave society from the descendants of the indentured servants who had preceded the black slaves. This article analyses the position of this anomalous group in the social and economic structure of slave society and the views of members of the white elite on what was widely regarded as the 'poor-white' problem.

In one of his Sunday sermons delivered on the eve of the slave emancipation act of 1833, Rev. E. Eliot, Archdeacon of the Bridge-town Cathedral, stated that the 'Blacks have, by their superior industry, driven the lower order of whites from almost every trade requiring skill ... and this at a time when a large white population are in the lowest state of poverty and wretchedness'.[1] He intended to outline for his multiracial congregation the large measure of social progress achieved during slavery in Barbados, as expressed in the fact that many black and coloured inhabitants had advanced above labouring whites within the social and material order. The Archdeacon was also aware that this development had long been the most controversial aspect of class and race dynamism within the colony. For him, however, it was not phenomenal that a section of the white community should find itself wedged beneath blacks and coloureds within a slave system which professed to be governed by the ideology of white racial superiority. Rather, it was irrevocable proof that in the organization of slave society property ownership, which conferred social respect and status, if not always formal political power, was also a primary determining force.

By the end of slavery in 1838 a heterogeneous white working class had fully developed, and society was characterized by an element of 'black over white' at its lower levels. This social condition was conceived by many white commentators as anomalous, and discussed generally as the 'poor-white problem'.[2] Its origins, however, lie in the formative stage of colonization when white indentured servitude, the founding labour institution, was undermined and displaced by black chattel slavery. Most indentured servants during the seventeenth century did not succeed in acquiring land, neither during nor after their five- to ten-year period of servitude, and as such the institution served the primary purpose of creating a wage proletariat rather than reproducing the planting community. In terms of class formation, white society was well developed by the mid-seventeenth century, and class conflict and struggle were an integral feature of social life; these took the primary form of landless whites expressing their hostility to the monopolizing tendencies of the planter elite. In turn, politically dominant planters resorted to the enforcement of harsh 'Master and Servant' codes, the first of which was enacted in 1661, designed for their economic management and political suppression. In addition, the planter elite manipulated the land market with the avid intention of ensuring the perpetuation of the labouring status of ex-indentured servants.[3]

In Barbados, where slaves outnumbered masters by the 1650s, society was also characterized by violent anti-slavery conflict. Much of this activity has been recorded as armed encounters between blacks and whites. White labourers were assigned a critical role within the white community's defence system against rebel slaves; they constituted the core of the militia regiments which were established for the maintenance of internal political stability. In spite of the expressed class grievances of these labourer-militiamen, planters expected them, none the less, to display enthusiasm in protecting the slave system. Although, in the first instance, this expectation might appear rather ambitious, it was solidly based upon a clear perception of the dynamics of white racial solidarity at the frontier. In spite of their material poverty and social oppression, white labourers shared the pro-slavery ideology and colonizing aspirations of the slavocracy. They were, therefore, keen to support the status quo in so far as it rewarded them with the valuable psychological and social benefits of legal freedom and membership of the politically dominant race.[4]

It is undoubtedly true, as Jordan has argued, that the social ideology which Englishmen used in structuring their New World colonial societies was expressed symbolically in terms of 'white over black'.[5] In Barbados, however, when oppressed white labourers supported the slave system they were in fact defending an institution which, in the long run, would prove to be their collective anathema. But under the day-to-day pressures of mere survival, few saw it this way. For them, black slavery was the only precursor for the fulfilment of their own colonial socio-economic fantasy; without slaves, no wealth – without wealth, no freedom. Also, by defending the slave system they hoped to protect the last remaining bastion of white labour privilege – monopoly of scarce skilled occupations. To continue as the aristocracy of labour within the slave economy was what they had finally settled for by the late seventeenth century, as their dream of entering the landed classes turned into a nightmare of economic failure.[6]

Such a racial division of labour, however, could be sustained only as long as the price of sugar remained sufficiently high to maintain super-profits, and the supply of servant labour adequate and reliable. None of these conditions was experienced by Barbados (or West Indian) planters towards the end of the seventeenth century. When they had existed in the earlier period, most slave-owners rationalized the whole-sale confinement of blacks to the field gangs in terms of their ascribed intellectual unsuitability for artisan crafts and other occupations that required minimal supervision. A minority of planters, however, notably those in close contact with slave traders, were aware that African slaves had been extracted from a technically complex labour force. These individuals did not defend their labour policy in the customary way. Instead, they argued that occupations which stimulated the minds of slaves would render them politically rebellious and therefore a danger to the entire social order.[7]

Between 1670 and 1690, the price of sugar on the European markets declined by 25–30 per cent from peak levels reached during the 1650s. Increased production in Jamaica, French Martinique and Guadeloupe, and Portuguese Brazil was the primary cause. The golden era of the West Indian sugar planter was over, as prices and profits were reduced to normal levels. Cost-cutting became the primary managerial response within the industry in an effort to rationalize production methods and labour ideologies. Of far-reaching significance was the policy pursued by most planters of training slaves into all plantation occupations – from skilled artisanal to petty managerial. The underlying economic calculation behind this policy was that it was cheaper and more efficient to employ slaves in all occupations, with the exception of the chief overseer post, than to pay higher remuneration to unreliable white labourers.[8] Planters made this decision on an individual basis which, though rational from that viewpoint, some considered irrational in terms of their collective interests. The long-term result was extensive unemployment among white labourers, with the consequences of their increased material impoverishment and loss of technical skills – a process, if anything, that was the obverse of that experienced by a significant section of the slave and free non-white population.

By the 1700s, successive governors had expressed their concerns about the socio-economic alienation of the white propertyless population, the more energetic of whom saw emigration as their only hope for colonial success. As Imperial administrators, they considered this condition as detrimental to the colony's security on account of its weakening of militia forces. Also, the increasing pauperization of this now distinct social group was considered by some governors as evidence of the humanitarian failure of the ruling planter elite. They pleaded with planters in the Assemblies and complained to metropolitan officials about the widespread 'white' poverty. During the mid-1690s, for example, Governor Russell made much of it in his correspondence to the Lords of Trade and Plantations. He stated that such impoverished persons could not 'be made more miserable than their countrymen and fellow subjects make them here'. 'Hundreds', he stated, are unemployed now 'for many years' and their former masters would not bestow on them 'a dram of rum' or 'a bit of fresh meat'.[9] Those who were fortunate to obtain employment as plantation overseers earned between £50 to £100 per year, but during the early eighteenth century the ranks of the unemployable white poor increased as slaves, free blacks, and free coloureds infiltrated and dominated the skilled occupations they once commanded.[10] In the mid-eighteenth century, this process of displacement continued, so that when Rev. Eliot made his social analysis in 1833, he was able to conclude 'that not one in twenty of the working shoemakers in Barbados', for instance, 'is a whiteman'.[11]

As the slave elite consolidated its position in the sugar industry during the eighteenth century white labourers found themselves caught in a cyclical trap from which no escape seemed possible. In 1744, the manager at Codrington estate noted that when whites seemed prepared to accept whatever work was offered, most managers turned them away on the pretext that they were unreliable and irritants to the slaves.[12] Denigrated as 'white slaves', many drifted into the urban communities in search of betterment.[13] There, the unhealthy and squalid conditions of ghetto life welcomed them as they prepared to hustle a living in any way possible. One observer of Bridgetown in 1824 noted: 'poor whites are the lowest and most degraded' of its inhabitants, most of them subsisting 'to their shame, let it be spoken, on the kindness and charity of slaves', while the 'free blacks and coloured people' display 'a strong contrast', of 'happiness' and well-being.[14]

Sheppard estimated that the number of white labourers who depended solely on wages for subsistence diminished from about 13,500 in 1680 to about 8,000 in 1834 – at all times the figure fluctuating between 40 and 60 per cent of the total white population.[15] Most of these were either fully unemployed or seasonally employed according to fluctuations within the sugar industry. The question which confronted prominent members of the white community who were concerned with issues of social welfare was what to do with these large numbers of uncompetitive, displaced workers. On the one hand, there was the matter of their basic political and social loyalty and importance to the slave system in terms of their militia duties, but for which planters were prepared to offer only nominal remuneration. On the other, slavery had degraded labour and labouring to the extent that many preferred unemployment, poor relief and begging in public places than to perform work associated with blacks and stereotyped as 'niggerwork'. Given their enhanced racial pride, derived from what a Guiana planter referred to as 'the conceit of the white blood', it became apparent to sympathetic institutions and individuals that the solution to 'the poor-white problem' must in some way be related to the removal of blacks and other non-whites, both slave and free, from certain types of occupations.[16]

From the outset, this line of reasoning encountered a number of difficulties. Planters considered it necessary to express a significant degree of social commitment to their slaves for personal economic reasons. It was in their class interest to keep their slaves, if not politically passive, non-violent at least. One of the politically sophisticated strategies used to this end was to respond positively to a number of the slaves' socio-material demands. One such important concession granted slaves, which was considered island-wide by the 1780s, was accessibility to skilled trades and low-level management occupations. Although the occupational elevation of slaves from the fields was initially the result of planter production rationalization, it soon became an integral part of slave resistance ideology and was conceived by them as a 'right'. Planter paternalism, then, excluded white labourers, and in the interest of social stability and high levels of productivity, slaves could not be removed from elite labour occupations.[17]

Furthermore, white labourers were seen by many planters as constituting a destabilizing force on the estates. Considered as an immoral and vicious group, they were accused, among other things, of commonly enticing slaves into drinking excessive quantities of alcohol, and sexually abusing female slaves. William Dickson, who resided in Barbados during the 1770s, wrote of the relations between plantation blacks and white labourers:

> The slaves are frequently robbed, cheated and plundered by these lesser whites who are protected under the law from any charge by Blacks. I am inclined to think that this is almost the only evil which slaves in Barbados suffer in a greater degree than those in the other islands, owing to the greater number of poor whites with which the island abounds. Nor do I see how under the present system of things, this grievance can be remedied.[18]

The solution which most planters found logical and acceptable was to exclude these offenders from the estates, and satisfy their sense of racial consciousness and public commitment by voting additional funds to the vestries for their poor relief. Meanwhile, the number of free blacks and free coloureds continued to increase, their material and social achievements rising above those of most poor-whites.[19]

White labourers who were unable to find steady employment, and were neither prepared to resort to the socially humiliating poor relief facilities, nor attracted to the isolation of back-country earth-scratching for subsistence, could earn a living by serving as plantation special militia tenants. This occupation entailed the constant policing of plantation slaves; retrieving runaways and suppressing rebels were also expected of these tenants. In most cases, they obtained 'a very scanty subsistence by cultivating, with their own hands, little odd skirts of land' which they held as tenants by this kind of military tenure.[20] These lands, according to Dickson, were generally 'located about the bushes and on the sides of gullies'.[21] The wives of these tenants, invariably also from poor-white stock, came under the influence of the Afro-Caribbean marketing culture of slaves. They were often seen on the way to markets walking 'many miles, loaded with the produce of their spots, which they exchange in the towns for such European goods' as they could afford to purchase.[22] Both male and female, according to Dickson, were engaged in marketing, and made 'a practice of buying stolen goods from the negroes, whom they encourage to plunder their owners of everything that is portable'.[23]

By the beginning of the nineteenth century, most rural poor-whites, with the exception of plantation militia-tenants, inhabited small villages located in the remote rab lands of the St. Andrew, St. Lucy, St. John, and St. Philip parishes – areas which the hegemonic sugar industry had rejected. These communities were quite distinct and visitors to the island, finding them rather slave-like in appearance, frequently commented upon their squalor and insanitation. In contrast, they made references to the high levels of material welfare enjoyed by large sections of the urban coloured and free black population, as well as the slave elite on the plantations.

One such visitor was Dr George Pinckard. He toured the West Indies with the military expedition of General Abercromby during the 1790s, and in his published notes on Barbados there are accounts of poorwhite settlements he investigated. First, he described their material condition:

> Besides the great number of hospitable mansions found on the plantations, in the different parts of the country – many humble dwellings attract the notice of the traveller .... They are the cottages of a poorer order of white people – of obscure individuals, remote from the great class of merchants and planters, and who obtain a scanty livelihood by cultivating a small patch of earth, and breeding-up poultry, or what they term stock for the markets. They are descended from European settlers, but from misfortune, or misconduct, in some of the race, are reduced to a state far removed from independence.[24]

In some instances, Pinckard stated, their condition is 'little superior' to that of free Negroes in the countryside, but was not comparable with that of established urban free coloureds and free blacks. Their houses, he described as 'small huts or cabins' in which large families live, located 'amidst the mountains, apparently shut from the world, and but seldom exposed to the intrusion of strangers'.[25] One household he visited in the back-lands of Mount Hillaby was six generations removed from an English settler. His family 'were poor, like the others, and compelled to labour much in full exposure to the sun. Like the negroes, too, their diet consisted chiefly of vegetables.'[26] In all, he visited three such households, of which members ranged from the fifth to sixth generation of British settlers. 'Only the abode of poverty' they know, and 'have been compelled to use a diet very similar to that of the Africans'.[27] Yet they remained fiercely attached to the colony, rather than the mother country, and would commonly confirm this by stating that they are 'neither Charib nor Creole, but true Barbadian'.[28]

Living in such close proximity with slaves, many poor-whites inevitably became partly creolized into elements of Afro-Barbadian culture, besides marketing. Pinckard provided evidence of the social aspects of this cross-cultural fertilization. He noted, for instance, the culture shock experienced by English travellers when they saw poor-white women carrying objects on their heads in the manner of the blacks. Also, quite striking was their acquired custom of carrying their young strapped to the 'hip, instead of seating them upon the arm'. This habit, he stated, they 'have adopted ... from the example of the negroes'. 'Seated upon the hip', he stated, 'the infant soon learns to cling, and in a great measure to support itself', while the hands of the mother remained free to conduct other affairs.'[29] In other ways, poor-whites were acculturized by slaves while they remained committed to the ideology of white social elitism. So that in spite of their expressions of white race solidarity, some prominent planters were aware that poor-whites were not only economically and politically repressed, but also socio-culturally alienated. For some, these labouring poor had become more Afro-creole than Euro-creole – and hence socially irretrievable.

In 1788, therefore, when the Colonial Office asked Barbadian planters if the poor-whites could take up the labour deficit on the sugar estates occasioned by the possible abolition of the slave trade, the answer it received was affirmative. Planters knew that in the formative years of sugar cultivation, 1643–50, white indentured servants working in field gangs were the back-bone of the industry. Indeed, on some remote estates gangs of poor-whites were still to be found in the cane fields. This fact posed no ideological problem for planters nor their managers, and the bulk of Barbadian whites had accepted that 'sugar and white labour' carried no fundamental contradiction – in spite of black slavery. As far as planters were concerned, these labourers were social failures and degenerates who deserved no paternal sympathy nor special consideration. Although, in planter political ideology, the principle of 'race first' was clearly articulated, it was not dogmatically applied at the lower levels of society, unless the integrity of the entire structure was endangered. That is, planter elitism was not offended, but confirmed, by the white working class's degeneration into a culture of poverty on the periphery of the plantations.

During the 1780s, however, Joshua Steele, a prominent planter and member of the London Royal Society of Arts, took measures to rehabilitate the lumpenized poor-whites who, for him, constituted a major social problem. He was primarily concerned by their unemployable condition. A survey in the 1780s revealed that the 'mechanical trades and occupations' were 'almost extinct' among the white population.[30] To reverse this deskilling process, Steele was instrumental in the establishment of the Society for the Encouragement of Arts, Manufactures and Commerce in 1781. This organization, dedicated to the provision of industrial employment for white labourers, functioned against the background of rapidly rising Vestry poor rates for the relief of whites.[31] The previous year, for example, the returns for the parish of St. Peter showed a total of 94 white persons, from a total of some 1,340, in receipt of poor relief – a parish with a relatively small poor-white population.[32]

In his campaign to assist poor whites, Steele made references to the comparative material living standard of free coloureds, free blacks, and elite slaves. These whites, his findings indicated, had members who represented the lowest levels of material life within the free community. Generations of unemployment, he stated, had removed from their consciousness the desire to labour, and as such they had to be persuaded by the offer of respectable and regular work that the possession of 'shoes, stockings or any more clothing than a ragged shirt or shift, with an Osnaburg breeches or petticoat, are worth' labouring for. Their habit of begging 'from house to house for victuals' and finding 'some Hovel to lie under at night' could be broken, he stated, but acceptable conditions and terms of employment had to be provided.[33]

First, Steele proposed that manufacturing industries, using local materials, be established so as to create artisan employment. Cotton goods, for example, could be locally manufactured using the home grown cotton which many small planters produced. Rather than importing cheap cotton items for slaves and poor-whites alike, an indigenous industry could meet market demands. Such a proposal, however, ran counter to the long established dictates of mercantilism which insisted upon a division of production that assigned to colonies the role of raw material exporter and that of manufacturer to the mother country. That not even a nail was to be made in the colonies was already a well-known dictum of English New World colonization, which in the previous decade had encouraged the mainland colonists into revolutionary opposition; an occasion on which the Barbadians (and other West Indians) remained loyal to the mother country. Some success was attained in providing work in the partially revived pottery industry and in fort construction, but the sum result of this initiative was disappointing.

Second, the Society pressed for legislative action in an effort to expand the employment range for white labourers. A bill was brought before the House in 1783 which aimed to encourage planters and merchants to employ the 'profligate' whites who live by 'vagrant beggary' and other forms of 'indolence'.[34] The bill was passed, but it had little positive effect upon either unemployment levels or poor law rates. These efforts were repeated during the 1790s, but to no avail, and in the early 1800s a visiting colonial official to the island noted that in 'no other colony is the same number of unemployed whites' to be met as in Barbados.[35]

William Dickson, though a close friend of Steele, did not share his enthusiasm for the upliftment of poor-whites. As a secretary to Governor Hay, Dickson arrived at Barbados in 1772 and resided there for some 13 years. Handler described him as 'one of the most useful and intelligent observers on the institution of slavery in Barbados'.[36] His 'letters of slavery' published in 1789, and a larger book, *Mitigation of*

Slavery which appendixed letters by Steele, published in 1814, elevated him as the leading literary authority on creole slavery in Barbados.[37] He dealt at length with the white unemployment, and on the whole, took a less sympathetic position. He was a critic of slavery, and supporter of abolitionism, but did not perceive the poor-whites' problem as constituting an ideological crisis for white society. For him, any policy which attempted to elevate them by means of systematic racist discriminatory action against hardworking and thrifty blacks and coloureds was not intellectually nor socially enlightened, nor in the interest of Barbados. He argued that the future stability and health of society depended upon the upliftment, emancipation and integration of blacks whose mental energies and abilities were suppressed by the arduous regime of field labour. The poor-whites, he implied, had their opportunity and wasted it, while non-whites were energetic in their pursuit of betterment.

Furthermore, for Dickson the liberal, the existence of poor-white communities at a social and material level beneath many free non-white inhabitants merely reflected social laws taking precedence over the colony's slave codes and official policies. These whites were in most cases, lazy and vicious, and therefore responsible for their own plight, he argued in a manner which became typical of mid-Victorian bourgeois social commentaries on the unemployed poor. His attitudes to the poor-whites are clearly outlined in this passage:

> The extreme ignorance of many of the poor white Barbadians, cannot justly be attributed to the want of opportunities and instructions, for there are schools in every parish, which I believe, were constructed for their betterment. Nor are the clergy blame-able for that ignorance. The free blacks and coloureds attend the schools and regularly attend divine service. The poor whites very seldom enter a church, except to observe elections and attend funerals, and are then, generally, in a state of intoxication.[38]

The outstanding defender of poor-whites after the failed efforts of Joshua Steele (who died in 1796), and the 'Society' he inspired, was John Poyer, a white creole historian, and intellectual pro-slavery ideologue. Elsa Goveia, in her now classic review of British West Indian colonial historiography stated in relation to Poyer's 1808 *History of Barbados*: 'There is one point to which he returns again and again – the need for encouraging the poorer whites ...'.[39] She was absolutely correct in suggesting that for Poyer the elevation of poor-whites was a critical aspect of his general defence of slavery. The slave system, Poyer stated, rests upon the 'natural' principle of white racial superiority, and hence the existence of blacks above whites within its structures represents a fundamental ideological contradiction, which, if not resolved, could erode the very conceptual apparati which held it together.

Poyer's theory of slave society, elements of which can also be traced back to the Jamaican historians, Long and Edwards, was most clearly outlined in an open letter addressed to the newly arrived Governor Lord Seaforth in 1801. Seaforth was, to some extent, a slave reformer. Among his objectives were the prevention of corporal punishment for female slaves, making slave murder by whites a capital offence, and the 'modernization' of the still valid 1668 slave code. For Poyer, he represented a threat to the ideological world of Barbadian slave owners, and so he took to pen in their defence. His 1801 open letter stated:

> In every well-constituted society, a state of subordination necessarily arises from the nature of civil government. Without this no political union can long subsist. To maintain this fundamental principle, it becomes absolutely necessary to preserve the distinctions which naturally exist or are accidentally introduced into the community. With us, two grand distinctions exist resulting from the nature of our society. First, between the white inhabitants and free people of colour, and secondly, between masters and slaves. Nature has strongly defined the differences [not] only in complexion, but in the mental, intellectual and corporal faculties of the different species. Our colonial codes has acknowledged and adopted the distinctions ... .[40]

This conception of social structure and race relations was popular among whites of all classes who objected to non-whites accumulating property beyond the petty level. In 1801, also, John Alleyne, absentee planter, in a letter to his estate manager, expressed the view that the effect of the rising material welfare of non-whites would be to undermine the social order and hence threaten the security of white rule:

> I am very sorry to hear of the large purchases made by the coloured people in our country of land and slaves: if it is permitted to go on without some check, we shall perhaps in no great distance of time find ourselves in the same situation that the neighbouring island of Grenada was in not long since. I am astonished that we are so blind to our own interest and safety.[41]

Poyer, then, with Alleyne's support, began a campaign calling for clearly defined and strictly implemented legal limits upon the ability of free coloureds and free blacks to accumulate wealth. Rather than reforming the social structure to make their social standing consistent with their economic value, it was proposed that their economic worth be reduced to make it correspond with the dictates of the ideological structure.

In the November 1803 sitting of the Legislative Council, John Beckles emerged as the leading opponent of the Poyer-inspired bill to reduce the material and social status of free blacks and free coloureds. He saw no concrete political benefits to the planter elite in linking the fortunes of these groups with the misfortune of poor-whites. Mature creole society, Beckles seemed to believe, could absorb and function effectively with some degree of inverse socio-economic movement of some whites and non-whites. He rooted his rejection of the property limitation bill to the primary political issue of the time – fear of coloured and black insurrection against whites. For him, it was more important for the perpetuation of slavery to win the support of free non-whites, many of whom were also slave-owners, than to attempt the amelioration of the poor-whites' conditions. It was the triumph of political pragmatism over ideological dogmatism. In his concluding speech, which carried the Council into opposing the bill, he stated:

> I am inclined to think that it will be politic to allow them to possess property. It will keep them at a greater distance from the slaves, and will keep up that jealousy which seems naturally to exist between them and the slaves; it will tend to our security, for should the slaves at any time attempt a revolt, the free coloured persons for their own safety and the security of their property, must join the whites and resist them. But if we reduce the free-coloured people to a level with the slaves, they must unite with them, and will take every occasion of promoting and encouraging a revolt.[42]

It so happened that Beckles' judgement was correct. During the 1816 slave uprising the free-coloured and free-black elite rallied to the support of whites and were commended for their keen military opposition to rebel slaves.[43]

Poyer also revived earlier ideas which called for the removal of blacks, both slave and free, from urban artisan occupations in order to throw them open to white labourers. It was the only way, he suggested, that respectability could be restored to traditional craft professions, thereby making them attractive to young labouring whites willing to become artificiers. This proposal was again defeated by an unconvinced planter class. For most estate managers, hiring out skilled slaves in the towns was a significant source of money income. Also, manumitters of favoured slaves took comfort in the knowledge that freedmen could make a living by selling their labour on the urban market. For them, poor-whites had only their loyalty to give at times of crisis; this was never questioned, nor highly prized.[44] The racist idealist world of Poyer, therefore, failed to move men more concerned with the practical matters of reducing cost of production, controlling slaves and manipulating the ambitions of free non-whites.

In the years following the abolition of the slave trade, free blacks and free coloureds continued to consolidate their social position. For Poyer, their advancement was at the expense of the labouring white poor, many of whom were forced to emigrate to the new frontiers of the English West Indies, such as Trinidad, Guyana, and the Windward Islands. He wrote:

> Many slaves are employed as tradesmen ... while the industrious

white mechanic is destitute of employment; or if he works, is ill-treated, and finds great difficulty in obtaining payment of his hard earned wages. No wonder that under such discouragements he is compelled to forego his fond attachment to his native soil, and emigrate to neighbouring colonies, where his skill and diligence are better rewarded.[45]

Undoubtedly, the political history of the remaining years of slavery was characterized by the gradual removal of civil and legal disabilities which had traditionally oppressed the free non-white population. In 1817, they won the right to give testimony in courts of law against whites, a benefit which they claimed protected their lives and properties from hostile poor-whites and their wealthier supporters. In 1831, they were declared the constitutional equals of whites.

The 1831 legislation, and final emancipation in 1838, brought to an end the long desired objective of many whites to see a strict racial divide of rich and poor, free and unfree. It was no longer possible to argue seriously for the rehabilitation of poor-whites by means of the displacement of non-white persons. Emancipation located the poor-whites outside of the realm of special legislative attention, at least as far as the internal social structure was concerned. Schomburgh, for instance, in his 1848 *History of Barbados*, disregarded them as a vicious and immoral lot, while stating that the future of the colony resided in the cultivation of a sober group drawn from the ranks of the coloured population.[46]. Emigration schemes sprang up from time to time with the intention of removing them to St. Lucia, Canada, and the Guyanas, among other places. Of those who remained behind, some were able to achieve social mobility via education and commerce, but it was an end to the serious consideration of social policy motivated by the ideology of white over black at the lower end of the society.

HILARY McD. BECKLES
University of the West Indies,
Cave Hill, Barbados

NOTES

*This article was first presented as a paper at the Caribbean Studies Seminar, Institute of Commonwealth Studies, University of London. I would like to thank participants who raised a number of issues and contributed to its improvement. Special thanks to Professor Shula Marks and Dr Richard Saville.

1. E. Eliot, *Christianity and Slavery: In a Course of Lectures preached at the Cathedral and Parish Church of St. Michael, Barbados* (London, 1833), pp.225–6.
2. In recent years little has been published on the white labouring poor of Barbados. The historiography remains mostly narrative in character and anthropological in perspective. See, for example, J. Sheppard, *The Redlegs of Barbados: Their Origins and History* (New York, 1977). This work gives a rather simple and

descriptive account of poor whites, or 'Redlegs' as they were called within the island's vernacular. See also T. Keagy, 'The Poor Whites of Barbadoes', *Revista de Historia de Americas*, 73–74, (1972). E. Price, 'The Redlegs of Barbados', *The Journal of the Barbados Museum and Historical Society*, 10 (1957). K. Watson, 'The Redlegs of Barbados' (unpublished M.A. thesis, University of Florida, 1970). For an attempt to bring some analytic rigour to the theme, see H. Beckles, '"Black Men in White Skins": The Formation of a White Proletariat in West Indian Slave Society', *Journal of Imperial and Commonwealth History*, 15 (1986), pp.7–21.

3. Although the literature on white servitude in colonial America has been increasing of late, much of it is not specifically related to the West Indies. The first major comparative work was A.E. Smith, *Colonists in Bondage: White Servitude and Convict Labor in America, 1607–1776* (Chapel Hill, NC, 1947). See also M. Jernegan, *Laboring and Dependent Classes in Colonial America, 1607–1783* (Chicago, 1931). More recently, see D. Galenson, *White Servitude in Colonial America: An Economic Analysis* (New York, 1981).

4. On the relationship between white servants and rebel slaves, see H. Beckles, *Black Rebellion in Barbados: The Struggle against Slavery, 1627–1838* (Bridgetown, 1984), pp.25–48. Also, 'Rebels and Reactionaries: The Political Responses of White Labourers to Planter-Class Hegemony in Seventeenth Century Barbados', *Journal of Caribbean History*, 15 (1981), pp.1–20. See also for background, J. Handler, 'Slave Revolts and Conspiracies in Seventeenth Century Barbados', *New West Indian Guide*, 56 (1982), pp.5–43. M. Craton, 'The Passion to Exist: Slave Rebellions in the British West Indies, 1650–1832', *Journal of Caribbean History*, 13 (1980), pp.1–21.

5. W. Jordan, *White Over Black: American Attitudes Towards the Negro, 1550–1812* (Chapel Hill, NC, 1968) Ch. 1. Also 'Unthinking Decision: Enslavement of Negroes in America to 1700', in T.H. Breen (ed.), *Shaping Southern Society: The Colonial Experience* (New York, 1976), pp.100–105. This view is clearly outlined and evaluated in R. Dunn, *Sugar and Slaves: The Rise of the Planter Class in the English West Indies, 1624–1713* (Chapel Hill, NC, 1972), pp.71–3. See also L. Ruchames, 'The Sources of Racial Thought in Colonial America', *Journal of Negro History*, 52, (1976), pp.251–73.

6. These themes have been discussed by the author at length elsewhere. See 'Black Men in White Skins', op. cit., 'The Economic Origins of Black Slavery in the British West Indies: A Tentative Analysis of the Barbados Model', *Journal of Caribbean History*, 16 (1982), pp.36–42. 'Plantation Production and White Proto-Slavery: White Indentured Servants and the Colonisation of the English West Indies, 1624–1645', *The Americas*, 41 (1985), pp.21–45.

7. Sir Peter Colleton, a prominent planter, argued in the 1680s that any intellectual stimulation offered slaves by developing their technical skills would 'impair their value' as 'uplifted Africans' are prone to scorn arduous labour. Also, it would 'endanger the island, in as much as converted negroes grow more perverse and intractable than others', *Journal of Lords for Trade and Plantations*, 8 Oct. 1680, *Calendar of State Papers, Colonial Series, America and the West Indies, 1677–1680*, f.611. (hereafter *CSPC*)

8. See R. Dunn, op. cit., pp.201–12. A.P. Thornton, 'Some Statistics of West Indian Produce, Shipping and Reserves, 1660–1685', *Caribbean Historical Review*, 4 (1954), pp.251–2. Anon., *A State of the Present Condition of the Island of Barbados* (n.p., 1689). J.H. Bennett, 'William Whaley, Planter of Seventeenth Century Jamaica', *Agricultural History*, 40 (1966), pp.113–23. Barbados Assembly, *A Moderate Calculation of the Annual Charge and Produce of a Plantation in Barbados*, 16 Sept. 1685, CO 31/3, ff.120–21. Also, Governor Atkins to Lords of Trade, 4 July 1677, CO 29/2, f.181. For Barbados' Sugar export and prices in the late 17th century, see Rawlinson Mss, B.250/61, 64, Bodleian Library, Oxford.

9. Governor Russell to the Lords of Trade and Plantations, 23 March 1695, *CSPC*, 1693–96, f.446.

10. R. Ligon, *A True and Exact History of the Island of Barbados* (London, 1657),

pp.114–15. Also, Representation of the Council and Assembly of Barbados, July 1696, *CSPC*, 1696–97, f.62.

11. E. Eliot, op. cit.

12. Manager Abel Alleyne to Society for the Propagation of the Gospel in Foreign Parts, Barbados, 4 April 1744, Codrington Plantation Correspondence, Society's Archives, Lambeth Palace Library, London.

13. Père Labat in his visit to the West Indies towards the end of the seventeenth century referred to field servants as 'white slaves'. See J.B. Labat (ed.), *Memoirs of Père Labat, 1693–1705* (London, 1970), p.125.

14. F. Bayley, *Four Years' Residence in the West Indies* (London, 1830), p.62.

15. J. Sheppard, op. cit., p.43.

16. Report of the Royal West India Commission, 1897, Part 1, appendix C, p.6. Also, in 1798, Dr. J. Williamson, a fellow of the Royal College of Physicians of Edinburgh, on a visit to Barbados described then as 'vain in ancestry', but 'as degenerated and useless a race as can be imagined'. J. Williamson, *Medical and Miscellaneous Observations Relative to the West India Islands* (Edinburgh, 1817), p.27.

17. This argument has been developed at greater length by H. Beckles and K. Watson, 'Social Protest and Labour Bargaining: The Changing Nature of Slaves Responses to Plantation Life in 18th Century Barbados', *Slavery and Abolition* (forthcoming 1988).

18. W. Dickson, *Letters on Slavery* (London, 1789; Westport, CT, 1970 edition), p.42.

19. For statistical data on the increase of the free coloured and free black population in Barbados, see J. Handler, *The Unappropriated People: Freedmen in the Slave Society of Barbados* (London, 1974), pp.7–29. H. Beckles, 'On the Backs of Blacks; The Barbados Free Coloureds' Pursuit of Civil Rights and the 1816 Slave Rebellion', *Immigrants and Minorities*, 3 (1984), pp.167–88. A. Sio, 'Race, Colour, and Miscegenation: The Free Coloured of Jamaica and Barbados', *Caribbean Studies*, 16 (1976), pp.5–21.

20. W. Dickson, *Letters*, op. cit., pp.40–41. The more privileged poor whites worked as fishermen, petty shop keepers, mechanics and clerks in the towns. But wages were generally low and irregular. Dickson notes: 'In consequence of this redundancy of white men ... their wages, as servants on plantations (and, indeed, as clerks in the towns) are pitifully low; and are, sometimes, paid in indifferent produce; ... their diet, in general, is both coarse and scanty, so scanty, indeed, that, in order to get victuals, they are sometimes obliged to connive at the villainies of the principal negroes on the estates', p.42.

21. Ibid., p.41.

22. Ibid.

23. Ibid.

24. G. Pinckard, *Notes on the West Indies, Vol. 2* (London, 1808), p.132.

25. Ibid., p.134.

26. Ibid., p.135.

27. Ibid., pp.136–7.

28. Ibid., p.133.

29. Ibid., p.395.

30. Quoted in J. Handler, *The Unappropriate People*, op. cit., p.124.

31. See D.G. Allan, 'Joshua Steele and the Royal Society of Arts' *Journal of the Barbados Museum and Historical Society*, 22 (1954), pp.84–6. See also J. Handler, *The Unappropriated People*, op. cit., pp.123–4.

32. This information is contained in the official population report for the St. Peter Parish, 1780, Barbados Department of Archives.

33. See D.G. Allan, 'Joshua Steele, op. cit., p.86. Also, S. Moore, *The Public Acts in Force, Passed by the Legislator of Barbados, from May 16, 1762 to April 8, 1800, Inclusive* (London, 1801), pp.226–7. K. Watson, *The Civilised Island Barbados A Social History 1750–1816* (Bridgetown, 1979), pp.56–7.

34. S. Moore, *The Public Acts*, op. cit., pp.226–7.

35. Anon, *Sketches and Recollections of the West Indies* (London, 1828), p.27.
36. J. Handler, *A Guide to Source Materials for the Study of Barbados History, 1627–1834* (Carbondale, 1971), p.52.
37. W. Dickson, *Mitigation of Slavery in Two Parts: Part 1, Letters and Papers of the late Hon. Joshua Steele ... Part II: Letters to Thomas Clarkson* (London, 1814), 528pp.
38. W. Dickson, *Lettters*, op. cit., p.58.
39. E.V. Goveia, *A Study on the Historiography of the British West Indies to the end of the Nineteenth Century* (Mexico, 1956), p.46. J. Poyer, *History of Barbados from the Earliest Discovery of the Island in the Year 1605, till the Accession of Lord Seaforth, 1801* (London, 1808).
40. [J. Poyer], *A Letter addressed to ... Lord Seaforth by a Barbadian* (Bridgetown, 1801). See also, his book, op. cit., pp.9–15. See also B. Edwards, *The History Civil and Commercial of the British Colonies in West Indies* (London, 1793), 2 vols. E. Long, *History of Jamaica* (London, 1774), 3 vols. For example, Long states that Africans were more related to the orang-utang than to whites. See Vol. I, Book III, Ch. One. Also Vol. II, p.253.
41. Quoted in K. Watson, *The Civilised Island*, op. cit., p.104. The reference to Grenada concerned the slave uprising of 1795 which was led by a group of free coloureds.
42. Minutes of the Barbados Council, 1 Nov. 1803, Barbados Department of Archives.
43. See for an account of the free coloureds and the Bussa rebellion, H. Beckles, 'On the Backs of Blacks', op. cit. Also, 'The Slave Drivers' War: The 1816 Barbados Slave Uprising', *Boletín de Estudios Latino Americanos y del Caribe*, No. 39 (1985), pp.85–111.
44. Dickson noted of poor white militiamen: 'Many of them have nothing to fight for, but the precarious possession of little spots of bad land, on which they barely exist. I may safely affirm, that they could not lose so much by a defeat .... The present white militia have no pay, and, when they meet with accidents, far from receiving any kind of compensation, they receive not so much as THANKS', *Letters*, op. cit., p.97.
45. J. Poyer, *A Letter Addressed*, op. cit., pp.20–21.
46. R.H. Schomburgh, *The History of Barbados* (London, 1848), p.196.

The Liberated Africans in the Bahamas, 1811–60

In the years 1811–60, Africans captured from slavers, bound for Cuba, were settled in the Bahamas. This article examines the initial response of the host society to these involuntary immigrants. It also discusses the evolution and operation of a system of long-term labour contracts for the recaptives which predated the more familiar one of the post-emancipation years. Although this system, described as a 'kind of modified slavery', was discontinued in 1838, it was reintroduced in 1860 in a form which constituted an officially-approved truck system.

In historical writing on liberated Africans in the British Caribbean, scholars have tended to discuss that immigrant group primarily in relation to the plantation colonies in the post-emancipation years.[1] Typical of that emphasis is K.O. Laurence's pioneering study on immigration into the West Indies in the nineteenth century which discusses the liberated Africans exclusively in the context of the labour demands of the plantation economy after 1834.[2] This article examines the experience of these involuntary immigrants in the non-plantation colony of the Bahamas between 1811 and 1860 and focuses on two main areas: their reception in the host society and the evolution and operation of a system of indentured labour predating the more familiar one which developed in the major sugar colonies after emancipation.

I

The settlement of the liberated Africans in the Bahamas was the direct result of British efforts to suppress the transatlantic slave trade. In 1807 Britain made participation in the slave trade illegal for its subjects. Until the end of the Napoleonic wars, British efforts had mainly involved stationing ships of the Royal Navy on the slave trading routes to intercept any vessels (British or foreign) which were suspected of transporting slaves. Such ships, with their cargoes, were brought to the nearest British port where the captain and crew were tried before a vice-admiralty court. If they were successfully prosecuted, the slaves were liberated. With the return of peace in 1815, these activities of the Navy were restricted to British ships. The British government subsequently persuaded the major maritime powers in Europe to abolish the slave trade and agree to a series of bilateral treaties which, in effect, permitted the British Navy to search their ships for slaves. Courts of mixed commission were established in West Africa, the Caribbean and Latin America to adjudicate on ships seized on suspicion of trading in slaves. Slaves on board ships condemned for engaging in the slave trade were freed.[3]

Despite these efforts, the transatlantic slave trade was not effectively suppressed until the close of the 1860s. Although the Spanish government agreed to prohibit the slave trade north of the equator in 1817 and south of the line after May 1820, these agreements did little to slow the trade to the Spanish colony of Cuba where the rapid expansion of the sugar industry sharply increased the demand for slave labour. According to Philip Curtin, approximately 550,000 slaves were imported into Cuba.[4] Slavers bound for Cuba were intercepted by ships of the British Navy but the number of slaves seized and liberated was small in comparison with the number which was successfully imported into that colony. As the most active participant in the search and seizure of slave ships, Britain was responsible for disposing of groups of African recaptives who could not normally be repatriated. Those Africans liberated in the Caribbean were settled in colonies like British Guiana, Trinidad, Jamaica and the Bahamas.[5]

The transference of liberated Africans to the plantation colonies in the 1840s and 1850s was regarded as a possible solution to the labour problems experienced especially by British Guiana and Trinidad.[6] The primary reason for settling liberated Africans in the Bahamas, however, was its position on the main shipping route used by slavers between the African coast and Cuba. The Bahama islands, as one colonial official aptly remarked in 1811, were 'The Turnpike Road to the market of Cuba'.[7] In a similar comment, the Legislative Council and the House of Assembly in a joint petition to the King in Council in the same year, accurately predicted the role of the colony as a 'reception depot' for liberated Africans:

> ... as the Bahamas are situated immediately on the high Road between the African Coast and the only Places where the Slave Trade can now find a Market in the West Indies, there appears but too much reason to apprehend that a very large portion of such Vessels as may be hereafter selected, on this side of the Atlantic, unlawfully engaged in that traffic, will also be brought hither. ...[8]

Between 1811 and 1860 approximately 6,000 Africans were landed in the Bahamas from 26 slave vessels, flying either the Spanish or Portuguese flag, which had been captured by British ships or were wrecked on the rocks and reefs surrounding the islands.[9] Once liberated, the Africans were, by the provisions of an Order in Council of March 1808, employed either in the West India Regiment or in the Navy or were apprenticed to 'prudent and humane masters or mistresses' in the colony by the Customs Office.[10]

II

As early as 1811 when the liberated Africans were first settled in the colony, members of the white population expressed fears about the impact which their presence could have on the stability of Bahamian society. In a petition presented to the President of the Council, William Vesey Munnings, in August 1811, a group of inhabitants voiced their misgivings about the recent introduction of recaptives into the island of New Providence and the possibility of further arrivals. These developments as the petitioners pointed out, provided 'a just ground of serious apprehension for the lives and properties of the Inhabitants'. They were especially concerned that the influx of Africans would increase Nassau's free non-white population, many of whom were unemployed and thus, they believed, likely to resort to criminal activities. The petitioners also noted that the free people of colour already formed at least three-fourths of the 'Parish Poor' in New Providence.[11]

In protesting against the policy of introducing recaptives into the colony, the petitioners also resorted to constitutional arguments. Although they did not question the right of the Imperial Parliament to legislate for the colony, the petitioners took the view that the details of the operation of any imperial law should be modified to reflect local interests. They asserted that the right of West Indian colonies to regulate their internal affairs, with royal approval, had been long admitted and was 'indisputable' and that the introduction of recaptives despite local opposition would represent a violation of that constitutional right.

Pleading the urgency of the situation, the petitioners requested Munnings to reconvene the House of Assembly to consider the matter and take further action. He expected that the members of the Assembly (15 of whom had signed the petition) would impose a tax on the holders of African apprentices which would discourage other inhabitants from accepting them. Since such an action would run counter to imperial legislation, Munnings assumed that the Assembly would include the tax in the annual revenue bill. This, as he noted in a despatch to the Earl of Liverpool, would force him to give his assent to the bill with its objectionable clause, in order to prevent the loss of a considerable portion of the colony's revenue.[12]

Contrary to Munnings' expectations, the Assembly did not introduce a tax on holders of apprentices but joined the Legislative Council in addressing a petition to the King in Council in November, to press for restrictions on the further entry of recaptives into Nassau. The petitioners pointed out that three slave vessels had recently been captured and 451 Africans emancipated by the vice-admiralty court in Nassau. Although 91 Africans were recruited for the military and naval services, the remaining 360 had been distributed, under indentures ranging from seven to 14 years, to the inhabitants of Nassau. They claimed that if the Africans were prepared to hire themselves out as agricultural labourers, after their indentures expired, there would be little reason to regret the introduction of the recaptives. However, they argued, in the West Indies free people 'of all descriptions' were unwilling to work as field labourers at the prevailing wage rates and concentrated in the towns where few found regular employment and many turned to begging and crime 'to eke out a precarious subsistence for themselves and their Families'. The petitioners were convinced that the liberated Africans, like other free non-whites, would 'readily fall into all these habits and notions which already render their Brethren unfit for the pursuits of Husbandry and averse to them'. They also warned that the presence of the Africans would lead to increased demands for poor relief which were already proving a financial burden to the community. Given these circumstances, the petitioners maintained that the unrestricted introduction of recaptives, without the development of 'new and unexpected sources of Industry', held the prospect of 'terror and dismay' for the colony. Finally, they claimed that since the Africans were not British subjects and therefore had no right to residence in any British territory, any imperial legislation which attempted to confer that right in the West Indies, contrary to the wishes and interests of the colonies, was a contravention of their constitutional privileges.[13]

Both petitions were explicit about the social problems which the continued influx of the recaptives into the colony was expected to create. However, more immediate concerns were unexpressed in those petitions. First, the petitioners must have been aware that the further introduction of recaptives would upset the delicate balance between free non-whites and whites in the town of Nassau and its environs. In New Providence, before the arrival of the first liberated Africans, the free non-whites were already challenging the numerical predominance of the whites. In a census of the population which was taken in that island in December 1810, whites numbered 1,720 and the free blacks and free coloureds combined, 1,074. However, as the officials who conducted the census admitted, the figures for the non-whites underrepresented their numbers.[14]

The second of these concerns was economic, for slave owners objected to a scheme which threatened to depress the value of their slaves by allowing the recaptives to compete on the urban labour market. This consideration remained important in shaping the attitude of white colonists towards the introduction of liberated Africans throughout the slavery era. Writing in 1836, Dr John Richardson referred to the early 1830s as 'a period when the prejudices of the Colonists were exceedingly opposed to the introduction of Africans as free labourers who might come into competition with their slaves'.[15] These anxieties are best explained by an examination of the nature of the Bahamian economy and the state of the labour market in the early nineteenth century.

With the collapse of the cotton-based plantation system by 1800, slavery ceased to be vital to the agricultural economy. Slave owners found themselves with a steadily increasing and underemployed labour force to maintain.[16] In the stagnating agricultural economy of the Bahamas, with no crop of commercial importance to replace cotton, slaves were permitted to hire themselves out in the island of New Providence where there was a market for their labour services. For the slave owners, the system of self-hire became a method of profitably reassigning slaves whom agricultural activities could not keep adequately employed. Self-hire seems to have become widespread in the first decade of the nineteenth century. In 1808, for example, an act was passed which made mandatory the registration of slaves who hired themselves out to work 'either on board of vessels or on the shore, as porters or labourers'.[17] By 1832, the system of self-hire, as a comment by Governor Sir James Carmichael Smyth in that year indicates, was firmly established:

> ... it has long been a custom in this Colony to permit the more intelligent of the Slaves, & more particularly Artificiers, to find employment for themselves & to pay their owners either the whole or such a proportion of what they may gain as may be agreed upon between the Parties.[18]

The effect of the liberated Africans on the labour market in Nassau was clear by 1815. Appearing as a witness before a select committee of the House of Assembly on a proposal for a general registry of slaves in December of that year, John Stephen, the rector of Christ Church, suggested that the introduction of free Africans had further depressed the value of slaves:

> As far as I have been able to learn from conversation, I have clearly understood that the value of Slaves in this colony has decreased during the last seven years; which may be owing to various causes, and chiefly to a superabundance of Slaves, to the exhausted state of the soil, and to the Introduction of several Cargoes of Africans seized at Sea, and condemned as lawful Prize, which have been let out to the Inhabitants upon Indenture.[19]

In the years after 1811, some white colonists came to regard the liberated Africans as subversive of the system of slavery. This was a fear largely explained by the perceived impact, on a normally quiescent slave population, of ex-slaves freed by the provisions of an imperial law rather than by the normal process of manumission. In his evidence before the select committee of 1815, Theodore George Alexander, one of the editors of the *Royal Gazette*, expressed the opinion (undoubtedly more widely held) that the presence of the recaptives together with the publicized activities of the abolitionists led slaves to believe that their own emancipation was imminent:

... the liberation and dispersion of a large number of Africans who have been brought here as Prize, and apprenticed out, serving to instill into the minds of the Slaves a spirit of insubordination, by creating the expectancy that their emancipation is at hand, and still more strongly impressed upon them by the known interference of a powerful influence in the mother country.[20]

The events of January 1816 must have confirmed earlier apprehensions of the threat to security posed by the liberated Africans. In that month, the black troops of the Second West India Regiment, to which many recaptives had been recruited and which was garrisoned in Nassau, threatened mutiny.[21] The white minority was alarmed by 'the flagrant impolicy and dangers of keeping so large a Body of Blacks in arms in so small a Colony'.[22] There was, however, an even greater feeling of insecurity created by the knowledge of the close links between the black troops and the wider black community, especially those Africans under indenture. In a despatch to Earl Bathurst, Governor Charles Cameron warned of the dangers which could result from 'the long residence of this Regiment in the Colony, their consequent habits of intimacy with the black population, particularly with the Indented Africans whose peculiar situation renders them very disorderly ...'.[23]

The white community's anxieties about the liberated Africans were expressed in a memorial, addressed to Governor Cameron, of July of that year. In this memorial they opposed the introduction of 300 slaves seized from a Spanish ship, bound for Cuba, which was wrecked at Green Turtle Key. In what was obviously a reference to the threatened mutiny, the signatories argued that the increase of the free African population 'would seriously contribute to the present insecurity of the peace and even existence of this Colony already but too much endangered by similar and other alarming causes'. Their main complaint, however, was that they exercised no firm control over liberated Africans who, in their words, existed in a 'state of total exemption from restraint and coercion'. It is not then surprising that the memorialists (reflecting the views of their caste) should have found the recaptives 'the most worthless and troublesome class of black people in the Town of Nassau and its vicinity'. Their difficulty in dealing with the liberated Africans was partly due to the fact that, unlike the slaves or freedmen, they had no clearly defined position in the slave society and were therefore something of an anomaly: 'Insulated from the rest of their colour by the novel and peculiar incidents of their actual situation and prospects, on terms of inequality with the Slave on one side, and the free-man on the other, they assimilate and associate principally with each other only'. Finally, the memorialists pointed out that the introduction of the recaptives would prove 'seriously burdensome' in a colony where both the slaves and the free labourers were already underemployed.[24]

The memorial was the first effort in an organized campaign to prevent the distribution of the Africans, under indenture, in the colony. On 9 July 'a great and numerously attended Meeting of the inhabitants', which was held at the courthouse in Nassau, adopted a resolution that if the Africans were introduced into the colony no one should accept them as apprentices.[25] It is clear from the complete text of the resolution that those attending the meeting regarded the continued introduction of liberated Africans into the colony as further evidence of the British government's tendency to interfere in local matters. The dispute between the colony's legislature and the executive over the proposed registration of slaves must have strengthened that idea.[26]

Despite the efforts of a section of the white population, the recaptives were introduced and distributed to the colonists in September of that year. In fact, 220 individuals applied for 597 apprentices, although there were only 218 to be distributed.[27] Whatever fears some whites might have harboured about the free Africans, there were others who were anxious to benefit from labour services without the capital outlay which purchasing a slave involved or without paying regular wages to a free labourer. As the signatories of the July memorial had predicted 'some individuals may conceive that the services of a few more negros [sic] *gratis* for a time might contribute to their private convenience'.[28] In an attempt to mollify the critics of the decision to bring the recaptives to Nassau, and to allay their fears, the Collector of Customs distributed only one-fifth of the apprentices in New Providence and allocated the rest to the outlying islands.[29]

Between 1816 and July 1831, when only 197 liberated Africans entered the colony, white fears subsided and were replaced by a resentment of the efforts, by members of the colonial administration, to improve the social and economic conditions of the recaptives. Most liberated Africans remained under indenture during those years but some were allowed to work on their own after 1825 when their indentures expired. In that year the Collector of Customs, Mr C. Poitier, purchased 400 acres of land in New Providence, from public funds for resale to those Africans whose apprenticeship had ended.[30] He had decided on this course of action because he realized that as apprentices, they had worked primarily as agricultural labourers.[31] This measure was received with hostility by slave owners who (as Poitier noted in a letter to Earl Bathurst) regarded the emergence of an African peasantry as undermining the structure of slave society:

> Your Lordship will be however no doubt aware, that a powerful interest in the Colonies is hostile to the advancement of these people in the scale of political rights; and consequently the jealousy with which my conduct is, begun to be viewed; and in truth as a considerable slave owner myself their ideas are brought home to my own feelings .... Neither my Lord, can it be expected that any man who considers it wise and fair ... to defend his right

to the property he has vested, under the sanction of law, in slaves
... should view with complacency, His Majesty's well clad free
Africans coming into our market, bending under the horse loads
of provisions, the produce of their voluntary labour, industry and
keen desire of acquiring property.[32]

During the administration of Sir James Carmichael Smyth, the
improvement of conditions in the settlement of Africans, which was
established by Poitier and was known as Head Quarters, became the
object of official interest and white resentment. Carmichael Smyth was
especially interested in establishing a school for the children of the
liberated Africans of that community and had appealed, without
success, to the Assembly for financial assistance in 1830. Members
of the Assembly had taken the view that such a project was the
responsibility of the metropolitan rather than the colonial government.
Although the British government acknowledged its financial obliga-
tion, there was a delay in the release of the funds by the Treasury.
Carmichael Smyth had, as a result, advanced £1,000 from his own funds
for the construction of the school. This concern for the liberated
Africans was, as Carmichael Smyth knew, widely resented in the white
community: 'The interest I took in the affairs of these free Africans
could not but be known and talked of in a small community like this, and
produced a sour sulky feeling amongst a number of the ignorant &
prejudiced white Inhabitants.'[33] Given Carmichael Smyth's reputation
as a militant abolitionist, his interest in the welfare of the Africans
would also have been regarded as another attempt to remove all
distinctions between the races – 'the levelling effect', as the *Bahama
Argus* observed, 'being a favourite one of his ...'.[34]

Writing in 1825, Poitier had also remarked on the creole slaves'
resentment of the attention shown by the colonial administrators to
the liberated Africans, despite official attempts to ameliorate their
condition:

The unmerited fortunate lot of these Africans, is an irritating
substantial cause of Dissatisfaction to the good intelligent creole
slaves, who with claims so very superior on public munificence,
see not one ray of hope to brighten the dark horizon of their fate:
for however modified; to a good intelligent man, slavery is a bitter
lot.[35]

In the West India Regiment too there was friction between the African-
born and the creole soldiers whose greater familiarity with European
ways (as a comment by Lewis Kerr in 1823 suggested) gave them an
advantage in securing promotion: '... there generally prevails in our
black regiments, a strong feeling of jealously of the Africans against the
Creoles; the latter more intelligent, and consequently possessing many
advantages in point of pretension to favor and promotion'.[36] There is,
however, no evidence of a sustained antagonism between the liberated

Africans and the creoles whether slave or free. The early tendency of the recaptives to keep to themselves (remarked on by the memorialists of 1816) was eventually succeeded by an easy relationship with the slaves. This can be partly attributed to the fact that (as our later discussion will show) they worked alongside each other, performing similar jobs, in the urban setting, on the plantations of the Out Islands and at sea. Even more important in establishing a pattern of amity was the widespread practice, among the liberated Africans, of choosing their sexual partners from the creole slaves. In 1827, for example, Governor Lewis Grant noted that many liberated Africans were 'connubially connected' with slaves and had families by them.[37] This trend was mainly a reflection of the preference in the transatlantic slave trade for adult males and children.[38] The imbalance between the sexes resulted in male Africans establishing liaisons primarily with slave women. These types of interaction must have minimized the cultural differences between liberated Africans of diverse ethnic backgrounds and a slave population which was by 1834 only 9.4 per cent African-born.[39]

The number of recaptives landed in the Bahamas peaked in the 1830s. Between July 1831 and December 1838 approximately 4,000 Africans entered the colony. This influx resulted in a renewal of the earlier anxieties of the white colonists about the economic competition for their slaves and the dangers of the free black presence. The arrival of the recaptives in large numbers also heightened the white community's awareness of the cultural differences between the creole slave population and the newcomers. These differences became more marked because, in the 1830s, incoming recaptives were increasingly settled in villages in New Providence rather than dispersed throughout the outlying islands.[40] In August 1831, the editor of the *Bahama Argus* commented after a visit to a new settlement of Africans at South West Bay:

> On Tuesday last, we were witness to a Levee held by the Collector of Customs, at which seven of these uncouth savages were the *dramatis personae*, all of whom were armed with machets, and most picturesquely attired in blankets. As these new candidates for *court favour* could not speak one word of English, it was truly gratifying to us to witness the profound knowledge of the Collector, in the Mandingo, Ebo and Koromantyn slangs.[41]

In September of that year, the editor once again called attention to the unfamiliarity of the Africans with European ways: 'It is really offensive to the eyes of a civilized community, to witness the wanderings of these barbarians, to the Custom House and elsewhere, almost in a state of nudity ...'.[42]

The 'strangeness' of the liberated Africans was especially apparent in a colony where the mainly creole black population had, by the 1830s, assimilated important elements of European culture. Language was a significant indicator of the extent to which creole blacks were culturally assimilated. In most British West Indian colonies blacks spoke a Creole which combined features of European and African languages. In the Bahamas, however, blacks spoke a vernacular which was closer to the English language, as contemporary observers noted.[43] In an editorial of 22 August 1835 on the 'Prospects of the Colonies', the *Bahamas Argus* commented: 'Thus may we justly contrast the Bahamas with the other colonies. Our labourers intelligent – speaking the English language, and not a miserable patios.'[44] In that same year Governor William Colebrooke, in a letter to James Stephen of the Colonial Office, suggested that the creole blacks' assimilation of English culture extended beyond language to include even facial expression:

> The language spoken here by whites & blacks, is the English language and with a great many superior to some of the common dialects in England. Another peculiarity with us is that many of the Black people except for the colour of their skins are as much Englishmen, as if they had been born & brought up in that country and the English expression of their Countenances is so marked that one really forgets the African feature in looking at them, so much is there the expression of the 'human face divine'.[45]

This evidence confirms Alison Watt Shilling's observation that there was probably 'a smaller percentage of pidgin speakers in the Bahamas than elsewhere in the Caribbean until the beginning of the nineteenth century, when there was an influx of Africans from the captured slave ships'.[46]

The unfamiliarity of the recently-arrived Africans with European culture was one of the reasons for the denial of full civil rights to them up to 1836. In 1833 an act was passed to remove the civil disabilities of the colony's free non-whites, with the exception of 'natives of Africa, or of the Islands contiguous thereto'. Although Africans were permitted to give evidence in the law courts, by the provisions of that legislation, they could do so after six years' residence and after producing a certificate from a clergyman or a justice of the peace that they were qualified to testify.[47] In the following year, civil rights were extended to the African-born except for those who had resided in the colony for less than seven years.[48] In 1836, liberated Africans with less than seven years' residence were unable to join the militia, vote at elections for members of the Assembly or for vestrymen and serve on grand or petty juries.[49]

The cultural argument was most clearly expressed in the discussions relating to the refusal of the Assembly in 1834 to admit Africans to the militia. This measure was directed at the newly-arrived Africans for, up to that point, those of 'old importations' had been allowed to serve.[50] Although Africans of long residence had, as James Walker, Collector of Customs, observed, 'not behaved improperly when trusted with Arms, and were now complete British Colonists in language and customs', the ban was extended to all recaptives.[51] This is explained by the panic which followed on the introduction of large numbers of Africans in the early 1830s when members of the Assembly attributed to the recent and culturally unassimilated recaptives a potential for violence. In a resolution to Governor Colebrooke in December 1835, the members of the House stated their reasons for excluding the Africans from the militia:

> Located as the Africans in this Island are, in communities or settlements, almost entirely distinct from the other inhabitants, and at a distance from any power which can act with promptness as a controlling force over them; and liable as we are to the arrival and settlement in the colony of an increased number, direct from the coast of Africa, and in a state the furthest degree removed from civilization the House cannot but view the enactment which prohibits the enrolment of such persons in the Militia of the colony, as a sound and wholesome provision, and one which cannot be abrogated without in some measure endangering the tranquillity of the colony.[52]

In the following year, however, the Assembly relented and allowed liberated Africans of seven years' residence to serve in the militia.[53]

The members of the House of Assembly might have regarded the liberated Africans as potentially dangerous but Governor Colebrooke, and eventually the Colonial Office, saw them as a group which would remain loyal to the British Crown in the face of United States' expansionism. During the 1830s, successive governors of the Bahamas had expressed concern about American expansionist tendencies. In 1830, for example, Sir James Carmichael-Smyth observed: 'Our near neighbourhood to America, and the anxiety already shewn by the American Government to extend their possessions in these seas, by their establishment at West Key, must not be lost sight of.'[54] Colebrooke, in 1836, also warned Colonial Office officials not to alienate the economic and political elite of a 'Community Connected as this is in so many ways with the neighbouring countries'. He noted that though the colony had been mainly settled by Loyalists from the southern states, their ties with the United States had been sustained by the 'influence of habit and Education and the effects of Constant commercial intercourse'. These ties had, he suggested, been strengthened by the abolition of slavery 'acting on the prejudices of the Old Colonists and their descendants'.[55]

In this context of uncertainty about the loyalties of white Bahamians, in the event of American aggression against the Bahamas, Colebrooke recognized the possibility of creating 'a class of devoted subjects' among the liberated Africans:

> If brought here after Capture they ought to be put down in favorable situations attended with care, and provided for till they can provide for themselves. Then indeed would our interference

be a blessing to them, and call forth their gratitude. They are peculiarly susceptible of kindness and in a short time become reconciled & eventually a most useful and valuable people. In a few years with the help of the Moravians and other Missionaries, & the Expenditure of a few thousand pounds, we could raise a rampart of them in this quarter, which would enable us to bid a bold defence to our American Neighbours – and we should reap a peaceful harvest from their labours.[56]

The evidence indicates that the Colonial Office endorsed Colebrooke's view of the importance of the liberated Africans in the Bahamas as a bulwark against American encroachment. In fact, Lord Glenelg, the Secretary of State for the Colonies, regarded them as being of central importance in the event of a maritime war against the United States. As James Stephen explained in a letter to Lord Fitzroy Somerset in March 1838:

... the Western Shores of the Bahama Channel being now entirely incorporated into the United States of America, might afford shelter to Ships of war and Privateers, which would be altogether unchecked in their operations against the British homeward Bound West India Trade, unless the Eastern Shores of the same Channel should be peopled by a race of persons attached to the British Crown and accustomed to a Maratime [sic] Life. Such a population, as it appears to Lord Glenelg, might be collected by due attention to the Africans who have recently been introduced from Portuguese & Spanish Slave Ships.[57]

III

As noted earlier, liberated Africans were either enlisted in the military and naval services or apprenticed to local residents by the Collector of Customs at Nassau who was (for most of the years under examination) directly responsible for their physical welfare, on first landing, and their eventual distribution. The main idea behind the system of apprenticeship, by which recaptives initially served an indenture of seven to 14 years, was that they should learn a skill or a trade in order to earn a living in the wider society once their term of servitude ended.[58] There was also an ideological justification for an apprenticeship. Abolitionists hoped that during those years the liberated Africans would be christianized and 'civilized', a process by which they would be introduced not only to the Christian religion but also to European social and cultural values. Based on an assumption of European cultural superiority, this idea was an aspect of what Howard Temperley has described as 'anti-slavery as a form of cultural imperialism'.[59] In an opinion prepared for the Earl of Liverpool in July 1811, James Stephen provides an insight into the reasons for the adoption of a system of apprenticeship, for 'condemned' Africans but not for captured creole slaves, in the Bahamas:

> Africans or new negroes, as they are called, neither being intelligent enough to protect their own freedom, nor able immediately to work for their own subsistence ... it was necessary in respect of them, to give, for their own sakes, the power of enlisting or apprenticing. But the same necessity did not exist in respect of Creole Negroes, i.e. negroes born in the West Indies. These therefore were to be restored to their freedom without any such temporary dangerous modification of it. Between the two descriptions middle terms might have been found, such as seasoned negroes, or negroes who have been long enough in the W. Indies to have learned some European tongue & some method of gaining a subsistence. But great difficulties would have arisen in drawing the lines between the sufficient & insufficient degrees of *Creolization*, if I may use the term (it would be an insult to these poor creatures to call it *civilization*) which might create fitness & unfitness for immediate freedom in that country; & as every doubt or pretence of doubt would be sure of a construction adverse to them in the Colonial Courts, it was thought best to take the broadest lines of distinction only giving to all Slaves not natives of Africa, the full and immediate benefit of the Act, subjecting native Africans to the powers of enlistment & apprenticeship.[60]

The objectives of the apprenticeship were reflected in the conditions, specified in the indenture contract, which the employers of the apprentices were required to meet. A contract, dating from 1833, stipulated that persons to whom apprentices were assigned should instruct them 'in some Art, trade, mystery or occupation'. Employers were also obliged to provide apprentices with 'sufficient, decent and comfortable food and clothing, medical assistance, medicines and other necessaries' during the period of apprenticeship. They were further required to ensure that the apprentices received instruction in the Christian faith and were eventually baptized. Employers were, moreover, expected to encourage the adults to attend church and apprentices under 21 years to attend Sunday school. This insistence on the employees' responsibility for christianizing the liberated Africans suggests parallels with the *encomienda* system of colonial Latin America. The indenture contract, between the Governor and the Collector of Customs, was in keeping with the contemporary official view that the recaptive (whether adult or juvenile) was not competent to protect his own interests.[61]

Despite these declared objectives, the system of apprenticeship became one by which employers extracted cheap labour from the liberated Africans providing few opportunities for acquiring further skills.[62] Like *emancipados* in Cuba, recaptives in the Bahamas were usually treated no better than slaves.[63] The direction in which the apprenticeship had developed was already clear to Governor Lewis Grant in 1825:

> ... but few of them have been brought up to Trades, a few of them also to the Sea, many a great many are working on the plantations & working indiscriminately with the Slaves and receiving similar treatment. Many are absolutely sent out on hire to work on the roads or to planters and Salt rakers and to be employed in labour which few proprietors would be willing to hire out their own Slaves (except the worst description) to perform.[64]

Grant's preliminary observations were later corroborated by the findings of a committee (on which he served) which investigated the 'state and condition' of the liberated Africans and reported in 1828. The report noted that African apprentices, like slaves, were usually employed in fishing, wrecking, cutting wood, raking salt, and agricultural and domestic tasks in New Providence and the Out Islands. In addition, female apprentices, like female slaves, were often sent out with trays of merchandise to hawk about Nassau.[65] Many holders of apprentices were no more than middlemen who sold the labour services of the recaptives to other employers on the self-hire system. Although the terms of employment for the apprentices on the self-hire system varied, the outcome of these arrangements was usually the same.[66] In an inversion of the conventional situation, it was the apprentice who paid regular 'wages' to his original employer, as the 1828 report noted: 'It is a matter of no consideration with the Holder where or how the Apprentice is employed whether he is raking Salt in the Ponds, felling Timber in an uninhabited Wilderness, or working on the Public Roads, the paramount object is the Wages.'[67] For many employers, apprenticing liberated Africans was a lucrative undertaking, especially in those cases where individual apprentices served more than 14 years under indenture.[68]

On the plantations in the Out Islands, the apprentices were exploited more thoroughly than the slaves of their holders. This is understandable for employers were interested in preserving their capital – the slaves – but had no such interest in the welfare of apprentices whose labour services they owned for a specified term. On that point the 1828 report commented:

> ... the feeling of sympathy which the Master or Proprietor may naturally be disposed to entertain for the Slave from his being under his special and exclusive protection does not seem generally to have been extended to the Apprentice. To get the labor and make the most of it during the time of the Apprenticeship, has been the paramount consideration with the Holder.[69]

Apprentices were also remunerated like slaves and thus given rations rather than cash, a practice which prefigured the truck system of the post-emancipation years.[70] Since the indenture contract failed to establish any minimum requirements for the apprentices' allowances, they were usually given those prescribed by law for the slaves. The official report noted, however, that on many plantations the supplies of food (which was limited to corn) and clothing were 'scant and precarious'.[71]

The responsibility of the employers for christianizing, and by implication 'civilizing', the liberated Africans was largely ignored. As the official report observed: 'The moral and intellectual improvement of the Africans employed in field or other labour does not appear to have been thought of by the Holders.'[72] Religious instruction for the apprentices was hindered by the fact that the activities of the Established Church were concentrated in New Providence. Liberated Africans tended to join 'various Sectarian Conventicles', for the Nonconformists had extended their proseyletizing efforts to the Out Islands.[73] By 1828, however, the influence of Christianity was still only superficial. Commenting on whether individual apprentices had been instructed in religion, the 1828 report most often noted: 'Can say his prayers.'[74] Even when the efforts to christianize were more assiduous, they did not always produce the desired result. In December 1816, J. Sullivan, the Collector of Customs for Crooked Island and Acklins observed, in a report on five African apprentices, with chagrin: 'These Africans are in good health, and well fed & Clothed, but make no progress either in Religion or Morals, Although they have Meetings where Prayers and Psalms are said and Sung, from whence they generally go either to Debauch their neighbours' Wife or Husband or Steal from them.'[75]

As early as 1825, Governor Grant recognized that the system of apprenticeship, with its long term of indenture, mainly benefited the holders of the apprentices. Noting the high level of demand for the services of the recaptives, even without a period of indenture, Grant instructed the Collector of Customs to bind the apprentices only for one year at a time. He took the view that these short-term indentures would allow officials to monitor more closely the treatment of the apprentices.[76] Although there is no evidence that Grant's arrangement for reducing the indenture persisted beyond his tenure in office, successive governors came to question whether the system of apprenticeship had achieved its original objectives. In September 1834, for example, Governor Blayney Balfour, in a despatch to the Secretary of State for the Colonies, Thomas Spring Rice, remarked: '... the system of Apprenticeship has had I conceive a fair trial and, where the negroes are not used by the Master as Domestic Servants, I am convinced that it is not beneficial to the African – he neither learns English, nor any useful occupation and is too often subject to harsh and cruel treatment.'[77] In the following year Governor Colebrooke also expressed the opinion that a long term of indenture was often of no benefit to the Africans. Referring to the distribution of 245 recaptives in August 1834 on seven-year indentures, Colebrooke observed that 'such engagements must constitute a kind of modified slavery, without advantage to the Africans in too many cases'.[78]

The reappraisal of the apprenticeship system, with its long term of indenture, was accompanied by experiments with alternative methods of preparing the liberated Africans for earning a livelihood. In 1836, for example, male adults from the Portuguese slavers *Vigilante* and *Criolo* were employed in public works in New Providence, under the supervision of overseers. Writing in July of that year, Colebrooke observed: 'The object has been to exact, until habituated to exertion, a moderate share of labour in useful works in return for subsistence, and thus to enable them to acquire the means of earning full wages; which they are generally doing.'[79] By November, he was convinced that a period of six months was long enough for adult Africans to acquire the experience necessary for earning a living. In a despatch to Lord Glenelg, Colebrooke stated that there was no need for a prolonged indenture for the recaptives:

> ... there can be no ground for withholding from them for any time, the full advantages of their industry on the plea of preparing them to provide for themselves. Indeed with the aid of their more experienced countrymen and encouraged by their example they readily acquire a knowledge of the value of their labour, and work most satisfactorily when their wages are paid to them weekly ....[80]

Colebrooke's views on the apprenticeship for adult recaptives were undoubtedly influenced by the conclusions of the African Board (to which responsibility for the liberated Africans had been transferred) after an investigation in 1835. The Board had reported that a system of indenture was advantageous to African juveniles 'in accustoming them by degrees to the habit of civilized life, and reclaiming them from nearly a savage state'. The members suggested, however, that the period of indenture should be shortened from seven years to five in cases where the apprentice was taught a trade and to three years when he was not. The Board also recommended that the same system of apprenticeship should not be used in the case of adult (and thus less impressionable) Africans. It pointed out that a brief apprenticeship of no more than six months would help the Africans to learn the English language.[81]

The changed views on the system of indenture were reflected in the instructions which were issued to the African Board by Colebrooke in August 1836. Adult Africans (defined as those above 15 years) were allowed to enter into voluntary agreements with their employers, which had to be confirmed by two members of the Board. These agreements, lasting no longer than 12 months, were consciously patterned on those which ex-slaves were being encouraged to make with their former masters. The Board was instructed to include in the agreements provisions for adequate food, clothing, lodging, medical aid in sickness, and wages of no less than one dollar per month for the first year and increases of a dollar per month in each of the next two years. The principle behind these specific provisions for wages, as Colebrook noted, was 'that the African is entitled to the full value of his labour from the employers for whatever period the engagement may be formed'. It was stipulated that those engagements made by the Board on behalf of minors should include provision for religious instruction and attendance at church.[82]

In 1838 Governor Francis Cockburn attempted to reverse the changes in the system of indenture which Colebrooke had introduced with Colonial Office approval. When 1,043 Africans, captured from Portuguese slavers, were landed in the colony in the first five months of that year, Cockburn, after consulting with his Council, decided to place the recaptives under indenture. He justified this course of action, to Lord Glenelg, by claiming that 'the expectations, entertained by my Predecessors, of the Africans being able to obtain a Living by their own exertions, had not been realized ...'. In these circumstances, Cockburn pointed out, it was felt that apprenticing the Africans would be 'the only reasonable mode of fulfilling the benevolent views of the British Government towards the liberated Africans'. He also noted that the need to protect the Africans from being 'enticed' to Demerara, by labour recruiters whose proposals 'they could in no way understand or enforce', had influenced this decision.

This decision, ostensibly based on humanitarian considerations was, in fact, a lightly disguised attempt to retain for the employer class, a labour force over which it could exercise a greater degree of control than over free wage labourers. The reintroduction of a long-term indenture for the liberated Africans must have assumed urgency since the Apprenticeship for the ex-slaves was in the last months of its existence. The concern for control was reflected in the articles of agreement by which adult Africans were indentured for four years and in which a penal provision was introduced. Any form of misbehaviour or violation of the articles of agreement by the indentured African was made punishable by the nearest magistrate, by imprisonment with hard labour, for a term not exceeding ten days or by confinement in the stocks.[83]

Cockburn's arrangements were short-lived for the Colonial Office had already decided to dispense with a system of apprenticeship for adult Africans. In a circular despatch to Governors of the West Indian colonies of 15 May 1838, Lord Glenelg stated that experiments, in some colonies, with allowing Africans to work for their living had 'tended to establish the conclusion that the restriction of an Apprenticeship is unnecessary and may be safely dispensed with'. The only exception to that ruling was African children, without mothers or relatives to provide for them, who would continue to be apprenticed for terms, not exceeding five years. In concluding his instructions, Glenelg noted that 'a complete and fair experiment' should be made to settle the Africans without recourse to an apprenticeship.[84] Cockburn was subsequently ordered to cancel the indentures of all adult Africans.[85]

In 1839, the House of Assembly attempted, with Cockburn's connivance, to circumvent the Colonial Office's ban on a system of indenture. The House used the technique of including an extraneous clause, which gave the Governor the power of 'disposal and control' of the recaptives, in a bill extending to them the privileges of British subjects. Supporting the need for this provision, Cockburn noted in a despatch to the Secretary of State for the Colonies, Lord John Russell in December of that year: 'Since the Indentures of Adult Africans were ordered to be cancelled the want of such a Power has been clearly proved. The Africans beleive [sic] me my Lord are not on their first arrival sufficiently enlightened to make agreements for themselves.' Such a measure, he pointed out, was also justified because there was the danger of Africans being enticed away to the slave countries in the vicinity. It was that possibility which, in Cockburn's opinion, made 'the limited control contained in the present Bill of paramount importance to the due Protection of the Africans'.[86]

Despite the display of concern for the Africans, the bill was disallowed. Colonial Office officials saw the granting of such wide powers of 'disposal and control' over the recaptives to the Governor as undue interference with their freedom of labour. In a despatch to Cockburn in March 1840, Russell stated the Colonial Office position on such an arrangement: 'As often as any Africans may be imported into the Bahama Islands you will take the necessary means for hiring them out to service for six or at most 12 months after their arrival, but beyond this you should not interfere with freedom of their labor.'[87]

In 1840, Cockburn was once again urging the need for reintroducing an indenture for the recaptives. On that occasion the object of his concern was the salt industry (then the main prop of the colony's economy) which was experiencing difficulty in attracting and retaining a labour force.[88] Cockburn saw the liberated Africans as a possible solution to the labour problem but he was aware that the working conditions in the salt ponds were no more acceptable to them than to the creole freedmen. Although the Africans worked in the salt industry, they were reluctant to sign any binding agreements with their employers. Their usual response to any suggestion that they should enter into such a contract was, 'No Sign Paper'. Writing to Russell in April of that year, Cockburn suggested that only a reinstatement of some form of apprenticeship could avert the problems which he anticipated from the Africans' reluctance to sign agreements:

This determination leads to the risk that when the salt-raking Season is over many of them may be discharged by their employers in which case they may for a time be exposed [to] that degree of want which I much fear would lead them to acts of Violence & Plunder. Nor am I aware of how the difficulty which I apprehend in this respect can be guarded against except by investing the Governor with a Power of making agreements and enforcing a compliance therewith both on the part of Employer and African. This I am aware would be in part a return to the apprentice System, but as I have before stated the Africans are in no way qualified to act for themselves at least Two or Three Years after their arrival.[89]

At the Colonial Office, officials remained opposed to interference with the African's freedom of labour and were reluctant to sanction any scheme which might be construed as a new system of slavery. In his response to Cockburn's despatch, Russell reiterated the Colonial Office's position on the question of a coercive system of labour:

> The disinclination which you observed on the part of the Liberated Africans to enter into written Contracts for Labor must not be encountered in the manner proposed. If authority were given to you to make such Contracts for them, the result would be to excite alarm & discontent & to create the necessity for a compulsory system of labor enforced by penalties.[90]

After 1841, the question of indenting recaptives in the Bahamas was not again a major issue until 1860, when 360 of them were landed in the colony following the wreck of a slaver on Abaco. Governor Charles Bayley assumed the responsibility for distributing them in the colony as apprentices: for two years in the case of adults and four years for juveniles. Prospective employers objected to that proposal on the grounds that 'they were liable to be deprived of their services just as the Africans were beginning to become useful'. As a result, Bayley eventually extended the period under indenture for children below the age of 14, to six years and Africans over 14 to five years. Neither group would receive wages during the period of indenture. Those older than 14 years were, however, to be paid 'the current wages usually paid to servants, or mechanics of similar proficiency, or capacity', after five years' service. The employers' main responsibility to the Africans under these arrangements was to provide them with food, clothing and, in the case of juveniles, religious instruction. Employers were also expected to give adult Africans 'every opportunity and facility for receiving instructions' in a trade.[91]

Although Bayley chose to represent these arrangements as being in 'the interests of the Colony and of the negroes themselves', they were clearly intended to benefit the colony's white employer class which dominated the local legislature. At that point, employers had neither the working capital to offer steady wage employment nor the ability to command occasional labour from a lower class which could survive without the sale of its labour power.[92] The African recaptives were eventually indentured to salt proprietors, and owners of fruit plantations and as domestic servants in the Out Islands. In Nassau, many of the recaptives were bound to joiners, carpenters, boat builders and blacksmiths.[93]

In October 1860, Colonial Office officials endorsed Bayley's re-introduction of a system of long-term indenture for the Africans. By that date, the Colonial Office, under pressure from the planters in the major sugar colonies, had accepted the necessity for long-term labour contracts for both Indian immigrants and liberated Africans.[94] Some officials expressed misgivings about aspects of the system of indenture which had been introduced. Sir Frederic Rogers, for example, in a minute of 16 October observed that the position of the liberated Africans in the Bahamas would be 'very much worse' than in other West Indian colonies. He pointed out that on their arrival in the other colonies, the liberated Africans could be indentured for three years or until the age of 18 'during that time they receive for the first year provisions – after that time – wages at the current rate – and always lodging'.[95] Despite Rogers' comments, there was no attempt to inter-fere with those features of the Bahamian system of indenture which he criticized. The major request for modifications to Bayley's arrange-ments was that the provisions for the indenture should conform to the guidelines set by Sir John Pakington in October 1852 and that legis-lation reflecting the changes should be introduced. In a letter to Bayley outlining the Secretary of State's views, Chichester S. Fortescue, then Under-Secretary of State, limited himself to expressions of disapproval about a system of indenture which made no provisions for the payment of money wages:

> ... the Secretary of State believes that the attempt in a free Country to retain the unpaid services of labourers after they have become aware of their usefulness, and while they see persons of the same class receiving a high rate of wages around them, will prove as fruitless (if not mischievous) in the Bahamas as it has proved in other places where it has been tried.[96]

In April 1861, legislation 'to provide for the fare of Africans brought to or otherwise arriving in the Colony from vessels engaged in the African Slave Trade' formalized the system of indenture. By its pro-visions, Africans under the age of ten could be indentured for a maximum of eight years, those between ten and 13 years of age for a term of six years, those between 13 and 16 for five years, and those older than 16 years for a term of no more than four years. Although the act provided for the cancellation of the indenture if the employer violated the agreement, it was weighted in his favour. First, Africans of all age groups were paid no money wages until after the end of the indenture. Second, unauthorized absence from work, unsatisfactory performance of the duties assigned, or 'misconduct' towards the employer could be punished, on conviction before a justice of peace, by imprisonment, with or without hard labour, for a maximum of 20 days. An anti-enticement clause also made it a crime, punishable by a fine, to hire or harbour Africans who were still under indenture.[97]

In 1862 and 1863, details of the 1861 legislation were amended but the basic framework for indenting liberated Africans remained unchanged.[98] After 1860, however, no more recaptives were introduced into the colony. Although there is no detailed information on the operation of this system of indenture, its existence must have reinforced the practice of payment in truck which already existed in the colony.[99] In effect, it constituted an officially-approved truck system.

IV

In the years after 1811, the influx of liberated Africans into the Bahamas roused the fears and apprehension of the white community and led to demands for their exclusion from the colony. For the whites, the introduction of large numbers of recaptives, especially into the town of Nassau, not only posed a threat to their lives and property but also provided competition for their slaves, working on the self-hire system, in the urban economy. Despite these initial fears about the liberated Africans, there were always individuals who were willing to employ them under the apprenticeship system. In theory, this system (with its emphasis on religious instruction and the acquisition of a skill) would prepare the liberated Africans for their integration into the Bahamian society and economy, after an indenture of between seven and 14 years. In practice, it functioned primarily as a system of labour exploitation in which the recaptives experienced, in Governor Colebrooke's words, 'a kind of modified slavery'. The system of long-term contracts was altered in the mid-1830s, and in 1838 all indentures for adults were cancelled. After rejecting proposals for a long-term indenture in the early post-emancipation years, the Colonial Office gave its approval for the reintroduction of such a system for the liberated Africans in 1860. As our discussion has demonstrated, the elaboration of a system of long-term indenture for immigrants in the nineteenth century dates from the period immediately following the abolition of the slave trade (in relation to the liberated Africans) rather than from the years after the abolition of slavery.[100]

HOWARD JOHNSON
The College of the Bahamas,
Nassau, Bahamas

NOTES

1. See, for example, Monica Schuler, *'Alas, Alas, Kongo': A Social History of Indentured African Immigration into Jamaica, 1841–1865* (Baltimore, MD, 1980); 'The Recruitment of African Indentured Labourers for European Colonies in the Nineteenth Century', in P.C. Emmer (ed.), *Colonialism and Migration; Indentured Labour before and after Slavery* (Dordrecht, 1986), pp.125–61; Donald Wood, 'Kru Migration to the West Indies', *Journal of Caribbean Studies* 2 (1981), pp.266–82. The exceptions are Peter T. Dalleo, 'Africans in the

Caribbean: A Preliminary Assessment of Recaptives in the Bahamas 1811–1860', *Journal of the Bahamas Historical Society* 6 (Oct. 1984), pp.15–24; D. Gail Saunders, *Slavery in the Bahamas 1648–1838* (Nassau, 1985), pp.193–204.
2. K.O. Laurence, *Immigration into the West Indies in the Nineteenth Century* (St. Lawrence, Barbados, 1971), pp.13–16.
3. Leslie Bethell, 'The Mixed Commissions for the Suppression of the Transatlantic Slave Trade in the Nineteenth Century', *Journal of African History* 7 (1966), pp.79–93.
4. Philip D. Curtin, *The Atlantic Slave Trade: A Census* (Madison, WI, 1969), p.234, Table 67.
5. Schuler, 'The Recruitment of African Indentured Labourers', p.128.
6. Laurence, *Immigration into the West Indies*, pp.13–16.
7. William Vesey Munnings to the Earl of Liverpool, 22 Aug. 1811. CO 23/58. Munnings was Chief Justice of the colony and President of the Council.
8. Enclosure in Munnings to Liverpool, 25 Nov. 1811, CO 23/58.
9. For estimates of the number of Africans landed in the Bahamas, see Dalleo, 'Africans in the Caribbean', p.24 and Antonia Canzoneri, 'Early History of the Baptists in the Bahamas', *Journal of the Bahamas Historical Society* 4 (Oct. 1982), p.9.
10. Quoted in D. Gail North, 'The Amelioration and Abolition of Slavery in the Bahamas 1808–1838' (B.A. dissertation Modern History, University of Newcastle upon Tyne, 1966), p.77.
11. Enclosure in Munnings to Liverpool, 22 Aug. 1811, CO 23/58. The terms 'liberated Africans' and 'recaptives' are used interchangeably throughout this article. For a discussion of this point see Christopher Fyfe, 'Freed Slave Colonies in West Africa' in John E. Flint (ed.), *The Cambridge History of Africa* 5 (Cambridge, 1976), p.181.
12. Enclosure in Munnings to Liverpool, 22 Aug. 1811, CO 23/58. The Earl of Liverpool was then Secretary of State for War and the Colonies.
13. Enclosure in Munnings to Liverpool, 25 Nov. 1811, CO 23/58.
14. 'An Account of the Population of the Island of New Providence taken in the month of December 1810'. Enclosure in Munnings to Robert Peel, 16 July 1812, CO 23/59. Cf. Ira Berlin, *Slaves without Masters: The Free Negro in the Antebellum South* (paperback edition, New York, 1981), p.209.
15. Richardson to William Colebrooke, 12 Nov. 1836. Enclosure in Colebrooke to Lord Glenelg, 15 Nov. 1836, No. 120, CO 23/97. Richardson was the surgeon to the Second West India Regiment which was stationed in Nassau.
16. For a discussion of this point see Howard Johnson, 'Labour Systems in Post-emancipation Bahamas' in B.W. Higman (ed.), 'Caribbean Economic History', *Social and Economic Studies* 37 (1988), pp.182–3.
17. B.W. Higman, *Slave Populations of the British Caribbean, 1807–1834* (Baltimore, MD, 1984), p.245. Higman provides an excellent discussion of systems of self-hire throughout the British Caribbean in the early nineteenth century.
18. James Carmichael Smyth to Viscount Goderich, 2 Aug. 1832, No. 163. CO 23/87.
19. Enclosure in Charles Cameron to Earl Bathurst, 24 Jan. 1816. CO 23/63.
20. Ibid.
21. Cameron to Bathurst, 24 Jan. 1816, CO 23/63.
22. Report of a committee of the House of Assembly, 9 Jan. 1816. Enclosure in Cameron to Bathurst, 24 Jan. 1816, CO 23/63.
23. Cameron to Bathurst, 24 Jan. 1816, CO 23/63. Earl Bathurst was then Secretary of State for war and the colonies.
24. Enclosure in Cameron to Bathurst, 12 July 1816. CO 23/63.
25. *Royal Gazette*, 13 July 1816.
26. Michael Craton, *A History of the Bahamas* (3rd edition, Waterloo, Ontario, 1986), pp.184–5.
27. Cameron to Bathurst, 12 Feb. 1817, No. 10, CO 23/64.
28. Enclosure in Charles Cameron to Bathurst, 12 July 1816, CO 23/63. Some of the

holders of African apprentices were free non-whites.

29. Alexander Murray to Bathurst, 27 Sept. 1816, CO 23/63.
30. C. Poitier to Bathurst, 8 Feb. 1825, CO 23/74.
31. Poitier to Bathurst, 4 March 1824, CO 23/73.
32. Poitier to Bathurst, 8 Feb. 1825, CO 23/74.
33. Carmichael Smyth to Goderich, 5 Feb. 1832, No. 137, CO 23/86.
34. Editorial in *Bahama Argus*, 7 April 1832.
35. Poitier to Bathurst, 8 Feb. 1825, CO 23/74.
36. Lewis Kerr to Lewis Grant, 3 May 1823. Enclosure in Lewis Grant to Bathurst, 3 May 1823, No. 16, CO 23/72. Kerr was a member of the House of Assembly.
37. Grant to Goderich, 26 Sept. 1827, No. 9, CO 23/76.
38. Paul Lovejoy, *Transformations in Slavery* (Cambridge, 1983), p.139.
39. Higman, *Slave Populations of the British Caribbean*, p.116. For a discussion of the diverse ethnic origins of the African recaptives in the Bahamas see Dalleo, 'Africans in the Caribbean', p.17.
40. For an extended discussion of this point see Patrice Williams, *A Guide to African Villages in the Bahamas* (Nassau, 1979).
41. *Bahama Argus*, 13 Aug. 1831.
42. *Bahama Argue*, 14 Sept. 1831.
43. For a parallel situation in Barbados see R.B. Le Page and Andrée Tabouret-Keller, *Acts of Identity: Creole-based Approaches to Language and Ethnicity* (Cambridge, 1985), p.41.
44. *Bahama Argus*, 22 Aug. 1835.
45. Colebrooke to James Stephen, 4 Oct. 1835. CO 23/94.
46. Alison Watt Shilling, 'Some Non-Standard Features of Bahamian Dialect Syntax' (unpublished Ph.D. dissertation, University of Hawaii, 1978), p.18.
47. 'An Act to relieve His Majesty's Free Coloured and Black Subjects of the Bahama Islands, from all Civil Disabilities', 4 Wm. 4, C.1.
48. 'An Act to amend an Act of the General Assembly of those Islands, entitled "An Act to relieve His Majesty's Free Coloured and Black Subjects, of the Bahama Islands, from all Civil Disabilities"', 5 Wm. 2, C.9.
49. See opinion by G. Birrell, Attorney General. Enclosure in Colebrooke to Glenelg, 12 March 1836, No. 23, CO 23/96.
50. James Walker to James Stephen, 12 April 1836, CO 23/98.
51. Ibid.
52. *Votes of the House of Assembly*, 1835–36, p.53.
53. Colebrooke to Glenelg, 2 June 1836, No. 52, CO 23/96.
54. Carmichael Smyth to Sir George Murray, 20 Feb. 1830, No. 36, CO 23/82.
55. Colebrooke to Glenelg, 3 Feb. 1836, No. 10, CO 23/96.
56. Colebrooke to James Stephen, 19 Aug. 1835, CO 23/94.
57. James Stephen to Lord Fitzroy Somerset, 10 March 1836. Bound with Francis Cockburn to Lord John Russell, 27 Feb. 1841, No. 92, CO 23/109. Somerset was then military secretary of the Horse Guards.
58. Cf. Johnson U.J. Asiegbu, *Slavery and the Politics of Liberation 1787–1861* (London, 1969), p.27.
59. Howard Temperley, 'Anti-Slavery as a Form of Cultural Imperialism', in Christine Bolt and Seymour Drescher (eds.), *Anti-Slavery, Religion and Reform: Essays in Memory of Roger Anstey* (Folkestone, Kent, 1980), pp.335–50.
60. James Stephen to Liverpool, 14 July 1811, CO 23/58.
61. Enclosure in Colebrooke to Glenelg, 5 Aug. 1835, No. 77, CO 23/94. For a discussion of the *encomienda* system see Immanuel Wallerstein, *The Modern World System I: Capitalist Agriculture and the Origins of the European World Economy in the Sixteenth Century* (New York, 1974), pp.92–3.
62. Cf. Berlin, *Slaves without Masters*, p.227.
63. Manuel Morengo Fraginals, *The Sugarmill: The Socioeconomic Complex of Sugar in Cuba 1760–1860* (New York, 1976), p.140; Rebecca J. Scott, *Slave Emancipation in Cuba: The Transition to Free Labor, 1869–1899* (Princeton, NJ, 1986),

p.70.
64. Grant to Bathurst, 5 May 1825, No. 13, CO 23/74.
65. 'Report on the State and Condition of the Liberated Africans', 10 Oct. 1828. Enclosure No. 7 in Grant to Sir George Murray, 10 Oct. 1828, No. 19, CO 23/79.
66. For a discussion of the terms of employment for the liberated Africans see Howard Johnson, ' "A Modified Form of Slavery": The Credit and Truck Systems in the Bahamas in the Nineteenth and Early Twentieth Centuries', *Comparative Studies in Society and History* 28 (1986), p.732.
67. 'Report on the State and Condition of the Liberated Africans'.
68. Grant to Goderich, 26 Sept. 1827, No. 9, CO 23/76.
69. 'Report on the State and Condition of the Liberated Africans'. Cf. David Galenson, *White Servitude in Colonial America* (paperback edition, Cambridge, 1984), pp.171–2.
70. Johnson, ' "A Modified Form of Slavery" '. - 732.
71. 'Report on the State and Condition of the Liberated Africans'.
72. Ibid.
73. Munnings to Bathurst, 21 Feb. 1826, No. 12, CO 23/75. Schedule B.
74. 'Report on the State and Condition of the Liberated Africans'.
75. J. Sullivan to Bathurst, 31 Dec. 1816, CO 23/63.
76. Grant to Bathurst, 5 May 1825, No. 13, CO 23/74.
77. Blayney Balfour to Spring Rice, 8 Sept. 1834, No. 5, CO 23/91.
78. Colebrooke to Earl of Aberdeen, 12 March 1835, No. 8, CO 23/93.
79. Colebrooke to Glenelg, 18 July 1836, No. 77, CO 23/97.
80. Colebrooke to Glenelg, 1 Nov. 1836, No. 105, CO 23/97.
81. 'Report of the committee appointed to inspect and report upon the condition and treatment of the Liberated Africans', 6 July 1835. Reprinted in *Bahama Argus*, 11 July 1835.
82. Instructions to the Members of the Board of Superintendence of Liberated Africans, 18 Aug. 1836. Enclosure in Colebrooke to Glenelg, 9 Sept. 1836, No. 92, CO 23/97.
83. Francis Cockburn to Glenelg, 19 May 1838, No. 75, CO 23/102.
84. Glenelg to West Indian Governors, 15 May 1838, CO 318/141.
85. Glenelg to Cockburn, 10 Aug. 1838, No. 79 (draft), CO 23/102.
86. Cockburn to Lord John Russell, 27 Dec. 1839, No. 8, CO 23/105.
87. Russell to Cockburn, 17 March 1840, No. 23 (draft), 23/105.
88. Johnson ' "A Modified Form of Slavery" ', pp.736–7.
89. Cockburn to Russell, 6 April 1840, No. 20, CO 23/107.
90. Russell to Cockburn, 30 May 1840 (draft), CO 23/107.
91. Charles Bayley to the Duke of Newcastle, 22 Aug. 1860, No. 82, CO 23/163.
92. For a discussion of this point see Johnson, ' "A Modified Form of Slavery" ', pp.735–6.
93. Bayley to Newcastle, 16 Nov. 1860, No. 107, CO 23/163.
94. For a discussion of changing Colonial Office policy towards long-term labour contracts for immigrants, see K.O. Laurence, 'The Evolution of Long-Term Labour Contracts in Trinidad and British Guiana 1834–1863', *Jamaican Historical Review* 5 (1965), pp.9–27.
95. Minute by Rogers, 16 Oct. 1860 on Bayley to Newcastle, 22 Aug. 1860, No. 82, CO 23/163. Sir Frederic Rogers succeeded Herman Merivale as Permanent Under-Secretary of State for the Colonies in May 1860.
96. Chichester S. Fortescue to Bayley, 23 Oct. 1860, No. 111 (draft). CO 23/164.
97. 24 Vic. C.2. Cf. Jonathan W. Wiener, 'Class Structure and Economic Development in the American South, 1865–1955', *American Historical Review* 84 (1979), p.974.
98. 'An Act to amend An Act, entitled An Act to provide for the care of Africans brought to, or otherwise arriving in the Colony, from vessels engaged in the African Slave Trade', 25 Vic. C.5; 'An Act to provide for the care of Africans brought to, or otherwise arriving in the Colony from Vessels engaged in the

African Slave Trade', 26 Vic. C.16.

99. Johnson, ' "A Modified Form of Slavery" ', pp.736–7.
100. For a different view, see Laurence, 'The Evolution of Long-Term Labour Contracts', p.9.

The Settlement of Chinese in Guyana in the Nineteenth Century

This article examines the process by which Chinese immigrant workers settled and adjusted to life in Guyana after slavery. It assesses their contribution to the plantation system and their efforts to establish independent economic enterprises after their indentureships. It also analyses the social and cultural adjustments imposed by the conditions of migration and plantation life. The Chinese, aided by patterns of residential segregation, were able to retain important aspects of their traditional culture to mould a distinct ethnic identity and group cohesiveness. The attendant problems of integration into the host society are also treated.

Chinese migration to Guyana during the nineteenth century was in direct response to the demand for labour by the sugar plantations after the abolition of slavery. The large-scale withdrawal of the ex-slaves from plantation work left a vacuum in the labour market which the planters sought to fill from any available source. Thus in 1843, the idea of recruiting labour from China was raised; but since the British government frowned on this plan,[1] nothing concrete materialized for a decade. By 1850, however, the planters were able to overcome the imperial government's objections to long-term labour contracts,[2] and thus cleared the way for the recruitment of Chinese immigrant workers. In 1853, the first 647 Chinese arrived in Guyana.[3]

Chinese immigration was always attended by problems, and thus China never became a permanent source of labour for the Guyanese plantations. After 1853, this migration was interrupted until 1859 when it was resumed. But within eight years, it was again stopped because of disagreements between the British and Chinese governments.[4] During that period, 11,282 Chinese went to Guyana. Subsequent efforts to recruit more Chinese were not very successful, and resulted in only two more shipments of a total of 903 immigrants in 1873 and 1879.[5] The Chinese immigrants, therefore, never formed more than 3.5 per cent of the colony's population, and their number actually declined by 46 per cent from 6,880 in 1871 to just 3,714 in 1891.[6]

Although most of the Chinese came from the southern provinces of Fukien and Kwangtung, they were not a homogeneous group. They were composed of two main ethno-linguistic categories, *Punti* and *Hakka*,[7] and were reputed to be either poor, or social outcasts on account of opium addiction. But it also seems that the *T'ai P'ing* rebellion may have contributed refugees to the pool of migrants.[8]

What was very striking about Chinese immigration into Guyana was the acute shortage of women. In 1863, at the peak of this migration, there were only 13.64 Chinese females per 100 males;[9] and even though the ratio improved slightly to 25.7 by 1880, it was far from adequate. Even then the ratio was just four females per 100 males among the Chinese indentured workers on the plantations.[10] As late as 1891, there were only 1,131 women out of a total Chinese population of 3,714 (that is, 30.5 per cent).[11] This generally low proportion of females was a major factor for the inability of the Chinese community to sustain its size by natural increase in the late nineteenth century.

The paucity of women among the Chinese immigrants was in part due to the suspicion with which emigration to Guyana and the Caribbean was regarded in China. The recruiting agents also attributed it to female infanticide and to the alleged custom of crippling the feet of women to make them unfit for agricultural labour and for loco-motion.[12] It is more likely, however, that these were merely rationalizations to explain away their own preferences for males who were considered far more suitable for the rigorous conditions of labour on the Guyanese plantations.[13]

In Guyana, the Chinese were distributed to plantations all over the country. Almost two-thirds were located in Demerara (mainly along the coast), about 21 per cent in Essequibo, and about 15 per cent in Berbice.[14] They, however, experienced grave difficulties in acclimatizing. Twenty-nine of the first immigrants in 1853 were hospitalized on arrival, and ten died soon after.[15] The mortality rate in that first year was 11.26 per cent.[16] This pattern reasserted itself when Chinese immigration was resumed in 1859, reaching a peak of 15.73 per cent in 1861. If even that was an unusually unhealthy year in the colony, and some Chinese may also have died from the effects of their addition to opium,[17] these are not sufficient to account for the generally high mortality from which they continuously suffered.

It is in fact quite clear that insanitary living quarters and poor medical facilities on the plantations contributed in no small way to the high mortality rates.[18] The location of plantations was also an important factor. Thus the highest mortality was experienced in the more humid Essequibo islands,[19] and the lowest on the dryer Corentyne coast in Berbice.[20] Generally speaking, however, the mortality rates declined once the surviving immigrants acclimatized. Thus during the 1870s, the rates were about two per cent per annum.[21]

On the plantations, the Chinese were provided with rudimentary quarters in a barrack building in the old 'negro yard'.[22] Though housed separately from other resident workers, they suffered from the general conditions of over-crowding, poor ventilation, poor sanitation, poor water supplies, poor and risky cooking facilities, and insecurity so prevalent on the Guyanese plantations.[23] Nevertheless they did try to add basic comforts to their otherwise spartan surroundings.[24]

All Chinese were recruited to work on the plantations as indentured workers. In 1864 their contractual period of service was increased from three to five years, with the 'option' of reindenturing for further five-year periods.[25] As indentured workers, they were subject to the general laws governing contract labour. Thus they were required to perform five tasks (worth five shillings) per week; and if they did not complete those tasks they were liable to be fined and/or imprisoned. Similar penalties were imposed for failure to attend the daily roll-call or to begin or finish work, for absence without leave, drunkenness at work, use of abusive of threatening language to plantation officials, and for bad behaviour on the plantation. Indentured workers could have their wages withheld for a number of reasons, and were not infrequently subjected to verbal and physical abuse. Because the laws were so weighted against the worker, there was not much chance of obtaining redress for any wrong.[26]

Despite the injustices and rigours of the indenture system, the Chinese made fine workers as long as they were not affected by opium. They were generally regarded as the best plantation workers in the colony 'for expertness and really natty work'. They worked mainly in the field as drain-diggers, drillers, stumpers and trenchers, shovellers and forkers. But they were not employed much in the factory,[27] even though they reputedly learned to operate the machinery more quickly than other workers.[28] Some planters thus preferred the Chinese to other indentured workers.[29]

The earnings of the Chinese do seem to reflect their high value as field workers. For instance, at Plantation Blankenburg in 1853, while 33 Chinese earned only $138.24 in their first six weeks (just 13 cents each per task), in the next four weeks they earned $183.52 (27.8 cents per task), and $105.96 in the next two weeks (32.1 cents each per task) – the statutory rate was 24 cents per task.[30] Likewise, in 1870 at Plantation Peters Hall, over a period of five weeks, 54 Chinese earned between $6 and $12 each. The average for the whole period was $5.44 or 22 cents per day.[31] Their ability and willingness to work, however, did not mean that they could be trampled upon. They were reputed to possess a keen sense of justice and were capable of strong resentment at anything that appeared unjust.[32] In such cases they were considered far more turbulent and refractory than the other immigrants.[33]

Although they were excellent workers, they were still open to exploitation and abuse. Disputes over wages from time to time led to several Chinese protests.[34] They were also physically abused by plantation staff.[35] So like other indentured workers, the Chinese resorted to sick-outs, work stoppages, strikes, incendiarism, assault and rioting in order to draw attention to their misfortunes. The 1860s in particular were rife with unrest among the Chinese.[36] This prompted the *Colonist* newspaper to assert that 'ordinary prison life seems to be nothing very unpleasant to the Chinaman'; and it observed that the number of Chinese incarcerated in the Georgetown gaol was out of proportion to their numbers in the colony.[37]

Throughout the period of Chinese indentureship, several attempted to desert the plantations altogether.[38] Though reliable statistics are not available, the press reports do suggest that desertion was very commonplace. While some Chinese deserters were apprehended by the police, several others were evidently successful and in some cases managed to escape to neighbouring Surinam, Trinidad and Cayenne.[39] For a few, however, escape took the form of suicide. Between 1865 and 1879, for instance, 29 Chinese committed suicide[40] through overdoses of opium.[41]

Most Chinese, however, tried to make the most of a situation that was far from ideal. Although the indenture system was quite oppressive, many Chinese found it financially rewarding to reindenture for more than one term. Some even commuted one term in order to reindenture. The main reason was the offer by the planters of a bounty of $50 to those who reindentured for a new five-year term.[42] This was an irresistable enticement, representing over 40 weeks' pay at the statutory rate. Thus many Chinese seized this opportunity; and between 1865 and 1870, for instance, 6,359 Chinese reindentured. Some cleverly absconded after receiving the bounty and went to other territories.[43]

While indentured on the plantations, some Chinese tried to supplement their meagre wages by cultivating cash crops in gardens around their dwellings and in the provision plots at the back of the plantations. This was a great boon to them. Where possible they cultivated these gardens intensively and were able to obtain good monetary returns from their efforts.[44] Several plantations, however, attempted to restrict this activity in order to prevent the Chinese from lessening their dependence on them. Thus in 1870, of the 97 plantations on which Chinese were located, more than half with over 2,000 of the 5,000 indentured Chinese, provided no garden plots at all. On the others, there was a total of 248 acres of gardens which the remaining 3,000 indentured Chinese had to share with their unindentured brethren. Of this total, 110 acres were located on two estates alone.[45] Some Chinese also reared livestock which was valued at $6,864 in 1870.[46]

To supplement their rations, many Chinese embarked on armed nocturnal raids of the provision grounds and stockyards of plantations and neighbouring villages. Large gangs of between 20 and 50 Chinese would roam the countryside armed with cutlasses fastened to long sticks, and terrorize plantation watchmen and village peasants. They used these weapons to such 'good' effect that several villagers and watchmen lost their lives in these nocturnal affrays. In 1861, the plantations were forced to arm their watchmen in order to combat these marauders, several of whom were in turn killed or wounded.[47]

Special laws were also passed in 1862 and 1865 to curb the Chinese gangs. The convicted offender was liable to a public flogging of up to 39 lashes;[48] but since the Chinese moved in such large numbers it was difficult to apprehend and punish many of them.[49] During the 1870s, however, these raids declined in frequency and intensity.[50]

For people who had migrated in the hope of acquiring some wealth, indentured labour on the plantations proved unfulfilling. No matter how industrious and frugal, their low wages did not enable them to accumulate real wealth. The only chance of doing so was by engaging in non-plantation economic enterprise.[51] But before the 1870s, such opportunities were very limited. Good arable land was not readily available because it was controlled either by the government or the planters, both of whom tried to restrict its accessibility to the ex-slaves and immigrant workers.[52] And retail trading and other service occupations were dominated by Portuguese immigrants who employed various tactics to keep out competitors.[53]

Nevertheless, by the early 1870s, the Chinese began to leave plantation work and to pursue alternative, independent occupations. This trend was accelerated after the practice of reindenturing came to an end.[54] Largely through missionary lobbying, the idea of granting land to promote the permanent settlement of Chinese immigrants gained favour among the colonial authorities.[55] The successful evangelical work of a Chinese missionary, Wu Tai Kam, among his fellow immigrants further helped to enlist the influential support of the Anglican bishop. Thus in 1865 the governor was eventually persuaded to make a grant of land at Camoenie Creek (22 miles up the Demerara river) for the settlement of Chinese who had completed their indentures. Called Hopetown, it was also the beneficiary of a government loan of £600 to facilitate the clearing, draining, and laying out of the land.[56]

Hopetown became the initial base of independent Chinese small-farming enterprise in Guyana. The pioneers, mainly Christian Chinese converts from Plantation Skeldon in Berbice, built thatched-roofed houses, cultivated a variety of crops (potatoes, ginger, vegetables, cassava, plantains, bananas, etc.), and reared cattle, pigs and poultry. Rice was grown on the freshly cleared ground before it was drained for other crops, and stone houses were used for husking and charring the grain.[57]

If agriculture, both for subsistence and for cash, was vital for the success of this settlement, it was mainly from the manufacture and sale of charcoal and shingles that the settlers derived most of their income. Within two months of settling, they had constructed 15 large furnaces or ovens for the manufacture of charcoal, with walls three to five feet thick, and with a capacity of 50–100 barrels.[58] With 40 such ovens by 1867, the impact on the local market of this small community of 170 Chinese was so great that they not only broke the Portuguese monopoly in the charcoal industry, but sold a superior product at 30 per cent less.[59] In order to market their products, they established a retail business in the capital, Georgetown,[60] which was also an important signal of their subsequent success in undermining the Portuguese dominance in that field.

Although the Hopetown settlement thrived for a few years, it eventually declined economically, partially because the distance from the Georgetown market was a great handicap, but more importantly because proper drainage proved too difficult to maintain without continued government assistance.[61] Hopetown thus faced the same economic stagnation as so many other villages in nineteenth century Guyana for want of government assistance. The settlement may also have suffered from the acute shortage of women which afflicted the Chinese community as a whole and made it impossible for it to maintain its numerical size.

Hopetown was by no means the only Chinese settlement in Guyana. Their establishment of several small agricultural communities was made possible during the 1870s and 1880s as a result of a new government policy of making lands available for the settlement of ex-indentured immigrants. Chinese immigrants thus settled along the Demerara river,[62] on the west coast of Demerara,[63] and on the Corentyne coast in Berbice. No. 72 village, Corentyne, for instance, was labelled 'Hong Kong' because of its essentially Chinese population which was engaged in a thriving rice cultivation.[64]

By the 1870s, the Chinese also began to infiltrate the licensed service sector, in particular the retail trade and transportation.[65] Starting out on a co-operative basis[66] to counter the aggressive Portuguese dealings, by 1870 some Chinese had set up small shops on several estates.[67] Already by 1877 one Chinese trading firm, Messrs. Kwong-san-Lung & Co., was importing most of its merchandise directly or indirectly from China.[68]

By the 1890s, the Chinese were well on their way to breaking the Portuguese stranglehold of the retail trade and, apart from numerous shops and stores scattered in the villages and plantations, they had established commercial bases in the Lombard Street area of Georgetown and along Main Street in New Amsterdam.[69] Indeed, both of these urban streets became virtual Chinese enclaves by the late nineteenth century. With respect to the former, the *Colonist* noted that, 'Lombard Street and the Southern end of Water Street, and all the little by-streets branching therefrom are alive with Celestials of every grade … in Lombard Street it will soon be the exception to meet men of any other race [than Chinese].'[70]

These small shops and stores both in town and country laid the foundation for the dramatic Chinese commercial expansion which took place after the turn of the century with the rise of chain-shop enterprises such as Ho A-Shoo Ltd., Hing Cheong & Co., and the vast commercial empire of Evan Wong, who by 1915 not only owned a vast chain of shops and stores, but also several plantations of rubber, cocoa, coffee and coconuts, balata and goldmining grants (including the rich Omai gold mines in Essequibo), sawmills, and shares in several companies in Georgetown.[71]

A few Chinese also engaged as butchers, druggists, 'traders in anything for which a market can be found', cart and cab owners, barbers and hairdressers, laundry-men, and skilled moulders and engravers of jewellery[72] of whom the best known was M.U. Hing.[73] The table below shows the number of licences held by Chinese in the service sector at the end of the nineteenth century.

LICENCES HELD BY CHINESE, 1899–1900[74]

Type	Number
Spirit Shops	25
Provision, butcher, drug shops/stores	425
Wine and malt	191
Opium and ganja	83
Hucksters	10
Donkey & mule carts, cabs and carriages	82
Horses, mules and donkeys	108
Batteaux, boats, punts, schooners, etc.	140

The successful Chinese penetration of the service sector was a major achievement. It was this which enabled them to accumulate wealth and improve their socio-economic status in the colonial society. They were reputedly industrious, self-reliant, and unobtrusive.[75] – a factor which was very crucial in averting the growth of overt animosity towards them as an ethnic group in a racially segmented society. In 1877, the *Royal Gazette* was obliged to comment on the growing opulence of the Chinese.[76] Apart from their commercial enterprises and stock-in-trade, their material prosperity was demonstrated by the amount of property they owned. By the end of the century, the Chinese owned property in Georgetown valued at $93,150, in New Amsterdam at $71,375, and in the rural areas at $24,056.[77] This was fairly substantial at existing land prices which generally ranged between $5–25 per acre.

Because the Chinese were not entitled to free or assisted return passages to China, most of them had no choice but to settle permanently in Guyana. A few, however, were able to accumulate sufficient money to pay their way back home. Some went to neighbouring territories such as Surinam, Cayenne, Trinidad, St. Lucia, Barbados, and even further to Jamaica. During the 1870s, the St. Lucian government encouraged Guyanese Chinese to migrate there by clandestinely paying their passages. The Guyana government, however, strongly disapproved of this[78] and, in 1876, passed legislation to forbid the issue of passports to immigrants who had not resided in the colony for at least five years unless they paid the Immigration Agent-General the equivalent of the cost of their introduction.[79] This was clearly intended to prevent the outflow of Chinese. By the 1890s, Chinese emigration had declined significantly.[80]

Permanent settlement, however, was not synonymous with socio-cultural integration. From the moment of their initial introduction as indentured workers, the Chinese immigrants were housed in relative isolation on the plantations and were thus kept apart from the local creole population centred in rural villages and towns. This tendency towards ethnic separatism was maintained after their indentureship was completed by the establishment of rural Chinese settlements and small urban enclaves. It was even encouraged by the colonial government, which in providing land for the Hopetown settlement, forced creole woodcutters to vacate the area to make way for the Chinese settlers.[81]

Indeed the integration of the Chinese was affected by attitudes of mutual suspicion between them and the creoles. All immigration was anathema to the creoles who were taxed to pay for the introduction of aliens to compete with them for jobs on the plantations and thus lower the price of labour.[82] By the late 1850s when significant numbers of Chinese began to arrive, large-scale immigration had already begun to lower wages and to make creole workers redundant.[83] Creoles made very little distinction between their dislike of the policy of immigration and of immigrants *per se*. Invariably this was expressed in racial terms.[84]

The Chinese, too, harboured racial prejudices towards the creoles and were not keen on mixing with them. They allegedly regarded 'all coloured races as barbarians who possess neither refinement nor education'. So deep-seated was their aversion towards the creoles that in 1861, the acting governor was obliged to advise plantation managers against employing blacks as 'drivers' or sub-overseers of Chinese work gangs.[85] Despite the severe shortage of Chinese women, these immigrants showed no inclination to develop intimate relationships with creole women.[86]

Although these strong prejudices and inhibitions may have been diluted with time (to the point where even the missionary, Wu Tai Kam, could develop an intimate relationship with a creole woman),[87] it is evident that intermarriage between Chinese and creoles was extremely rare in the nineteenth century.[88]

In general the relations between the Chinese and creoles were tarnished by small-scale violence. Chinese were the objects of insults and assaults by creoles in the streets. According to the *Guiana Times*, the most respectable-looking Chinese were compelled by mere numbers to submit to the greatest indignities in public while onlooking policemen refused to arrest the offenders. Some Chinese were also humiliated and dishonoured by having their 'tails' (plaited hair at the back of their heads) cut off without any excuse.[89] Occasionally such instances of unprovoked bullying even led to the murder of the unfortunate Chinese victim.[90]

On the other hand, when organized in gangs, the Chinese were themselves quite violent. Their nocturnal raids of plantation and village stockyards and provision grounds frequently resulted in the wounding and even the murder of intervening creoles. There were also a few instances of communal violence between Chinese immigrants and creoles as, for instance, in 1853 at Blankenburg-Den Amstel on the west coast of Demerara,[91] in 1863 at Plantation Zeelandia in

Essequibo,[92] and in 1866 at Plantation Bel Air on the east coast of Demerara.[93]

Fortunately, such instances of communal violence involving the Chinese were quite rare. As an ethnic group, they did not attract considerable adverse attention from the creole majority despite the existence of mutual racial animosity. This was in part due to the fact that they were a small minority who were not perceived as a major threat to creole interests. Even after their successful movement into the retail trade and their growing prosperity by the late nineteenth century, there is no evidence of a growing antagonism between them as a community of traders and the creole consumers.

This contrasts markedly with the case of the other major trading group in Guyana, the Portuguese, and indeed even with other Chinese communities in Jamaica and Trinidad.[94] The main reason for this difference is that whereas these other communities dominated retail trading in these colonies and were consequently considered 'secondary colonists' and 'an exploiter class', the Chinese in Guyana were the 'underdogs' struggling to compete against the firmly established Portuguese traders. Their participation in the retail trade was undoubtedly more favourably regarded because it resulted in lower prices to the consumer. If anything, therefore, it may have *weakened*, rather than intensified, creole hostility towards the Chinese community.

The Chinese nevertheless remained a distinctive ethnic minority with a strong sense of group cohesiveness based on a distinct racial and cultural identity. They were readily identifiable by their dress which generally consisted of a loose jacket and blue cotton trousers for both males and females. The women also wore chignons as headgear, while the men wreathed their 'pigtails' (plaited hair) round their heads and wore hats of their own making.[95] Females generally whitened their faces with cosmetics to enhance their beauty in accordance with Chinese aesthetic standards. Some brides continued to keep their faces whitened for a long time after marriage, but respectable widows never used cosmetics whatever their age. The women also adorned their heads with flowers and wore ornamental jewellery on their hands, necks and arms.[96]

Because of the severe female shortage, these immigrants could not easily reconstitute the traditional Chinese family in Guyana. Not surprisingly, the number of Chinese children was small,[97] and indeed the Chinese community could not maintain its numerical size during the nineteenth century. Nevertheless for those who could marry Chinese women and start a family, domestic life was generally characterized by a sense of decorum and good breeding in familial relations. For instance, no one ate meals before all were ready, and food was divided equally.[98] This, however, did not prevent the occasional 'wife-bashing' from occurring.[99]

The unavailability of historical data makes it extremely difficult to reconstruct the socio-cultural organization of the Chinese community in Guyana during the nineteenth century. But it is very probably that the nocturnal gangs alluded to before may have been manifestations of Chinese secret societies similar to those found in other overseas Chinese communities. In South-east Asia, these were known as the *Triad*, and were patterned on those in Fukien and Kwangtung. These societies provided the Chinese overseas with ethnic group organization in the absence of traditional territorial and kinship systems, and also served political and economic functions. But they were reputedly mainly criminal organizations whose overriding purpose was robbery and extortion.[100]

An important function of secret societies in South-east Asia was the operation of gambling and opium dens.[101] The fact that these were also prevalent among the Chinese immigrants in Guyana, both on and off the plantations, is further suggestive of the existence of similar societies there.[102] Some Chinese were such inveterate gamblers that it was not unusual for them to squander $50 to $100 in one night (equivalent to 40–80 weeks' wages at the statutory rate!). Until the 1880s when they were opened to the general public, these dens remained secret and exclusive only to the Chinese.[103]

That the Chinese gangs or secret societies in Guyana had criminal and economic functions, there is no doubt. Whether they were also intended to provide the immigrants with corporate organization and leadership in order to build a cohesive ethnic community in a racially hostile and alien social environment is difficult to determine. That, however, would have been the extent of their political significance. Because the Chinese were numerically too small to form an important political grouping, there was no need to enlist the support of these organizations as, for instance, in Indonesia.[104] On the contrary, the colonial authorities were distinctly hostile to these organized Chinese gangs and ruthlessly attempted to suppress them.

Since most traditional Chinese cultural events are family oriented, and because the severe shortage of women rendered it extremely difficult to reconstruct the Chinese family in Guyana, not many Chinese festivities appeared to have survived the crossing.[105] Further-more, the need to conform to the work routine of the plantations meant that the Chinese immigrants could only celebrate cultural events when granted time-off by the management. In addition, since many of them were (as will be shown) converted to Christianity, they had to give up some of their cultural customs. These conditions thus imposed serious limitations on their ability to practise their traditional religious and secular culture.

These immigrants, nevertheless, continued to celebrate their greatest cultural festival, the New Year. There is no evidence, how-ever, that in Guyana they were able to engage in the same type of elaborate preparations as in China where the activities lasted about one month, commencing at the beginning of the twelfth lunar month and reaching a climax in the last ten days.[106] This was partially due to the fact that the work routine on the plantations simply did not permit them the necessary time. And, in any case, because much of the traditional house-cleaning and religious observances in preparation for the festival are family oriented,[107] they were probably not strictly observed by this essentially single-male community.

The immigrants, however, did maintain the tradition of celebrating their New Year on the second new moon after the winter solstice[108] (that is, either in January or February) with a lavish display of food, fruit and drink.[109] As in China, the climax of the New Year festivities was reached on the fifteenth day of the first month with the lantern festival, *Cheng Yueh Shih Wu*. The display of lanterns symbolizes the brightness and good luck that the family hopes for, and the chasing out of the darkness and bad luck that they wish to avoid.[110] In Guyana, large Chinese processions paraded through the streets with lighted lanterns of various sizes, shapes and colours, depicting birds, fishes, etc. They were accompanied by the loud music of bagpipes, gongs, cymbals and tom-toms, and by the display of fireworks and crackers[111] as a manifestation of happiness, and to scare away demons.[112]

One of the factors which affected the ability of the Chinese immigrants to preserve their traditional culture in Guyana was the influence of Christianity. Euro-Christian ideology and dogma, disseminated in both church and school, were employed as a mechanism of social control, and were intended, *inter alia*, to instil notions of white superiority and to inculcate attitudes of deference and obedience to the white ruling minority.[113] Specifically in relation to the Chinese, the proselytization of Christianity was also expressly calculated to curb the growth and influence of secret societies among them.[114]

The receptivity of the Chinese to Christianity was enhanced by the fact that some of them had already been converted before emigrating to Guyana.[115] Thus on arrival they were keen to attend chapels.[116] On the recommendation of a German missionary, Rev. Lobscheid, several of these Chinese Christians were located at contiguous plantations on the Corentyne coast of Berbice (Skeldon, and Eliza and Mary) to facilitate their worship in the Chinese language.[117]

With the advent of the Chinese missionary, Wu Tai Kam, in 1864, the conversion of these immigrants was considerably accelerated.[118] In 1866 he was officially appointed Missionary to the Chinese immigrants on a government stipend of £300 per annum, and was instrumental in seeking the grant of land for the Chinese settlement of Hopetown.[119] It was, significantly, mainly the Chinese Christians from the Corentyne who formed the nucleus of the Hopetown settlers.[120] By 1867 when Wu Tai Kam left the colony, the groundwork had been firmly laid for the large scale conversion of the Chinese immigrants.[121] By the late 1880s, there were few Chinese who were not Christians.[122]

As a mechanism of social control, Christianity had positive effects among the Chinese. They were reportedly transformed as social beings,[123] and there was a noticeable correlation between their conversion and the decline in the nocturnal activities of the Chinese gangs. If this signified a dissolution of the secret societies, then it certainly was a highly successful process.

But although the Chinese converts were required to abandon certain aspects of traditional culture which were considered incompatible with Euro-Christian morality, their conversion did not seem to entail complete 'de-Sinocization' or an overt acceptance of white superiority. Christian worship was conducted in the Chinese language by Chinese catechists; and, during the 1870s and 1880s, the Chinese built their own ethnic churches in several parts of the colony.[124] Converts continued to celebrate the Chinese New Year by adding special church services to the traditional practices.[125] In this context, the process of Euro-Christianization was not as complete as may have been hoped for.

Towards the end of the nineteenth century, the Chinese community was a permanent, integral, albeit distinctly separate, component of Guyanese society. In 1891, with two-thirds of its membership still foreign-born,[126] it showed very little sign of integrating fully into the host society; and since women still composed only 30 per cent of its members,[127] its inability to sustain its numerical size meant that the Chinese were increasingly becoming an endangered species. Nevertheless their impact, especially in the economic sphere, far exceeded their numerical strength. By 1900 this small ethnic group had not only made an important contribution to the agricultural economy of the colony, both as plantation workers and as small farmers, but had also become very influential in the commercial sector as well.

BRIAN L. MOORE
*University of the West Indies,
Mona, Kingston, Jamaica*

NOTES

1. K.O. Laurence, *Immigration into the West Indies in the Nineteenth Century* (St. Lawrence, Barbados, 1971), p.36.
2. See K.O. Laurence, 'The Evolution of Long-Term Contracts in Trinidad and British Guiana, 1834–1863', *Jamaica Historical Review*, 5 (1965). In 1848, three-year contracts were imposed on all immigrants, and in 1864 Chinese immigrants were subjected to five-year contracts.
3. Laurence, *Immigration into the West Indies.*
4. Ibid, pp.36–8.
5. Colonial Land and Emigration Commissioners (hereafter CLEC) to Herbert, 22 and 24 March 1873, CO 318/271 and Kortright to Hicks Beach, 19 Jan. 1880, No. 13, CO 384/128.
6. Decennial censuses, 1861–1891.
7. Enclosure 4 in Walker to Newcastle, 19 Nov. 1861, No. 83, CO 111/332; Mundy to Carnarvon, 4 April 1866, No. 37, CO 111/362. According to Fried, the difference between these two groups is essentially linguistic. See M.H. Fried, 'Some Observations on the Chinese in British Guiana', *Social and Economic Studies*, 5

(1956), pp.61–2.
8. See C.C. Clementi, *The Chinese in British Guiana* (Georgetown, 1915), pp.333–49.
9. Hincks to Newcastle, 4 May 1864, No. 89, CO 111/345.
10. Report of the Immigration Agent-General (hereafter IAG), 15 Oct. 1881, in *Administration Reports, 1880*.
11. Decennial census for 1891.
12. Barkly to Grey, 31 Oct. 1851, No. 152, Parl. Papers, 1852–53, LXVIII.
13. The strong preference for male workers is much better documented in relation to the larger migration of Indians, but essentially the same considerations would have prevailed in the recruitment of Chinese.
14. Clementi, op. cit., Table VI (appendix).
15. Blair to Barkly, n.d. Enclosed in Barkly to Newcastle, 26 Feb. 1853, No. 32, CO 111/294.
16. Enclosure in Wodehouse to Grey, 21 July 1854, No. 41, CO 111/301.
17. See, for instance, Hincks to Newcastle, 21 May 1862, No. 78 and enclosures, IAG reports of 9 May and 25 Nov. 1862. The medical reports of the Immigration Department reveal consistently high mortality rates among the Chinese: in 1859 – 7.95 per cent; 1860 – 8.97 per cent; 1861 – 15.73 per cent; and 5.41 per cent between Jan. and June 1862. Between 1863 and 1867, the annual rate varied between 4.75 per cent and 6.61 per cent.
18. Lobscheid to Walker, 19 July 1861. Enclosed in Walker to Newcastle, 19 Nov. 1861, No. 83, CO 111/332; and enclosures in Hincks to Buckingham and Chandos, 20 Feb. 1868, No. 16, CO 111/366.
19. Reports of the IAG enclosed in Hincks to Newcastle, 21 May 1862, No. 78, CO 111/334. In 1861, for instance, the mortality rate among the Chinese was 30.61 per cent in Leguan, and 39.57 per cent in Wakenaam.
20. All the reports of the IAG during the 1860s clearly indicate that the Corentyne experienced far less mortality than other parts of the colony.
21. See the reports of the IAG for the period 1873–80. In 1873, the mortality rate among the Chinese was only 1.84 per cent, in 1874, 1.98 per cent, and in 1880, 1.64 per cent.
22. Report of Dr Shier, 23 May 1865 in *Colonist*, 1 June 1865.
23. See my 'Social and Cultural Complexity in British Guiana, 1850–1891' (unpublished Ph.D. thesis, University of the West Indies, 1973), pp.200–205.
24. Barkly to Newcastle, 7 April 1853, No. 54, CO 111/294.
25. See Ordinance No. 4 of 1864.
26. Moore, op. cit., pp.210–29.
27. Anon, The Overseer's Manual in *Argosy*, 5 April 1884.
28. Report of the [1870] Commissioners (ms.), sec. 13, CO 111/379.
29. Barkly to Newcastle, No. 54, loc. cit.
30. Enclosure in Barkly, No. 54, loc. cit.; and enclosure in Barkly to Newcastle, 3 May 1853, No. 73, CO 111/294.
31. Report of the [1870] Commissioners (ms.), appendix C, CO 111/382.
32. Report of the [1870] Commissioners (ms.), sec. 13, supra. cit.
33. Enclosure 3 in Walker to Newcastle, 8 July 1853, No. 29, pp.1852–53, LXVII.
34. *Creole*, 16 and 19 May 1860; Hincks to Newcastle, 22 March 1862, No. 40, CO 111/334.
35. *Creole*, 7 Nov. 1860.
36. See note 31. Also *Creole*, 25 July 1860; *Royal Gazette*, 11 July and 1 Oct. 1861; *Colonist*, 12 Dec. 1866, 24 March 1868, 18 Sept. and 22 Nov. 1869.
37. *Colonist*, 28 June 1866.
38. Report of the [1870] Commissioners (ms.), sec. 13, supra cit.
39. *Colonist*, 6 Jan. 1864, 16 Jan. 1868, 1 Feb. 1869, 4 Sept. 1875; *Royal Gazette*, 4 June 1872; *Creole*, 16 and 27 June 1873; *Demerara Daily Chronicle*, 27 Aug. 1882.
40. Report of the [1870] Commissioners (ms.), sec. 22, CO 111/380.
41. *Creole*, 5 May, 7 and 18 July 1860; *Colonist*, 3 Oct. 1860 and 22 Oct. 1864; *Berbice*

Gazette, 19 Aug. 1865; *Demerara Times*, 20 Aug. and 6 Sept. 1875.
42. CLEC to Merivale, 17 Feb. 1857, No. 1526, CO 318/215.
43. Report of the [1870] Commissioners (ms.), sec. 13, supra cit.
44. Enclosure in Scott to Kimberley, 4 April 1873, No. 48, CO 111/397; also report of the [1870] Commissioners (ms.), appendix c, supra cit.
45. Report of the [1870] Commissioners (ms.), sec. 24, CO 111/380.
46. Report of the [1870] Commissioners (ms.), sec. 3, CO 111/379.
47. The newspapers of the 1860s are replete with reports of such incidents. See also Cox to Austin, 18 Aug. 1867, enclosed in Mundy to Buckingham and Chandos, 22 Aug. 1867, No. 114, CO 111/363.
48. Enclosure in Hincks to Newcastle, 16 Dec. 1862, No. 212, CO 111/337; and enclosure in Hincks to Cardwell, 1 Dec. 1865, No. 189, CO 111/353.
49. See *Colonist* of 11, 24 and 26 July 1866, 12 Sept. 1866, and 10 July 1867; Report of the [1870] Commissioners (ms.), sec. 25, CO 111/380; and Hincks to Buckingham and Chandos, 21 Nov. 1867, No. 161, CO 111/364.
50. *Royal Gazette*, 20 Jan. 1874 and 26 Oct. 1875; also *Colonist*, 14 Aug. 1875.
51. Wodehouse to Newcastle, 25 Feb. 1860, No. 31, CO 111/326.
52. See my 'Social and Cultural Complexity', pp.103–4.
53. See my 'The Social Impact of Portuguese Immigration into British Guiana after Emancipation', *Boletín de Estudios Latino Americanos y del Caribe*, No. 19 (1975).
54. This practice was priced out of existence after 1875 when the bounty reached $200.
55. The German missionary, Lobscheid, was the first to advocate granting land to the Chinese for settlement, and this was later taken up by the Chinese missionary, Wu Tai Kam, with the support of the Anglican bishop. See Lobscheid to Walker, 19 July 1861 in Walker to Newcastle, No. 83, loc. cit.; and Hincks to Cardwell, 21 Feb. 1865, No. 27, CO 111/350.
56. Hincks, No. 27, loc. cit.
57. Enclosures in Hincks to Cardwell, 19 Sept. 1865, No. 155 and 18 Dec. 1865, No. 200, CO 111/353; Report of the [1870] Commissioners (ms.), sec. 24, supra cit.; *Guiana Times*, 1 March 1866; and G.S. Jenman, 'Model Settlers: A Lesson in the Small Industries', *Timehri*, 2 (1883), pp.99–101.
58. Ibid.
59. *Colonist*, 13 Feb. 1867; and Report of the Crown Surveyor, 16 Feb. 1881 in *Administration Reports* for 1880.
60. *Colonist*, 13 Feb. 1867.
61. Jenman, loc. cit.; Scott to Kimberley, 30 Aug. 1872, No. 114, CO 111/391; F.O. Low, 'The Hopetown Chinese Settlement', *Timehri*, 6, No. 23, 3rd series (1919), pp.66–7.
62. *Argosy*, 5 April, 1884.
63. Report of the IAG, 4 Aug. 1882 in *Administration Reports* for 1881.
64. *Colonist*, 14 April, 1881.
65. Report of the [1870] Commissioners (ms.), sec. 24, supra cit.
66. *Creole*, 12 Jan. 1866.
67. Report of the [1870] Commissioners (ms.), appendix C, supra cit.
68. *Colonist*, 16 Aug. 1877.
69. Ibid.; J. Heatley, *A Visit to the West Indies* (London, 1891), p.42; A. Hardy, *Life and Adventure in British Guiana* (London, 1913), p.85; L. Crookall, *British Guiana* (London, 1898), pp.104–5.
70. *Colonist*, 16 Aug. 1877.
71. Clementi, op. cit., pp.333–49.
72. Heatley, op. cit., p.41; *Colonist*, 16 Aug. 1877.
73. Clementi, loc. cit.
74. Report of the IAG for 1899–1900, CO 114/87.
75. *Colonist*, 16 Aug. 1877; Crookall, loc. cit.; Heatley, loc. cit.
76. *Royal Gazette*, 15 Feb. 1877.
77. Report of the IAG for 1899–1900, supra cit.

78. Longden to Carnarvon, 6 Sept. and 8 Oct. 1874, Nos. 165 and 190 respectively, CO 384/103. In 1874, 135 Chinese went to Surinam, 60 to St. Lucia, ten to Trinidad, ten to Jamaica, and two returned to China.
79. Longden to Carnarvon, 1 Dec. 1876, No. 259, CO 384/111.
80. See the reports of the IAG for 1892–1900, CO 114/57–87.
81. Trotman to General Secretary, 1 May 1867, No. 316, MMS/W.v/5.
82. Light to Stanley, 27 Sept. 1844, No. 98, CO 111/213; Light to Stanley, Nos. 203, 204, and 207, of 4 Oct. 1844, CO 111/214; and enclosure in Light to Stanley, 1 Feb. 1845, No. 22, CO 111/220.
83. Report of the [1870] Commissioners (ms.), sec. 26, CO 111/380.
84. Foreman to Tidman, 24 Sept. 1858, LMS 8/2 (Bce); Bleby to Boyce, 22 Oct. 1868, MMS/W.v/2; Creole, 28 Jan. 1874.
85. Enclosures in Walker to Newcastle, No. 83, supra cit.
86. Ibid.; Report of the [1870] Commissioners (ms.), sec. 13, supra cit.; Scott to Kimberley, 18 July 1871, No. 106, CO 111/386; H.V.P. Bronkhurst, The Colony of British Guiana and its Labouring Inhabitants (London, 1883), p.124.
87. Hincks to Buckingham and Chandos, 18 Dec. 1868, No. 177, CO 111/369; Report of the [1870] Commissioners (ms.), sec. 13, supra cit. Although he was married and had a family in Singapore, Wu Tai Kam contracted an intimate relationship with a coloured woman who became pregnant. He consequently decamped from the colony in hurried secrecy.
88. Enclosure 4 in Walker to Newcastle, No. 83, supra cit.; Report of the [1870] Commissioners (ms.), sec. 25, supra cit.
89. Guiana Times, 28 July 1866.
90. Royal Gazette, 28 April 1877; Demerara Daily Chronicle, 22 Aug. 1883.
91. Barkly to Newcastle, 20 Feb. 1853, No. 32, PP, 1852–53, LXVIII.
92. Royal Gazette, 28 May 1863.
93. Ibid., 19 Feb. 1866.
94. See my 'The Social Impact of Portuguese Immigration', supra cit.; also H. Johnson, 'The Anti-Chinese Riots of 1918 in Jamaica', Immigrants and Minorities, 2 (1983); and J. Levy, 'The Economic Role of the Chinese in Jamaica: The Grocery Retail Trade', Jamaican Historical Review, 15 (1986).
95. Bronkhurst, op. cit., pp.114 and 209; E. Jenkins, The Coolie: His Rights and Wrongs (London, 1871), p.64.
96. Bronkhurst, op. cit., pp.211–212.
97. Report of the [1870] Commissioners (Georgetown, 1871), p.137; in 1871 children under 15 years amounted to only 9.2 per cent of the Chinese population.
98. Barkly to Newcastle, 26 Feb. 1853, No. 32, PP, 1852–53, LXVIII.
99. Colonist, 25 Aug. 1864.
100. M. Freedman, 'Immigrants and Associations: Chinese in Nineteenth Century Singapore', Comparative Studies in Society and History (hereafter CSSH), 3 (1960), pp.30–35; and M. Topley, 'The Emergence and Social Function of Chinese Religious Societies in Singapore', CSSH, 3 (1961), pp.62–3.
101. Freedman, loc. cit., p.37.
102. Report of the [1870] Commissioners (ms.), sec. 13, supra cit.; Bronkhurst, op. cit., pp.114–15; Argosy, 5 April 1884.
103. Argosy, 4 Nov. 1882; Daily Chronicle, 11 and 30 May 1888; Heatley, loc. cit.
104. L.W. Crissman, 'The Segmentary Structure of Urban Overseas Chinese Communities', Man, 2 (1967), pp.197–8.
105. W. Eberhard, Chinese Festivals (London, 1958), p.4.
106. M.C. Yang, A Chinese Village (London, 1948), p.90.
107. Ibid., pp.90–92.
108. Eberhard, op. cit., p.32.
109. Anon., loc. cit.
110. Yang, op. cit., p.95; Eberhard, op. cit., pp.62–3.
111. Royal Gazette, 24 Feb. 1880; Colonist, 23 Jan. 1879 and 11 Feb. 1880; Argosy, 2 Feb. 1884 and 14 Feb. 1885; Bronkhurst, op. cit., p.365; Heatley, loc. cit.

112. Yang, op. cit., p.94.
113. See my 'The Problem of Stability in a Racially Segmented Society: Plantation Guiana after Slavery', seminar paper, History Department, UWI, Mona, 1983, pp.8–10.
114. Walker to Newcastle, No. 83 and enclosure 4, supra cit.
115. Lobscheid to the Bishop, 20 Dec. 1859, SPG/E.6; Report of the [1870] Commissioners (ms.), sec. 25, supra cit.; Daily Chronicle, 2 March 1889.
116. Rattray to Tidman, 25 Jan. 1853, LMS 7/8 (Dem); Barkly to Newcastle, No. 32, supra cit.
117. Report of the Guiana Diocesan Church Society for 1861 (Demerara, 1862), p.15; extract from The Guiana Magazine, SPG/E.14; Shrewsbury to the General Secretary, 2 April, 1860, MMS/W.v/5.
118. Enclosure in Murdoch to Rogers, 10 April 1865, No. 3340, CO 318/245; Austin to Bulloch, 20 Aug. 1866, SPG/D.28.
119. Hincks to Cardwell, 21 Feb. 1865, No. 27, CO 111/350; Mundy to Cardwell, 3 Aug. 1866, No. 30, CO 111/360.
120. Hincks to Cardwell, No. 27, loc. cit.; Report of the [1870] Commissioners (ms.), sec. 24, supra cit.
121. Colonist, 19 Nov. 1869; Bridger to Secretary, 30 Dec. 1873, SPG/E.28; Royal Gazette, 6 May 1879; F. Josa, Tale of a Roaming Catholic (London, 1920).
122. Josa to Secretary, 31 Dec. 1887, SPG/E.42.
123. Colonist, 25 April 1876; Josa, Tale, supra cit.
124. Longden to Carnarvon, 4 Dec. 1875, No. 249, CO 111/406; Royal Gazette, 4 Dec. 1875, and 9 Feb. 1878; Demerara Times, 12 Nov. 1875; Colonist, 10 Feb. 1876; Demerara Daily Chronicle, 13 June 1884; Argosy, 5 July 1884; Daily Chronicle, 16 Nov. 1886.
125. Demerara Daily Chronicle, 10 Feb. 1883; Argosy, 6 Feb. 1886.
126. Decennial census for 1891.
127. Ibid.

The Madeiran Portuguese and the Establishment of the Catholic Church in British Guiana, 1835–98

The Madeiran Portuguese first arrived in British Guiana as indentured immigrants on 3 May 1835, bringing their agricultural expertise and their Catholic faith. This article documents the contribution of these immigrants to the growth and expansion of the Roman Catholic Church in the colony. As a result of their presence, new churches were built along the east coast, Demerara, where most of the Portuguese immigrants were concentrated. Private schools, which taught in Portuguese, were also established in Georgetown. The Christmas novena and the guilds and societies of the Madeirans eventually became part of the Catholic culture in British Guiana.

The Catholic Church in Guyana, today now numbering approximately 86,619 adherents,[1] owes its existence, expansion and growth to the Portuguese who first came to British Guiana in 1835 as indentured emigrants to satisfy the labour hunger of the planters.

Although previously there had been intermittent visits of Catholic priests to the territory, it was not until 9 December 1825 that the building of the first Roman Catholic church was begun, and opened by the Rev. J. Hynes, OP in 1827. There is little indication that during the years following the church made much headway. Then in May 1835, the first batch of 40 Madeirans arrived on the *Louisa Baillie* to work on the estates of La Penitence, Liliendaal and Thomas. The agricultural expertise of the Madeiran peasant, born and bred on a small mountainous island of 286 square miles where every inch of soil was precious, was early noted by both the planters and the press. In the first month of their arrival, it was stated that they were proving to be industrious workers, giving 'great satisfaction to their employers'.[2] Unfortunately, in those first months they over-exerted themselves and, subjected to deficiency in diet, poor accommodation and work in an enervating climate, suffering and death resulted. Yet neither suffering nor death deterred others of their countrymen from coming to Demerara. Thirty of the original emigrants had returned to Madeira, encouraging in turn their relatives and friends to cross the ocean and seek their fortune in a land that was being viewed as an 'El Dorado'.

In Madeira, in the 1830s and 1840s, and through the 1880s, poor economic conditions accelerated the exodus of Madeirans who were migrating, not only to Demerara but to Brazil, the West Indies, Africa and the United States of America. Moreover in the eighteenth century, when Madeira's affluence had declined with the downfall of sugar, Madeirans began to emigrate to Brazil in search of 'uma vida melhor'. Between 1835–55, it was estimated that 40,000 left the Madeiran archipelago.[3] In the 1830s, the Agent-General of Madeira reported that there were listed almost 2,000 names of unemployed all eager to set off for British Guiana. The local authorities, deeply concerned over this 'internal haemorrhage' with its resultant crippling effect on the island's agriculture, precarious as it already was, placed obstacles in the way of the emigrants. Information regarding ill-treatment aboard ship and in Demerara was spread. When emigrants tried to leave clandestinely, tight supervision in the Bay of Funchal and around the island was enforced. Other deterrents in the obtaining of a passport, a certificate of baptism, a certificate of exemption from military service were aimed, among others, at curbing emigration.[4]

Regardless of obstacles, the Madeiran emigrants continued to arrive in Demerara. In July 1841, Governor Henry Light wrote to the Colonial Office that the influx from Madeira was considerable and more were expected. The *Blue Book* of 1841 recorded the arrival of 7,600 in February alone. The later introductions seemed to be of a better class and Light felt sanguine that they would acclimatize more easily. Yet 1841 proved to be a bad year for the immigrants. Yellow fever was raging in British Guiana and among the children measles had spread rapidly with fatal results. Concerned over what he claimed was a 'fearful mortality', Governor Light proposed to the Court of Policy that Madeiran emigration be stopped; this proposal in turn was sanctioned by the Colonial Office in 1842.[5] Despite the mortality and resultant suspension of emigration from Madeira, more than 1,200 Portuguese trickled into Demerara between 1842 and 1845 when large-scale bounty immigration was resumed. In 1846, the largest number ever to come to British Guiana in one year arrived – 5,975. By then, many had moved off the plantations into small farming in the villages and into the huckster and retail trade.

From Madeira the Portuguese had brought not only their agricultural and commercial skills, but their devotion to their religion – the Catholic faith. Every writer of Madeiran history agrees that they are a profoundly religious people. As early as 1514, Pope Leo X had created Funchal, the main town of Madeira, a bishopric, and in 1539 raised it to an archbishopric with spiritual jurisdiction over all the newly-discovered lands of the Portuguese. The roots of their faith went deep; their devotion was marked by the simplicity and exuberance of a folk religion, characteristics that, in British Guiana, would be misunderstood and criticized by those belonging to an Anglo-Saxon culture; their faith would be branded a 'Madeiran type of Catholicism – far from perfection in many ways'.[6] The devotion of the Portuguese people to their Church, their God, the Mother of God and the Saints found expression in a multitude of annual *festas*. Their most loved and renowned festival was that of *Nossa Senhora do Monte*. Very early in the history of the island a church to Our Lady of the Mount was built on the spot where, according to legend, many miracles had been performed. Through the years, Madeirans attributed their protection from famine and flood to Our Lady. Daily pilgrimages were made to the shrine, especially by sailors before sailing across the sea. In 1819 one writer, obviously English, noted the celebration of the annual festival thus:

> A grand festival is holden annually in honour of the saint; it begins on the fourth and lasts till the fifteenth of August; during this period the Church is decorated externally with flags of every nation, while drums and fifes are playing throughout the day in the portico of the church, and every evening the temple is superbly illuminated, when a great display of fireworks is exhibited; on the fifteenth day which is called the day of the Lady of the Mount, there are generally collected about twenty thousand persons from all parts of the Island, being attended with a vast deal of bustle and confusion, not unlike the appearance of an English fair.[7]

I

The desire of these people, so far away from their island home, for the religious *festas*, was naturally sharpened. In an alien society speaking only an alien tongue, the need for the security and familiarity of their devotional services and celebrations, both cathartic and cohesive, became even more intense. This need was communicated to the Portuguese government, and through the Agent-General of Immigration, a request was made to Rev. William Bates, then Vicar-General of the Roman Catholic Church, to introduce Portuguese clergymen to supply the spiritual wants of the increasing numbers of Portuguese in British Guiana. Consequently, Rev. Bates petitioned the Court of Policy for three clergymen from Madeira, observing that 1,300 Roman Catholic immigrants had recently arrived from Madeira.[8] The Commission of Inquiry into the Condition of Portuguese Immigrants on the Arabian Coast, 1841, had highlighted this need. Commenting on the high rate of mortality reported by the Commission, the Colonial Office noted that it seemed that a quarter of the Portuguese had died 'without the consolation of their Religion which by adding to their dejection increased their danger'.[9] Governor Light, sensitive to the situation, gave whole-hearted approval to the introduction of the Portuguese clergymen with the approval of Lord Stanley.[10] But it was most unlikely that the Portuguese government would have obliged by sending priests to Demerara, for after the Proclamation of the Constitutional Charter on 5 June 1834 in Madeira, the Church had been suppressed and monasteries disbanded. In Demerara, neither the Court of Policy nor the Combined Court agreed to the recommendation. As far as they were concerned, salaries for such clergymen would mean an additional burden on the finances of the colony. This adamant stand caused Governor Light to complain of injustice towards the Portuguese and to observe the Courts' refusal would surely have caused the Portuguese government to oppose emigration had the suspension not occurred earlier.[11]

With the increasing and urgent need to provide for the spiritual wants of the Portuguese, members of the Catholic Committee wrote a strong petition to the Governor and the two Courts, reminding them, among other things, that the Catholic inhabitants, one-tenth of the population, contributed 'a full quota to the public burdens of taxation' and that the Committee had applied for financial assistance only *once in nineteen years*. Above all, the Courts had failed to honour their pledge to provide for the Portuguese emigrants. The Committee warned that were this pledge not fulfilled, a valuable group of emigrants might well withdraw themselves and their capital, resulting in a check and possible suppression of emigration from Madeira.[12] This petition left the Courts unmoved. Why, they argued, should they grant monies for Portuguese clergymen when, in their calculation, there were only 4,000 Portuguese in the Colony?[13] No doubt the Courts felt it was time that the Portuguese learnt to speak the Queen's English.

Later in the year, to the intense joy of the Portuguese, Bishop Hynes brought out, from Lisbon, Senor Joaquin Antonio Correa de Natividade whom he ordained a priests on 5 October 1845. So ten years after their arrival the Portuguese heard for the first time a sermon preached in their own language. No wonder that they wept for joy.[14] This joy was short-lived as Fr. Correa asked to return to Europe, discouraged at the poor results of his efforts among the Portuguese settlers on the Essequibo coast. One Jesuit writer observed that the faith among the Portuguese was no more than skin-deep and that their 'moral sense was defective',[15] yet he fully acknowledged that the Portuguese constituted 'the backbone of the Church in this Colony'. After a ten-year span in the reception of the Sacraments and the sharing in religious services due to the absence of Portuguese-speaking priests, religious decline and apathy might well be expected. Yet what were later dubbed 'superstitious pietistic customs' by the English Jesuits were still kept alive and bridged the gaps left by the absence of religious devotions. It is recorded in the annals of the Society for the Propagation of the Gospel, that in areas such as Wakenaam in the Essequibo and Beterverwagting on the east coast of Demerara where there was no Catholic priest, the Portuguese, avid for religious instruction and services in their own language, attended the Anglican chapels where the ministers spoke Portuguese[16] – an early ecumenical move arising out of need.

In the 1850s many of the Portuguese had become 'the wealthiest and only ready money people' through their industry and careful habits, as the press noted. Portuguese merchants had begun to charter their own ships to bring in emigrants to work in trade.[17] In the meantime, through the request of Bishop Hynes and the intervention of the Portuguese Minister in London, the Combined Court had been moved to give additional grants to the Roman Catholic establishment which included a stipend for an additional priest speaking the Portuguese language.[18] In 1853 the annual allowance for Catholic priests was raised from $720 to $940 each, on condition that three out of the eight clergymen had knowledge of the Portuguese language.

II

A majority of Portuguese had settled on the east bank of Demerara at Meadow Bank, Ruimveldt and Agricola. This considerable settlement had caused Bishop Hynes in the 1830s to make Meadow Bank the centre of the church and it was in this village on 24 March 1857 that the Catholic Mission of British Guiana was handed over to Fr. James Etheridge, the first Jesuit Superior. This marked the beginning of the 'Jesuit Phase in British Guiana'. Fr. Etheridge had brought with him Frs. Aloysius Emiliani, SJ and Clement Negri, SJ who knew Portuguese. In November six more priests arrived, including Fr. Benedict Schembri, SJ who founded Meadow Bank Church and would become known as 'a real apostle of these people' (the Portuguese). Fr. Schembri, a Maltese, had previously worked in Brazil and learnt the Portuguese language.[19] It was vital that priests coming to work among the Portuguese knew the language, as the Portuguese knew very little English.

From 1857 with the arrival of the Jesuits, above all, of Portuguese-speaking Jesuits, the work of the Roman Catholic Church in British Guiana advanced rapidly. The English Jesuits were aghast at the weakened state of the church and the magnitude of their responsibility to the Portuguese Catholics whom they estimated between 5,000–6,000 in Georgetown alone. They voiced concern over the paucity of baptisms, were loud in condemnation of concubinage and illegitimacy, and could not believe that there was 'scarce a Confession'.[20]

Had the people, so long without the services of a Portuguese-speaking priest, lost the habit of going to confession? With the efforts of Fr. Schembri, a first-rate Missioner, the 'most indefatigable Fr. Pavarelli', the great favourite Fr. Negri, and Fr. Emiliani, 'an active Missioner in Portuguese', a great revival of Catholicism took place. The preaching of the Portuguese-speaking priests drew the Portuguese back to the church in great numbers, the services were packed and Easter communions jumped from 100 in 1857 to 1,000 in 1858.[21] Bishop Etheridge, witnessing this growth, realized his own need to learn the Portuguese language also, and as a result reaped success for his efforts. The other English Jesuits balked at learning the language although this militated against their hearing confessions. Yet Fr. Sherlock attributed the progress in the church to the Italian fathers, expressing the hope that the English would get on with the learning of the Portuguese language.[22] Bishop Etheridge complained that Fr. Walker could neither speak Portuguese nor even understand it, nor would he do so.[23] Frs. Jones, Walker and Wollett were decidedly anti-Portuguese, and this caused much conflict in the apostolate with the Italian and Maltese priests who were more attuned to the customs and religious practices of the Madeirans. Bishop Etheridge observed to the Father Provincial in England: 'Good Fr. Walker cannot conceal his dislike of foreigners and their ways' and was concerned that Walker's attitude 'would offend the prejudices of the Portuguese'.[24] Etheridge was a realist and quite rightly saw that where there were no Portuguese-speaking priests, 'the Churches would be as empty as we found them and the Sacraments except Baptism nearly out of use'.[25] Etheridge's realism did nothing to change the attitude of most of the English Jesuits who hardly ever saw eye to eye with the Italian priests in their policy towards their Portuguese congregation. It seems that their annoyance increased because of what they considered over-protection and prominence given to the Portuguese. It was felt that this favouritism was causing the creole population to fall off in their attendance at mass. A particular irritation was the delivering of sermons in Portuguese. In 1859, only three years after the riots when the creole population, urged on by the 'Angel Gabriel', John Sayers Orr, vented their anger against the Portuguese shopkeepers, such an irritation was understandable. One could agree, in this instance, with Fr. Wollett that it would have been more diplomatic to have the Portuguese sermons after, instead of during, the mass.[26]

III

Fr. Schembri's argument, which did bear some weight, was that in order to revive the Catholic faith and practices that had declined through the barren years, it was imperative for the Portuguese to hear sermons and have instructions in their own language, and to be exposed to religious practices similar to those in Madeira, their hymns and devotions to be encouraged and learned. It is not surprising that he stressed the need for special treatment and, above all, for a special church for the Portuguese, where everything would be in their own language 'without fear of criticism – even from the English clergy'.[27]

In 1858 it was estimated that there were about 35,000 Portuguese in British Guiana and mostly all were Catholics. There was then only one church in Georgetown, one in New Amsterdam, one at Essequibo and one at Victoria on the east coast. Shortly after his arrival in British Guiana in 1857, Bishop Etheridge had notified the Father Provincial in London that if all the backsliders among the wealthy Portuguese, so generous to the poor and needy, so eager to attend baptisms, marriages and funerals, came to mass, their church (Brickdam) 'would be far too small'.[28] Fr. Sherlock also observed that 'at Georgetown, our congregation is more substantial than any I know in England'.[29] With this growth of the Portuguese population, there arose the corresponding need for a church where they would feel at home in their religious customs. Bishop Etheridge gauged the mood of the Portuguese correctly; in April 1860 land was bought in Main Street for $1,000 and a new church at the cost of $1,200 was begun under the direction of Fr. Schembri. By completion, the cost amounted to $18,000. Bishop Etheridge may have taken into consideration Fr. Wollett's concern regarding a schism, for he astutely circumvented such a possibility by legally securing the property to himself and his successors.[30] The church was built against a background of controversy – Fr. Schembri allegedly claiming that the Bishop intended the church for exclusively Portuguese services while the other priests claimed the opposite.[31] A few years later Bishop Etheridge, constrained to make a case for a separate Portuguese Church, noted the precedents of the Italian Church in London and the French Church in Rome. He argued that the objection to the Portuguese Church on the part of the English-speaking Jesuits was partly one of economics and partly one of culture. It was obviously felt that the English-speaking church would lose revenues to the Portuguese church, but this proved a groundless fear. Indeed Etheridge showed much fairness and openness of mind in dealing with such a sensitive matter. Although himself English, and therefore naturally veering towards English habits and practices, he noted English priests were in the minority, two to seven, and thus he could not 'prudently in conscience let the English *domineer* on House or Church'.[32] Controversy notwithstanding, the Church of the Sacred Heart, Main Street, was blessed at Midnight Mass in December 1861 by Fr. Schembri, Bishop Etheridge being out of the country at that time for reasons of health.

In Malgretout the Catholic Church had been established in 1845 but there had been no regular priest until the arrival of Fr. Pavarelli on the west bank, Demerara, in 1857, when he began his work, not only among the Portuguese but also with the East Indians and blacks on the sugar estates in the region. He soon built a school and in the years that followed reaped much success in improvements at mass attendance, communion and attendance at school and religious instructions. Other churches began to rise all over the colony. In March 1861, a small house was bought for $400 to serve as a chapel near Malgretout. Previously the priests and bishop used the house of a Catholic manager in the neighbourhood to say mass. Throughout the country, before the building of churches, this pattern was followed. It was often noted that masses were said and confirmation held in private houses along the east coast, Demerara, and Berbice, in managers' and doctors' houses or over Portuguese shops. Much attention was given to the foundation of the church along the east coast because of the proximity to Georgetown by railway.[33]

It was, therefore, a natural development when the Church 'stations' followed the expansion of the railway which extended to Plaisance in 1848, to Buxton and Belfield in the 1850s and to Clonbrook and Mahaica in the 1860s. When the Portuguese ceased to work on the estates, they settled in the newly-established villages along the east coast; so too did the non-indentured who joined relatives and friends there. Thus temporary church 'stations' mushroomed along the coast at Beterverwagting, Buxton, Belfield, Clonbrook and Mahaica as the Portuguese evinced their need for the comforts of their religion. By 1866 Victoria had its church and by 1870 Plaisance a chapel-cum-school. Fr. Mark Messini, considered a genius at raising money, had bought land and a house for the use of both chapel and school and this was blessed by Bishop Etheridge on 29 May 1870. Later, on the Feast of St. John the Baptist, the patron saint, the interior and exterior of the chapel were spectacularly illuminated. For the first time in the annals of the colony, a special train was put on to transport the Portuguese from Georgetown and along the coast to join in the Plaisance celebrations.[34] This was the beginning, not only of an age of excursions to attend grandiose church celebrations all along the coast where the train served, but marked an era of spectacular and sometimes over-boisterous festivities in Plaisance village. Under the direction of Fr. Aloysius Casati (1875–1910), Plaisance Church would become one of the leading churches on the east coast. In 1877 the new church was opened there and two years later Fr. Casati established in Plaisance a boys' orphanage – St. John Bosco Orphanage – which is still in existence. He was also responsible for the church at Beterverwagting, St. Peter's, dedicated in 1875 shortly after he went to Plaisance.

Until his death in 1877, Bishop Etheridge delighted in attending the many celebrations – a confirmation, a pontifical high mass, the Thirteen Days' devotion, a plethora of processions and, above all, the grand celebrations held at Plaisance in honour of St. John the Baptist when, as he reported, the church was 'crushed to suffocation' with an almost exclusive Portuguese congregation.[35] The Portuguese outdid themselves in the exploding of fireworks, the *sine qua non* of all their ecclesiastical and secular celebrations. On the Feast of St. John the Baptist, they carried out the custom of making and jumping over large bonfires. This custom brought from Madeira was especially dear to unmarried boys and girls who leaped over the fire in the belief that it would bring them a happy marriage during the coming year. The boisterousness which accompanied this custom did not delight the other Plaisance villagers who considered the noise a nuisance and the bonfires a danger.[36] Bishop Etheridge greatly encouraged the growth of the church among the Portuguese by his presence. He was indefatigable and anxious to see that the work begun by the Italian priests would be carried on. When Fr. Mosca died in 1877 at Malgretout leaving the mission in excellent order, Fr. Casano was immediately sent to succeed him and serve the new mission at Hague.[37]

IV

The Madeiran Portuguese had a long tradition of Catholicism. Their 'folksy' type of Catholicism was the earthy expression of islanders living close to their environment; it was an exuberant type of religion, far different from the staid, conservative Anglo-Saxon expression. Not only did the English Protestants in the colony, but also the English priests, consider them 'un-English in birth and religion'. This difference in outlook would cause much misunderstanding within the Church. In Madeira, the profoundly religious Madeirans celebrated their religious *festas* with joyful abandon and with much pomp and splendour. They gained their greatest pleasure from the many Church festivals, coming from all parts of the island to walk in procession carrying shoulder-high life-size images of Christ, the Virgin Mary and the Saints, accompanied by the clergy, the military and bands of music. To round off the celebrations, shots were fired and fireworks exploded. Writers on Madeira gave eye-witness accounts of these processions, namely: 'The religious processions in Funchal are an institution. The statues of the various saints are carried in line along the streets on the shoulders of uniformed bearers and the military occupy a prominent place in the ranks.'[38] Also:

> 'Festas', or church festivals, take place throughout the year in various parishes, and each Church usually celebrates at least half a dozen ... the church and churchyard are gaily decorated with flags and flower-decked poles. There are booths and stalls in plenty, and a considerable amount of money changes hands. Fireworks play a great part in the entertainment, large numbers being let off for the sake of noise, which is often deafening. There is usually a long procession, which is sometimes quite elaborate ... Women may be seen walking with bare feet in the processions, and climbing up the Mount Church on bare knees at the great festival on August 15th.[39]

The Feast of *Nossa Senhora de Monte* was one of the greatest feasts and, like all other festivals, was preceded by a novena. Other special feasts were those of St. Peter, St. John the Baptist, St. Anthony, the Feast of Pentecost and, above all, the Feast of Corpus Christi (Body of Christ). The procession on the Feast of Corpus Christi was ordered by law of the country to commemorate the institution of the Blessed Sacrament and held at public expense; in it took part all the ecclesiastical, civil and military authorities and all confraternities of the Blessed Sacrament.[40] The Feast *par excellence* was the Feast of Christmas, for which the novena preparation was a unique one. The *Missa do Galo* (Midnight Mass) and the *Missa dos Pastores*, the mass following the Midnight Mass, were celebrated with great pomp and joy.

Love for their church created a bond, strengthening the feeling of communion with their relatives in Madeira and giving the immigrants a sense of unity with each other in their adopted land. So in British Guiana, these feasts were also celebrated with equal joy, pomp, splendour and extravagance. Bishop Etheridge saw this need of the Portuguese to express their faith in celebration as vital. He wrote: 'Portuguese ... *must be*, and *can only be* kept in any sort of a way to Church and their duty by ceremonies and practice something like what they have been accustomed to in Madeira'.[41] Others sneered at what they thought to be 'superstitious practices'. For emigrants settling in a foreign land, this continuation of their tradition through an expression of customs and culture in their own language enhanced their sense of security and offset the cultural alienation so strongly felt. Their exuberant celebrations were life-sustaining. On the other hand, they were seen by non-Portuguese observers as 'Saturnalia'; it was noted with derision and, possibly with an undercurrent of jealousy, that 'great devotion meant greater drinking'.[42]

Yet these *festas* brought in their train help for the needy. In 1858, the *Royal Gazette* reported the celebration of the Feast of Pentecost at the Royal Hotel, Main Street. Coupled with the religious celebration went charity to the poor, either preceding or concluding the occasion with a dinner and a supply of clothing. This was not, the *Gazette* stated, 'the only occasion where the wealthier classes of the Portuguese have extended the hand of charity to the poor of the city'.[43] After the distribution there was a procession to the Royal Catholic Cathedral where mass was celebrated. On the east coast, at Victoria, as at other churches, this feast was solemnly celebrated; the church hung with banners and flags, the Portuguese band in attendance, and after the usual procession a hearty dinner was served to the poor, who were each given a suit of clothes, a few shillings, a plate, bread and a towel to commemorate the occasion.[44]

In British Guiana, as in Madeira, during the nine days preceding the Feast of Pentecost, the *emperador* visited all the Catholic homes of the poor and the sick in his parish/village carrying with him a dove, representative of the Holy Spirit, and a crown in which people placed their gift to be used in the celebration of the feast. Agostinho De Freitas, *emperador*, advised through a notice in the press that at Malgretout the feast would be celebrated with all pomp and brilliance, with mass and procession and the '1st of December' band in attendance.[45] Special steamers were run to accommodate the Portuguese faithful from across the Demerara River.

In 1875 the new church at Meadowbank, location of the early Madeiran arrivals, was built. It was dedicated to Our Lady of the Mount, the patroness of their island, Madeira. To honour the occasion, a statue of Our Lady had been presented to the church by Manoel Fernandes Camacho, merchant and shipowner, as well as Portuguese consul in Georgetown. With great pomp and solemnity the statue was carried in procession two miles from Brickdam to Meadowbank – all very 'delightful' to the Portuguese, according to Bishop Etheridge who presided and blessed the statue.[46] Meadowbank church was the scene of many religious festivals and all seasons of the Church's year were highlighted. Young and old fully enjoyed the Feast of St. Peter which they fittingly celebrated by carrying small boats in procession and singing to the accompaniment of their bands. There was always a dramatic touch. On Passion Sunday, four Stations of the Cross were erected in the churchyard; two processions formed up, one with a full-sized waxen figure of Christ carrying His cross, the other of the Sorrowful Mother. The proceedings culminated in a ceremonial meeting of the two groups of the fourth Station. It was also a tradition that certain Portuguese families coveted the honour of providing the 'angels' with wings and the 'mourners' with purple drapes.[47]

A favourite feast was that of St. Anthony when again the poor were remembered at the distribution of what came to be known as St. Anthony's bread, a custom which is still carried on in Guyana today. This feast was flamboyantly celebrated at the Church of St. Anthony in Buxton which had been built in 1871. The feast of St. John the Baptist was beloved by the young Portuguese who indulged in many customs which, according to their supercilious neighbours, smacked of superstition. They broke eggs in glasses of water to find out their destiny: the shape of the egg would determine their fate – a church, marriage; a ship, travel; a star, success. They built large bonfires over which they jumped in competition, causing great consternation among the villagers in Plaisance.[48] The Church of St. John the Baptist in Plaisance was the scene of many a boisterous *festa*. In the late nineteenth century the mission there was strongly Portuguese. There are innumerable reports, both in Church annals and in the daily press, of novenas to a plethora of saints, pontifical high masses and processions, all capped with a dinner for the poor and that *sine qua non* of their celebrations – fireworks.[49] Unfortunately, some of these festive celebrations got out of hand and ended in broils, to the intense annoyance of the other villagers who complained to the police that the peace of the village was too often disturbed.[50]

Yet all villagers in different areas throughout the country were one in the celebration of the Christmas novena, attended not only by the Portuguese, but also by other ethnic groups, by non-Catholics as well as Catholics. Every novena service was packed with all classes even though this meant rising at an early hour for the 3.00 a.m. service. This novena was another Madeiran custom dear to the people. For the nine days preceding Christmas they attended mass at early dawn. Before mass they sang praises to the Mother of God in the hymn 'Benidita Sejaes'; a special sermon appropriate to the season was preached and the mass concluded with Benediction. There were varying additions at some churches. At Victoria, Fr. Baroni would sit before the altar holding the image of the Infant Jesus and the whole congregation would bow to it.[51] Of all the religious customs brought into the country by the

Madeiran Portuguese, the Christmas novena continued to hold sway in the heart of all Catholic Guyanese. It was correctly observed: 'So long as it thrives, there will be no one in the Colony who will be able to regard Christmas merely as a public holiday.'[52] Thus much gratitude is due to the Portuguese whose fervour in preparing for the feast of Christmas continues to enhance the religious aspect of it in the eyes of the Guyanese.

The Portuguese also contributed much to the penchant for celebration among the Guyanese. They never lost an opportunity to rejoice, whether over a secular or religious occasion. Like their Madeiran countrymen, they merged a holy-day into a holiday and their *festas* were combinations of 'religious fervour and innocent amusement'.[53] Portuguese converged on the churches at Plaisance, Buxton, Beterverwagting, and Victoria by special trains which were laid on and pilgrims made an excursion of it, singing to the accompaniment of their bands, each feast marked by the firing of firecrackers and rockets.

An outstanding and memorable festival took place in 1893 when the Portuguese in British Guiana joined whole-heartedly with Catholics throughout the world in celebrating the Golden Jubilee of Pope Leo XIII. Celebrations were held from May to November throughout the country. The grand illuminations of Sacred Heart Church with 3,000 lights were the talk of the town and considered the finest ever witnessed in the country. A special night train was put on to enable villagers along the coast to come and view the illuminations. Newspapers gave wide coverage to the event which was succinctly and strikingly described by the *Daily Liberal* thus:

> There are going to be grand doings today and tomorrow at the Church of the Sacred Heart in Main Street in honour of the Jubilee of His Holiness the Pope. At six o'clock this morning the fête will be ushered in by a grand peal of bells, followed by a display of fireworks, and music by a brass band. At 11 o'clock there will be a Pontifical High Mass. At five o'clock in the afternoon the *Te Deum* will be sung by the choir and the First of December band will play a program of music in the porch. Tomorrow there will be a big gathering of school children in Highbury House, Thomas Street, where refreshments will be distributed and speeches delivered, relative to the feast. At five o'clock the scholars will march in procession through the streets and bow to the likeness of His Holiness Pope Leo XIII .... At eight o'clock sharp, there will be an instantaneous display of 270 electric lamps in and around the church, the Band simultaneously starting the Pope's hymn, the words of which will be taken up by the Choir .... The Committee of Management earnestly ask all Catholics throughout the colony to illuminate their residences tomorrow night, and they also ask all Catholic merchants to close their offices and stores at 3 o'clock tomorrow afternoon so as to allow their employees to take part in the rejoicings.[54]

The day of solemn thanksgiving and praise at Plaisance, ending with illuminations, was described as 'a long-to-be-remembered and a gala day'. Flags and buntings streamed from private residences and stores and even from the shanties. Chinese lanterns and fairy lamps were everywhere and the whole village was 'filled with mirth and rife with a spirit of holiday making and amusement'.[55] The joyous mood of the day even negated rivalry and trade competition. All business places, except of course the rum shops, were closed. All barriers to culture and class came down.

The celebration at Friendship was dubbed 'an imposing spectacle'; at Victoria, 'the Jubilee of the Pope ... the grandest ever seen on the east coast'. At Buxton, the societies, guilds, and confraternities turned out in full in their colourful regalia, bearing banners in procession. In the evening, the illuminations and fireworks brought delight to all. The lavish decorations of the church, the singing of High Mass, the accompaniment of the *Primeiro de Dezembro* band, the processions of banners borne by the various societies, the illuminations of the church by hundreds of fairy lamps, were all repeated at the Victoria celebrations. Though a similar celebration at Henrietta on the Essequibo marked the close of the Papal Jubilee celebrations in November, those held at the Brickdam Cathedral in early October were made specially memorable by the attendance of the Most Rev. Dr Flood, Archbishop of Trinidad, who preached the panegyric on Pope Leo XIII, seeing him as a man of deep knowledge, faith and zeal, a writer of encyclicals.[56] The services of the day were imposing, culminating with an artistic illumination of the cathedral.

Playing a very prominent role in the Papal Jubilee celebrations were the numerous guilds, confraternities and societies established at all the churches. Here again was another link with Madeira where each church and each district abounded in societies, guilds and fraternities. Fr. Schembri helped to fill this need and, in the 1860s, established at Sacred Heart Church guilds and societies for men, women and children. A favourite among the young ladies was the St. Philomena Society. At Meadowbank there was fittingly a Society of *Nossa Senhora do Monte*; all the churches had their special societies, the Society of St. Aloysius for young men, the Confraternity of the Blessed Sacrament, the Society of the Rosary, the Confraternity of the Sacred Heart, Guild of the Holy Ghost, the Children of Mary and the Society of St. Vincent de Paul which still continues to play a meaningful role among the poor and needy in Guyanese society today.

Apart from the church-oriented societies, the Portuguese founded others to express the bonds of charity among themselves in a more concrete way. Like the *Assosciacão de Beneficiencia de Funchal* founded in 1862, the Portuguese Benevolent Society of British Guiana, established ten years later in their adopted home and confirmed as a friendly society by Ordinance No. 5 of 1875, held similar goals for 'the encouragement of industry and charity among the Members'. It was

composed exclusively of 58 male Portuguese who joined together for
mutual support in sickness, unemployment, old age, imprisonment,
for the relief of widows and orphans and for funeral expenses. They
also pledged to fund schools for the education of the children of the
members.[57] Great hopes were held out for this society which from the
outset signalled the pride of the Portuguese, who in less than a quarter
of a century had risen to economic prominence, and who now assured
the colonial government that their aim was to have 'no Portuguese
among the inmates of the Alms House'.[58]

It seemed that the aims of the society exceeded its funds and in 1887 it
came to a standstill in order to pay off large numbers of pensions to
widows, as well as to settle membership arrears. In November 1887, the
Society was revivified and reorganized under a new title, *Fraternidade
Portugueza of British Guiana.*[59] Unfortunately, the Society came to an
end a year later on the heels of a court case.[60]

V

One of the aims of the Portuguese Benevolent Society had been the
establishment of schools for the children of their members. As the
business of the societies, as well as their trade with Madeira, was
transacted in Portuguese, it would follow that the Portuguese were
concerned for the preservation of their language, and for the implant-
ing of knowledge. Throughout the nineteenth century the majority of
the Portuguese continued to speak their language among themselves;
their songs, their drama recitals were in Portuguese. There were five
Portuguese newspapers in the colony, *A União Portugueza, O Voz
Portuguez* and *Chronica Semanal*; two, *The Watchman* and *The
Liberal* reported in English and Portuguese. These newspapers kept
the Portuguese businessmen in touch with the economic situation in the
colony as well as with events in Madeira and Portugal. The accounts of
such events, political and historical, often expressed the pride of
the Portuguese in their heritage. It is also a fact noticeable among
immigrant groups that their language is, for them, an oasis in the desert
of another language. As business grew between Madeira and British
Guiana, transactions were carried on both in Portuguese and a smatter-
ing of English picked up through daily contact with their English-
speaking customers. Above all, possibly in the belief that God understood their prayers best in Portuguese, they held on to the language for
all church services. They had been starved of sermons in their language
until Fr. Correa arrived in 1845, and continuously requested Portuguese priests so that they could, in confidence, go to the sacraments. It
should not have been, therefore, a matter of surprise and concern to the
English priests that the Portuguese wished to maintain their language –
medium of their faith and their culture. It should have been less
surprising that they wished to attend schools in which the Portuguese

language would be taught – Portuguese schools as they came to be known.

On 29 June 1847, at the request of Bishop T. Hynes, OP, then officially Vicar-General for British Guiana, the Ursuline Sisters arrived in the colony to establish schools to provide Catholic education for the children of Portuguese immigrants.[61] The separatism of schools for the Portuguese and schools for the Creoles was the *bête noire* of Fr. Walker, who objected to the opening of a Portuguese Catholic Church and who anticipated a continuance of this separatism in the educational field. Portuguese children were not encouraged to go to the already-established Catholic schools, much to the chagrin of the English Jesuits. The reason for this, as offered by Fr. Schembri, was the fear of the children losing their language in the English-speaking schools; worse still they would be exposed to reading 'bad English books thus becoming corrupt and losing their religion'.[62] There is no evidence of this corruption or loss of faith as a result of attending English-speaking schools, but in the years ahead there was eventually a loss of their language and with it much of their culture. By the end of the century Bishop Galton wrote that 'the rising generation and the majority of the younger Portuguese had lost the Portuguese language'.[63]

By the mid-nineteenth century the Madeirans had become very education-conscious. In Madeira, private and public schools sprung up offering reading, arithmetic, Portuguese, geography, history, English, French, music, dancing and, last but not least, Christine doctrine.[64] There were notable schools for destitute children and night schools were seen as necessary for enhancing literary attainments.[65] Although, by and large, the early indentured immigrants from Madeira were illiterate, later groups were not. With the exception of the wealthier Portuguese who claimed that they had gained their success in business ventures without a formal education, by the 1860s many Portuguese began to express a desire for secular as well as religious education. With the movement of the Portuguese away from the plantations to the shops, there was a growing need for literate clerks speaking English. Yet at the same time there still existed the desire to hold fast to their language, a natural desire among an alien group for whom use of their own language served both as a bond as well as a bulwark against strangers.

In 1862 a Portuguese Female School was opened in Brickdam under the tutelage of Miss C. D'Oliviera. At the same time Fr. Schembri was being criticized for his wish to have a separate school where nothing but Portuguese would be spoken. Fr. Walker complained that Portuguese children were not encouraged to come to the English-speaking Catholic schools and 'consequently there are many little schools for boys and girls up and down the town'.[66] There was also a Portuguese Female School in Water Street as well as one for Portuguese boys in the area, which had been established because of an objection to their attendance at Fr. Baldini's school where catechism classes were held mostly for girls.[67] Although there seemed to have been a period of stagnation after Fr. Baldini's absence from the Sacred Heart Parish, 1867–69, in November 1867 under Fr. Mosca, the lower area of the presbytery was boarded up and became a grammar school – the beginnings of the present Sacred Heart School.[68] In 1869, a Portuguese master was sought in order to attract Portuguese boys to the school.[69] Where Fr. Baldini's interest centred on the girls, Fr. Messini's was on the boys. Not keen on the grammar school, he closed it and started a school for boys. On Fr. Baldini's return to Sacred Heart, he improved the Girls' School in 1871 by erecting a large schoolroom between the wings of the former and added two rooms to the Boys' School. By then the school had received an English-speaking headmaster who, by teaching English, qualified the school for a government grant in 1870.

In asking for an increase of priests in 1870, Bishop Etheridge particularly stressed 'no more Englishmen'.[70] Was he considering mainly the Portuguese element in Church and school? If so, he must have been aware of the increasing number of Portuguese immigrants,[71] which in turn meant an increase of the congregation in the churches. In his reports on confirmation he observed that of the 270 confirmed at Sacred Heart alone 'all but 2 were Portuguese'.[72] In 1875, with the promulgation of the reports of the Longden Commission on Education and the furore concerning denominational education in the colony, Etheridge must have felt that a major argument for the continuation of Catholic schools was the fact that Portuguese children were being sent to regular schools where religious instruction was made optional. Possibly then, this was the reason for the support of private schools in the 1870s teaching both Portuguese and English. Mrs Clothilde Reis De Sousa at 48 Regent Street was a well-known schoolmistress who taught her pupils Portuguese, English, piano, dancing, reading, writing and arithmetic.[73] This same versatile lady also ran a craft school for girls at the corner of Charlotte and King Streets where were taught 'fancy needlework, bead work, crochet and embroidery fit for a London exhibition'. Other aspects of culture were not neglected. Mrs De Sousa's pupils and teachers played the piano and sang in English, Portuguese and Italian. It was observed that they were 'being well prepared to advance and add lustre to our colonial well-being'.[74]

At the Philharmonic Hall, Mrs Carvalho's school displayed the talents of the pupils in drama and music at an annual exhibition. Mr F.A. Reis ran St. Edward's school at King Street where, besides art and craft, both English and Portuguese were taught as being useful in the business world.[75] In the 1870s both the Sacred Heart Boys' School and the Catholic Grammar School had Portuguese masters, Joseph John De Freitas and Signor Machado respectively; Miss C. D'Oliviera now served as Mistress at the Girls' School, Sacred Heart.[76] By then a new type of Portuguese immigrant had been arriving – the labouring class was in the minority and young lads were coming into the country to serve as clerks in the many Portuguese business houses.[77] Both at the secular and the Sunday schools Portuguese boys were doing well. For their smart appearance at the Sacred Heart Sunday school and for their knowledge of the Portuguese language at the end-of-year examinations they were specially praised.[78] In 1888 the Ursuline Sisters started a school for Portuguese girls.

In 1890 a Portuguese College giving a classical-type education was established and directed by E. de M. Brito Nobrega. The college obviously met the need for the training of future Portuguese business-men. Bishop Butler fully supported this college, agreeing with the view that 'To bring up children in their own language was best'. Moreover, in his praise of the work done at the college in turning out 'intelligent young businessmen', he observed that merchants in Water Street found that 'the boys educated at the College made better clerks than those educated in Madeira',[79] a very obvious point as the boys educated in British Guiana had the advantage of being bilingual. Not to be out-done by the success of the girl scholars at the Ursuline Convent (it was felt that the girls should not think themselves superior to the boys in talent and literary abilities), it was decided that examinations at the Portuguese College would be conducted by a committee of distinguished gentlemen who were *au courant* with the official pro-gramme of the Portuguese government, and that examination papers should be sent to Portugal for approval.[80] The standards were kept very high; the accent was on quality, not quantity, though Bishop Butler deplored the paucity of students, numbering less than 60.[81] It seemed that the Portuguese College was eventually closed, its place having been taken in September 1898 by a Portuguese Catholic School giving daily lessons in Portuguese and in business-related subjects.[82] This was probably the result of Bishop Galton's concern regarding the loss of the Portuguese language by the younger generation. He was not at all happy that the 11 Catholic elementary schools at the end of the nineteenth century were entirely supported by government grants. They had lost the Catholic atmosphere as even the schoolmasters were only nominal Catholics.[83] The Portuguese schools had taught not only secular subjects, but religious instruction as well.

The issue regarding the teaching of the Portuguese language had long been a heated one among the clergy, exacerbated by the differing views of the English and Portuguese elements within the church. This difference of opinion had militated against the forging of a clear-cut policy for the growth of the church. It is true that the rapid progress in the establishment of churches triggered by the need had somewhat softened the issue but, according to the press, it had only been deferred. It was catapulted back into prominence thus:

A movement is on foot amongst the Portuguese in the colony with the object of establishing a new Roman Catholic Church under priests of their own nationality. A large sum of money has already been subscribed towards the object, and arrangements have been made for bringing out of Madeira three priests attached to one of the orders there.[84]

The two main grievances among the Portuguese were the lack of priests of their own nationality and the fact that the education of their children in Portuguese was, to some extent, neglected. These complaints were viewed sympathetically, for it was observed that the non-Portuguese-speaking priests were unable to communicate with their flock and were not 'en rapport' with them. The objection to the Portuguese children being taught English was a real grievance. Although the local press tried to be conciliatory, it was difficult at this point in the history of the Portuguese, almost half a century in a British colony, to support fully the argument for more Portuguese-speaking schools or a specifically Portuguese Catholic Church. Ironically, those arguing for Portuguese schools and church were of the wealthier class who pointed out that ignorance of the English language had not been a deterrent to their economic success. The Portuguese were not at all anxious to set foot into the political arena,[85] although in the late 1880s prominent business-men joined the reform movement to assert themselves as *bona fide* citizens and to further their business interests against the all-prevailing plantocracy. In order to take a greater part in politics it was necessary for the Portuguese to master the English language, but even those few who eventually entered the field adhered to their language when among their own. The Catholic governor, Lord Gormanston, over whose arrival in the colony in 1888 the Portuguese were most euphoric, seemed to think very poorly of the Portuguese whom he considered 'devoid of true ambition' in not taking any interest in politics.[86] Indeed, between extending their businesses and helping to build churches, the middle-class Portuguese had little time for politics on a grand scale.

VI

Emigration from Madeira continued on a reduced scale in the 1870s, and by 1882 ended with the government's suspension of its annual vote. This development in no way halted the growth of churches under the auspices of the Portuguese. Over the 1870s and 1880s the population of Bartica, the hub of gold miners at the conjunction of the Essequibo and Mazaruni Rivers, had expanded. Many of the Portuguese at Bartica were involved in gold mining and nearly half of the inhabitants were Roman Catholics. By 1892 the acute need for the building of a Roman Catholic church was discussed by a number of zealous and prominent Portuguese gentlemen, together with those of other ethnic groups, who agreed to set in action plans for raising the necessary funds.[87] After years of hearing mass in Mr A.J. D'Amil's hotel and Mr M.F. Da Silva's cottage, the Church of St. Anthony became a reality with the laying of the foundation stone on 10 October 1897. Education of the children was not neglected and attention had already been paid to the opening of a Catholic school.[88] Indeed this church–school combination was the hallmark of all missionary endeavours, not only in British Guiana but in all parts of the world. Robert Ricard summed it up well: 'Nothing is more evident in the stabilization of the Church than the importance of the school.'[89]

By the end of the nineteenth century, churches were dotted along the east coast and west coast, Demerara, in Essequibo and Berbice. These churches were the scenes of lavish and spectacular celebrations of the favourite feasts of the Portuguese and were given full coverage in the local press. The Portuguese love of music, a well-known trait of the Madeirans, was expressed in their singing of *Missas Cantatas* (Sung Masses), and in most of the churches there were trained choirs.[90] The famous *Primeiro de Dezembro* band, established in 1876, was in constant demand and in attendance at most of the religious festivities and excursions all over the country. So too were 'the little musicians of Father Casati's Orphanage', Plaisance.[91]

Throughout the nineteenth century the Catholic Church was closely identified with its Portuguese congregations. The building of the churches in the villages had been mostly financed and supported by the Portuguese. They could well afford it as by the 1880s they 'owned the bulk of the property of the Colony outside the Sugar Plantations'; they also collected and paid the excise revenue amounting to $600,000 annually.[92] In nineteenth-century British Guiana the rise of the Portuguese to economic prominence was notable indeed. They were prominent in both business and church affairs, and there is much evidence to prove that they contributed to the support of the Church both back in Madeira and in their adopted land. In other respects Portuguese culture began to wane. The movement away from the language had begun and, although a number of wealthy Portuguese continued to return to Madeira on visits to relatives or to see their ancestral home for the first time, the trend was to send their sons to Britain for further education in the professions.[93] Returning doctors and lawyers brought back their skills and the Anglo-Saxon culture as well, which influenced home and church. By the early part of the twentieth century church celebrations had begun to lose their early exuberance. This was a result not only of the new breed of Portuguese and of priests, but of the burgeoning cosmopolitan nature of the Catholic church embracing other ethnic groups through example and the influence of the schools.

Much of the religious legacy, however, lived on and was passed on – in the Christmas novena, in the guilds, confraternities and societies which continued to make an impact on Catholic life. There is no doubt that the growth and expansion of the Catholic church in British Guiana owed much to the Madeiran emigrants who brought to the colony not only their agricultural and commercial expertise but also their deep and joyful faith.

SR. M. NOEL MENEZES, RSM
University of Guyana

NOTES

1. *Population Census of the Commonwealth Caribbean, 1980–1981*, 'Guyana', Vol. 2, p.474.
2. Governor James Carmichael Smyth to the Earl of Aberdeen, 25 May 1835, Guyana National Archives (hereafter GNA).
3. Luis de Sousa Melo and Susan E. Farrow, *Impressions of Madeira in the Past* (Funchal, 1983), p.19.
4. Ibid.
5. See Governor Henry Light to Lord Stanley, 22 Nov. 1841, No. 157 and Lord Stanley to Light, 17 Feb. 1842, No. 56 in *Papers Relative to the West Indies, British Guiana*.
6. BG/15, Fr. Walker to Fr. Provincial, 6 Nov. 1861, f.481, Jesuit Archives, London.
7. *An Historical Sketch of the Island of Madeira* (London, 1819), p.27.
8. Minutes of the Court of Policy, British Guiana, 5 Aug. 1841, GNA.
9. Previously James Stephen had stated that the Portuguese government should be notified of the willingness of the Colonial Office to make arrangements for the reception and accommodation of a Roman Catholic priest if they wished to send one. See enclosure in Light to Lord Russell, 13 Oct. 1841, No. 129, CO 111/183.
10. Lord Stanley to Governor Light, 27 Dec. 1841, No. 47, CO 111/183.
11. Light to Stanley, 24 Jan. 1842, No. 73, GNA.
12. Members of the Catholic Committee to Governor Light, the Court of Policy and the Combined Court, 17 March 1845, GNA.
13. Minutes of the Court of Policy, British Guiana, 22 March 1845, GNA.
14. *Daily Chronicle*, 15 June 1893. In October 1841, an Irish priest, Rev. Kelly, was commissioned to work among the Portuguese in Essequibo. However, his inability to speak the Portuguese language was an obstacle to communication and little progress was made.
15. BG/22, 'The Jesuit Phase of the History of the Catholic Church in British Guiana to the death of Bishop James Etheridge, SJ on 31 Dec. 1877', pp.17–18, typescript in Jesuit Archives, London.
16. M.B. Johnson to Rev. E. Hawkins of SPG, Wakenaam, 24 Dec. 1855, Box 1789, 'British Guiana', also Charles Conyers to Secretary, USPG, 14 Jan. 1856, Box 1769, 'British Guiana', United Society for the Propagation of the Gospel, London.
17. Editorial in *Royal Gazette*, 30 Dec. 1854.
18. Minutes of the Combined Court, British Guiana, 6 April 1846, and H.G. Howard, H.M. Chargé d'Affaires at Lisbon to Viscount Palmerston, 28 March 1850, CO 111/278.
19. *The Missionary Magazine*, III, No. 17 (Oct. 1939), p.89.
20. BG/11, Bishop J. Etheridge to Fr. Provincial, 10 July 1857, f.335, Jesuit Archives, London.
21. BG/12,Etheridge to Fr. Provincial, 9 April 1858, f.350.
22. BG/12, P. Sherlock to Fr. Barrow, 25 May 1858.
23. BG/17, Etheridge to Fr. Provincial, 22 June 1863, f.597.
24. BG/18, Etheridge to Fr. Provincial, 6 July 1864, f.618.
25. BG/17, Etheridge to Fr. Provincial, 9 March 1863.
26. BG/9, Fr. Wollett's Notes, 16 June 1859, f.215.
27. BG/22, 'The Jesuit Phase of the History of the Catholic Church', p.35.
28. BG/11, Etheridge to Fr. Provincial, 10 July 1857, f.335.
29. BG/12, Fr. Sherlock to Fr. Barrow, 25 May 1858.
30. BG/8, Bishop Etheridge's Diary, 14 April 1860, p.43.
31. BG/15, Fr. H. Loud to Fr. Provincial, 23 Nov. 1861.
32. BG/19, Etheridge to Fr. Provincial, 1865, f.634.
33. Immigration Agent General to W.B. Wolseley, Acting Government Secretary, 5 Dec. 1850, CO 111/277.
34. BG/22, 'The Jesuit Phase of the History of the Catholic Church', p.71.
35. BG/8, Bishop Etheridge's Diary, p.71.
36. *Daily Chronicle*, 14 July 1898.

37. BG/8, Bishop Etheridge's Diary, pp.75–86.
38. Anthony J. Drexel Biddle, *The Land of the Wine, being an Account of the Madeira Island at the Beginning of the Twentieth Century* ... (Philadelphia, 1901), II, 72.
39. Charles A. Le Power, *Power's Guide to the Island of Madeira (The Pride of Portugal)* (London, 1951), p.11.
40. Charles Thomas Stanford, *Leaves from a Madeira Garden* (2nd edition, London, 1909), p.249.
41. BG/17, Etheridge to Fr. Provincial, 9 March 1863.
42. 'The Jesuit Phase of the History of the Catholic Church', p.40.
43. *Royal Gazette*, 22 May 1858.
44. *The Watchman*, March 1874.
45. *Chronica Semanal*, 14 de Maio de 1898.
46. *The Watchman*, 17 Dec. 1875, also BG/8. Bishop Etheridge's Diary, p.83.
47. 'The Jesuit Phase of the History of the Catholic Church', p.81.
48. *The Reflector*, 25 June 1892; *Daily Chronicle*, 14 July 1898.
49. Portuguese stores sold rockets, bombs and coloured stars. See advert of A.C. De Faria, 14 Croal Street in *The Daily Chronicle*, 5 June 1892.
50. *The Echo*, 25 July 1896.
51. *Daily Liberal*, 31 Dec. 1893.
52. *The Missionary Magazine*, Vol. 1, No. 2 (April 1935), p.45.
53. Stanford, p.233.
54. *Daily Liberal*, 23 July 1893.
55. Ibid., 2 Aug. 1893.
56. *Daily Chronicle*, 17 Oct. 1893.
57. Ordinance No. 5 of 1875 (British Guiana).
58. *The Watchman*, 28 May 1875.
      In 1875 the Alms House, a dwelling for the poor and destitute in the colony, was in the process of building. It was designed by the well-known Italian architect, Caesar Castellani, a former Jesuit lay-brother, later civil engineer in the colony, who was also responsible for the Victoria Law Courts, New Amsterdam Hospital and other fine structures.
      In 1887 there were 35 Portuguese out of the 541 inmates in the Alms House while at the Orphan Asylum there were only two out of 106.' Report of the Poor Law Commissioners, 1887' and 'Report of the Orphan Asylum, 1887' in British Guiana *Blue Book*, 1887, pp.141 and 213.
59. *Demerara Daily Chronicle* (Mail Edition), 10 Dec. 1887.
60. Not as prominent as the Portuguese Benevolent Society was the Dona Maria Society founded in the 1880s.
61. *Ursuline Centenary Booklet* (Georgetown, 1947), p.1.
62. BG/15, Fr. Walker to Fr. Provincial, 6 Nov. 1861, f.479.
63. BG/20, Bishop Galton to Fr. Knight, 11 Nov. 1897, ff.721–2.
64. *As Novidades* (Funchal), 2 Dec. 1867.
65. *A Ordem* (Funchal), 9 July 1856 and 16 April 1859.
66. BG/15, Fr. Walker to Fr. Provincial, 6 Nov. 1861, f.479.
67. 'The Jesuit Phase in the History of the Catholic Church', p.68.
68. Ibid.
69. BG/19, Etheridge to Fr. Provincial, 3 Feb. 1869, f.653.
70. BG/19, ibid., New Year's Day, 1870, f.657.
71. Between 1851 and 1871 the number of Portuguese in the Colony fluctuated between 9,000 and 7,000. In 1851 of 9,938 Roman Catholics, 7, 928 were Madeirans (*Results of the Decennial Census of the Population of British Guiana, 1851*, p.17).
72. BG/19, Etheridge to Fr. Galloway, 10 March 1875.
73. *The Watchman*, 15 Sept. 1876.
74. Ibid., 24 Dec. 1875.
75. Ibid., 22 Dec. 1876.
76. *The British Guiana Directory, 1877*, pp.103 and 132.
77. British Guiana, *Annual Administrative Report* – Alex M. Cameron, Health Officer,

1880.
78. *Daily Chronicle*, 15 Aug. 1882 and *The Demerara Daily Chronicle*, 22 Dec. 1882.
79. *Daily Chronicle* (Mail Edition), 10 Jan. 1894.
80. *Daily Liberal*, 5 April 1893.
81. *Daily Chronicle*, 10 Jan. 1894.
82. *Chronica Semanal*, 3 Sept. 1898.
83. BG/20, Bishop C.T. Galton to Fr. Knight, 11 Nov. 1897, ff.721–2.
84. *Colonist*, 4 Dec. 1882.
85. *A União Portugueza*, Sabado, 7 Junho 1890.
86. Ibid.
87. *Daily Liberal*, 9 March 1892.
88. *Daily Chronicle*, 23 Dec. 1893.
89. Robert Ricard, *La 'Conquête Spirituelle' du Mexique* (Paris, 1933), p.249.
90. *Daily Chronicle*, 28 May 1887.
91. *Daily Chronicle*, 27 April 1888 and 2 May 1888.
92. W.F. Haynes-Smith to the Earl of Derby, 24 May 1884, No. 141, GNA.
93. *Daily Chronicle*, 20 and 26 Aug. 1888.
    Among others, Caesar Augusto Faria studied medicine in Paris and England; Casmiro Joaquim Gomes gained his M.D. at Edinburgh University. Dr João Gomes D'Aguiar, father of a prominent business magnate in Guyana today, Mr Peter D'Aguiar, studied medicine in London. In the annals of law, Chief Justice G.J. De Freitas, a London bar graduate, was renowned; he was considered a 'true gentleman of Portugal' as well as one 'devoted to his King (English) and Country'. See *Daily Chronicle*, 20 July 1938.

British West Indians in Haiti in the Late Nineteenth and Early Twentieth Centuries

Using primarily Foreign Office records, this article examines the hitherto-ignored West Indian immigrant community in Haiti in the late nineteenth and early twentieth centuries. It discusses their economic and political activities as well as their relations with the host society. It argues that in a black republic the successes or failures of these immigrants had less to do with the colour of their skins than with the political and economic problems of Haiti.

'For a century', wrote James Leyburn a trifle inaccurately, 'Haiti saw no foreigners except the few traders at seaports, an occasional Wesleyan missionary, a limited number of consuls and ministers, certain travelers interested in odd corners of the earth, and, after 1860, Catholic priests and sisters'.[1] He did, however, note that black Americans had during that time gone, either singly or in groups, to settle there. Benoit Joachim presents a rather different picture. Stating that about a quarter of the Haitian population is descended from people who did not live in Saint Domingue before 1804, he too notes the various attempts to attract black Americans but points to the much greater numbers of immigrants from the Caribbean. Many of the recently freed people of Guadeloupe and Martinique emigrated to Haiti from the 1850s, settling in 'the towns and establishing there some of the most important merchant houses in the capital. They penetrated into the interior where they carried on various trades. Likewise it should be noted that at the end of the century the majority of coachmen in Port-au-Prince came from Jamaica.'[2] There were few British West Indians in Haiti in the nineteenth century but they were all neither Jamaicans nor coachmen. Forming a small part of the contemporary emigration to places outside of the British West Indies, these emigrants provide a unique opportunity to observe British West Indians in a country not ruled by whites, where the successes and failures of the emigrants had little to do with the colour of their skins and much to do with the political and economic problems of Haiti. Hence the discussion ends in 1915 with the American occupation, though there continued to be both a transient and a resident British West Indian population in the 1920s and the 1930s.[3]

There are two major problems in estimating the number of British West Indians in Haiti during this period. First, Haitian censuses after 1864 were unreliable;[4] second, the immigrants tended not to register with the consulates, usually only resorting to them with complaints about the Haitian authorities.[5] The population of Haiti according to the most commonly accepted estimates was somewhat more than one million in the 1870s and about two million by 1915.[6] West Indian immigrants at their peak in the 1880s probably numbered no more than 3,000. This can be no more than a tentative estimate though there exist in the records a number of references to the size of this population.

Some British West Indians had been living in Haiti since the 1850s as registers of British subjects in Haiti show; Spencer St. John, the British representative there, referred to the repatriation of some in the late 1860s and commented in 1872 on these problems:

> The relief of destitute Colonial subjects, I may add, is a matter which sometimes causes me considerable embarrassment, inasmuch as applications to Colonial authorities for the sanction of any expenses in such cases invariably meet with unfavourable replies.[7]

The British West Indians in Haiti at this period formed part of the early emigrations to places outside of the British Empire. People had moved to Panama to build the railway in the 1850s and to St. Croix in the Danish Virgin Islands from the early 1860s onwards to work on sugar plantations. In 1873–74 'a great number' of British West Indians were brought to Tortuga Island (Ile de la Tortue off the north coast of Haiti) to work on a British financed concession. This rapidly failed due to political opposition but some of these workers probaby remained in Haiti.[8] By 1875 the British consul commented that 'the number of British subjects residing here is considerable', explaining that 'for years' they had been 'arriving here from Jamaica and other places in search of employment'.[9] Early in 1881 when the Haitian government was unable to provide an estimate of the number of British subjects in Haiti, the consulate hazarded a guess of its own. Estimating about 2,000 in Haiti (and 500 in the Dominican Republic) the official cited the failure to register as one reason for having to make a rough estimate but pointed to the nature of the migration as being another: 'Their numbers in both states are continually varying, because they come and go according to the fluctuations of employment. At present they would seem to be diminishing, as few arrive while a good many are leaving.'[10]

The receipts for the various consular offices provide some indication of where these immigrants lived. In order of size in the early 1880s, the main areas are Port-au-Prince, Les Cayes, Petite Goave, Jacmel and Cap Haitien. Of course consular offices were not receiving money from British subjects alone but other evidence suggests the importance of these areas (except Petite Goave) as areas of settlement for immigrants.[11] In 1885 an estimate of 'at least fourteen hundred British subjects' resident on the north coast in the Cap Haitien and Fort Liberte areas was made by the vice-consul serving the area. Since the vice-consult, John Dutton, was resigning because of his complaint that over 20 years expenses had exceeded receipts by £2,500 to £3,000, he may have been exaggerating to improve his case.[12] The failure to replace him resulted in about 300 people signing a petition in 1887 asking for a replacement since they claimed that about 900–1,000 British subjects lived in that part of the country.[13] If we accept Dutton's estimate and that of the petition we come to two tentative conclusions: given that Port-au-Prince was the main place of residence of British West Indians at least as many probably lived there, hence our estimate of about 3,000. Second, the earlier opinion that the numbers were diminishing may simply refer to an annual fluctuation but by the late 1880s the numbers of immigrants were falling. By 1899 'there were a few Jamaican negroes and a Vice Consul ... at Cape Haytien' was the dismissive comment of the acting consul-general on this once important area.[14] The twentieth century references are consistent with the earlier impressions of declining numbers. In 1907 about 60 people 'all negroes, or coloured West Indians' lived at Les Cayes on the south coast;[15] a petition in 1913 gave the same figure though the consular estimate was about 30 to 40.[16] In 1909 'only about 40 natives of the West Indies in poor circumstances' were reported as living at Jeremie on the northern coast of the southern peninsula.[17] Four years later about 20 was the estimate with 'practically none' at Jacmel on the south coast and 'some few' at Gonaives on the west.[18]

British West Indians in Haiti, despite the early group of agricultural workers on the Ile de la Tortue, were mainly urban residents in a variety of occupations. Some idea of these occupations can be gleaned from two sources. In 1888 the occupations of 23 residents of Port-au-Prince were given. These were people who had claims against the Haitian Government for losses suffered in fires (there were about 80 claims and no discernible reason why the occupations of these 23 and not those of the others should be provided). The largest group, mainly women, was in domestic service: four laundresses, a dyer and cleaner, a seamstress, a cook and two servants. The next largest was connected with the coach business: three carriage builders, three coachmen, and a farrier. There were also two shoemakers, a mason, a carpenter, and a schoolmistress and her daughter. The twenty-third is illegible but is probably another laundress. From the size of the claims made – mostly for a few hundred dollars – these were the respectable poor of the West Indian community in Port-au-Prince.[19] The upper reaches of the community signed the 1905 petition against the proposed Anglo-Haitian Nationality Convention. Thirty-three lived in the capital, 14 in Cap Haitien. Omitting the two Wesleyan ministers (the senior was certainly from the Channel Islands) we have 44 occupations given. Commerce and the building trades lead the way: there are eight merchants and two clerks; a contractor, a bricklayer, a painter, and seven carpenters and cabinet-makers. There were five tailors. Three signatories gave their occupation as coach builder, one as coachmen. There were two engineers and a mechanic, two teachers, two storemen, a stevedore, a seaman, a sexton, a deacon, a veterinary surgeon, a trained agriculturalist, and a traffic manager.[20] Compared to the previous list there are two notable differences. First, just over half have fairly high status occupations, compared to about a quarter on the previous list. Second, women are absent. The first is readily understandable. The petition was designed to show that 'many British West Indians residing in Haiti are gentlemen of education and culture, filling good and responsible positions, such as pastors of Churches, Merchants, Agents of Steamship Lines, Agents of Life Assurance Companies, Consuls and Vice Consuls etc.'. The second may be connected with the first: the exclusion of low status jobs would exclude women. It may also reflect the decline in the number of immigrants generally and the tendency of British West Indian men to marry Haitian women.

The best known of these gentlemen in the late nineteenth century was J.R. Love, who was a medical doctor and an Anglican parson in the Haitian Church under the Afro-American Bishop Holly. After a famous dispute he turned his attention to Haitian politics, becoming an ally of General Manigat.[21] In 1886 he inspired a petition which was signed by people of similar standing: Arthur N. Crosswell and Frederick B. Coles, involved in finance and commerce, and a few years previously charged with fraud in a complicated case, and Dr A.J. Pairman who lived in Jacmel.[22] Later in the century there was George Duncombe, a coloured Jamaican who owned a bakery and in 1901 acted briefly as consul-general.[23] The records also reveal some of the humbler members of the community: a number who served in the Haitian armed forces like Samuel Burnet employed as a fireman on the Haitian gunboat *Dessalines* and Elijah Daniel who described himself as a 'buss driver'.[24] A petition from the residents at Les Cayes (1913) described some of the signatories as architects, builders and contractors.[25] The occupations of the majority of poor West Indians cannot be ascertained. They were sometimes described as 'very low and depraved … not more so than the corresponding classes living in large cities in Great Britain' (by the petitioners of 1905) and as living in slums or being 'gaol birds' by the violently prejudiced consul-general of that time Vansittart. In calmer mood, he stated that they 'are chiefly Cabmen, Cooks, Servants etc. …' which confirms the impression given by the 1886 claims.[26]

Differences in wealth and class are confirmed by other evidence. Of the 80 claims for compensation for losses incurred in the 1886 fires only three amounted to substantially more than $1,000: one for $15,000, a second for $4,000, and a third for $3,506. The rest were all in the range of $100 to $1,000 with the majority being below $500. Men like Dr Love, Crosswell and his brother, and Coles had claims against the Haitian Government for tens of thousands but more typical of West Indians were people like Albert Lyons from Jamaica and Raoul Louisy from St. Lucia. Lyons died in 1906 leaving a small house consisting of one room and a courtyard and £200 and Louisy died in 1910 leaving a house in Port-au-Prince, 'one or two boats' and building stores.[27]

Compared to the Haitian population British West Indians lived almost always in coastal towns. There is one reference to an inhabitant of Petite Riviere, an internal market town.[28] Much less than ten per cent of Haitians lived in urban areas. As a consequence, the occupational structure of the immigrants differed markedly from that of the local population since nearly all the rural Haitians were engaged in agriculture. Some West Indians, like the people hired by Mrs Maunder to work her late husband's concession in the Ile de la Tortue might have originally arrived to work on the land but if this was so they must have drifted quite rapidly to the towns. In origin the immigrants may not have been very dissimilar to other contemporary emigrants from the West Indies but they differed in their predominantly urban destinations. Velma Newton describes the social composition of the early twentieth century migration to Panama in these terms:

> Although hundreds of artisans, office workers, other 'indoor types', the unemployed and fortune hunters of about every stream in life formed the departing crowd, it is possible to draw a picture of the emigrant whose type was most frequently seen in the migration stream. The typical emigrant was a black man. He was usually an agricultural labourer or unskilled town dweller, between twenty and thirty five years old, and was illiterate, or had gone to elementary school for only a few years.[29]

Bonham Richardson's study of the Barbadian migration to Panama confirms the impression that it consisted mainly of labourers, though the rather better than West Indian average Barbadian education system made it unlikely that illiterates predominated.[30] Franklyn Knight in his study of Jamaican migrants to Cuba, using Cuban records, gives a figure of ten per cent professional and artisan classes among the 1927 migrants, and repudiates the suggestion that the migrants as a group were illiterate.[31] From the petitions and surviving letters to the consulates in this period we can made two observations. The 300 signatories to the 1887 petition all signed rather than making their mark and of the various complainants only Samuel Burnet made his mark. There seems to be no other evidence available on this point to refute or validate Vansittart's allegation that the majority of urban slum dwellers was illiterate. The fluctuations in numbers of immigrants suggest that Bonham Richardson's conclusion about emigration from St. Kitts and Nevis applies with slight modification to Haiti: white and coloured West Indians have tended to migrate permanently, while the black worker class tended to migrate temporarily.[32] In the case of Haiti the class difference seems to hold while black middle class people, blocked by colour bars and the declining British West Indian economies, seemed to have found permanent homes in Haiti.

In their religion the British West Indians differed greatly from the host community. Spencer St. John estimated that in the 1880s there were about a thousand Anglicans 'and the majority of these are probably American and English coloured immigrants'.[33] The cause of the Anglican Church could not have been helped by the conduct of

Joseph Robert Love. Born in Nassau, Bahamas in 1839, he left for the United States in 1866 where he was ordained in 1876 and qualified as a doctor in 1879. In 1881 he left for Haiti, where he served, at first very successfully, under Bishop Holly. By September 1881 Love and the Bishop were in dispute and Love was dismissed a year later. Other Protestant Churches had less turbulent histories. The Wesleyan missionaries, St. John thought, had 'as many as 1400' members, though in 1915 there were just over 1,100 members who included as well as professional Haitians 'political refugees from Cuba and economic ones from Jamaica and other islands'.[34] It should be noted that the signatories to the 1905 petition were headed by the superintendent of the Wesleyan mission and another Wesleyan minister. There were also some Baptists. In March 1885 the Rev. Alexander Von Papengrath applied for authority to celebrate marriages between British subjects at the Baptist Missionary Society chapel at Jacmel, writing that 'in consideration of the number of British subjects residing there I would like to suggest that a licence be granted'. He explained that 'in this town there is only our Baptist Chapel for all protestant religious purposes' and that he had had several applications from 'men who were deprived of means & inconvenienced to travel elsewhere'. Morality would benefit if the application were granted, 'since it will ultimately spread a good moral influence in this place, which in most cases, without a possibility of honourable legal union, does only degrade our protestant people & casts a sad gloom ever these British subjects out here'.[35] The 1887 petition from the residents of Cap Haitien included a Baptist missionary among its signatories but little else appears in the records about the Baptists in Haiti. The Haitian elite were mainly Roman Catholic, and some were freemasons (Bishop Holly once conducted a funeral service for a prominent freemason when the Roman Catholics would not); the religion of the majority of the Haitian people was Voodoo. St. John's conclusion that 'the Protestants have not had much success in Hayti' was true, since the majority of Protestants seemed to have been immigrants. There were probably some Roman Catholics among the British West Indians in Haiti, since we have the names of at least two emigrants from St. Lucia. On the whole, however, in religion, as in residence and occupation British West Indians were unlike the host population.

Little appears in the records about any organizations of West Indians. From the prominent role of the clergy in various petitions we can deduce that the churches formed the basis of organized activity. Vansittart in 1905 complained that over the nationality question 'the whole *Black* and *Mulatto* colony is up in arms against me. I regret to say they are headed by the Wesleyan missionaries in this island, who appear to be the most venomous.'[36] Love who had tried to set up his own church after being dismissed in 1882 was the originator of the 1886 petition outlining the grievances of various prominent West Indians. The 1887 petition included one Baptist and one other missionary (of unspecified denomination) among its 300 signatories. Events of imperial importance were celebrated by events organized by prominent British subjects. In 1887 there was a procession of British residents in celebration of the fiftieth anniversary of Queen Victoria's accession to the throne; the 1905 petition refers to a number of similar activities.[37] In 1897 a special English service was held to celebrate the diamond jubilee of the Queen; in 1901 'suitable letters' were forwarded on the death of the Queen and the accession of Edward VII; and collections were made for the widows and orphans of the South African war. A hint at more secular activities is found in a consular letter to the Foreign Office in 1910. It dealt with the case of Charles Lloyd, accused of making frivolous complaints against the police:

> In 1908 Lloyd got up a British Benevolent Society with himself as treasurer; the society ran for six months or so and then collapsed. No payments were made for any benevolent purpose and Lloyd never gave any account of money received. After that he run a sort of life insurance business among his friends, and having collected a certain amount of money in premiums disappeared.[38]

The records do not show whether there were other friendly societies or rotating credit associations (for this is what the 'sort of life insurance business' sounds like). Given the widespread existence of both types of organization in the British West Indies, Lloyd was probably not alone, even if seemingly less honest than others involved in such organizations. Fluctuating levels of population at the beginning of the period and declining numbers later must have made it difficult to sustain many organizations.

What were relations between Haitians and British West Indians like? Clearly large numbers came to Haiti looking for work and then moved on, hardly staying long enough to establish any relations with the local people. Mrs Maunder, a Haitian lady with good social connections, the widow of a Liverpool merchant, worked her concession for a year from 1873 with workers from the neighbouring British islands. The workers had little time to adjust to Haitian society, living as they were in the enclave they had created in an island off the north coast of Haiti, before Mrs Maunder was forced to flee Haiti for Jamaica in 1875. The arbitrary working of Haitian law remained a major theme in subsequent relations between Haitians and British West Indians. In 1885 the consul proposed the appointment of M. Pascher Lespes to the post of unsalaried legal adviser 'to prevent the poorer classes of the British Colony here, from being robbed as they at present are, by the petty lawyers to whom they have recourse'.[39] Love and his fellow petitioners considered that these problems were 'the logical consequences of a systematic antagonism, based upon nationality, and operating in great measure against all foreigners, but in a greater degree and in a more significant manner, against British subjects'. Love and his friends may have mistaken antagonism against themselves (for reasons we shall examine shortly) for a more generalized antagonism against British subjects but the complaints about the denial of justice in the courts detailed in the petition seem well founded. Nathaniel McGhie, for instance, had been arrested in 1884 for smoking a pipe at the door of his home in Petite Riviere when a general was passing, despite his objection that being a British subject he had a perfect right to smoke in his own home. Dr Pairman claimed that he had been falsely accused of running down a woman with his horse. Love's specific complaint was the government's refusal to honour its own debentures and the courts' refusal to give him any redress. This seemed rather more soundly based than his allegation of a lack of press freedom.[40]

Being arrested by the police could be hazardous. The police force was described by the unfavourably disposed St. John as 'certainly the worst ... of all the institutions of Hayti'.[41] The Haitian government in 1887 issued a circular designed to end the ill-treatment of arrested persons, a common practice.[42] False arrests and beatings did not stop. Fernando Stines, chief clerk of the Atlas Company, a resident in Haiti since 1875, complained of being falsely arrested for theft in 1895; Melville Mathurin, from St. Lucia, similarly falsely accused of theft was beaten by the police and imprisoned; by way of variation it was the soldiery who beat Samuel Burnet, the fireman on the gunboat, in 1898.[43] Vansittart, whose prejudice occasionally entangled him in contradictions, had previously written that the brutal police, disregard for the law and the autocratic powers of the President 'render the position of foreigners a very unenviable one', boldly decided in 1906 that West Indians usually provoked the police and thus deserved the beatings, hoping then to get rich through winning compensation: the problems all arose from a difference in character 'The Haytian negro is miles ahead of the British one, and he is invariably polite, altho' his rascality is undoubted. But his British colleague has the rascality combined with impudence'.[44] His comment on West Indians in Les Cayes was similar: '(with few exceptions) of a singularly turbulent disposition, constantly clashing with the authorities'.[45] Beyond the racism there lies, perhaps, a grain of truth. As in the United States where they had nót been moulded into the deferential conduct of native black Americans and could be disruptive of customary relations between black and white Americans so in Haiti British West Indians were not habituated to the extreme deference to authority demanded, usually physically, by the powerful and when in conflict with the authorities demanded rights which they identified with their British nationality. A different interpretation of British West Indian behaviour was offered by Vansittart's successor who argued that 'the British subjects at Jeremie ... like most British subjects in Hayti [are] as a rule better behaved than the local population'.[46] Incidents continued to occur to the end of the period. For example, in 1911 Samuel Lewison, a keeper of livery stables, complained of maltreatment at the hands of the Haitian authorities and two years later the British Foreign Office re-established unpaid vice-consuls at Cap Haitien and Les Cayes 'to protect the coloured British subjects who reside in the republic'.[47]

Love in his petition had also complained about the denial to foreigners of access to the press. This plainly had much to do with his involvement with politics. In this he was not alone for in 1885 the reason for not appointing native Haitians or coloured men from the West Indies as vice-consuls in Jacmel was the same: 'their partial conduct in revolutionary movements'.[48] The Press Law of 31 October of the same year had decreed that all journals or periodicals should have a responsible manager and that the manager should be Haitian, enjoying full rights of citizenship. Clearly this was an attempt to block the political activities of people like Love, regarded by at least one Haitian president as subversive. In 1888 Love was serving with rebel forces and 'liable to severe punishment if captured'.[49] In 1891 Love with one of his political allies General Manigat had written a book 'in which', according to the acting consul, 'nothing is new, excepting the extraordinary statement (repeated all through the book) that Dr Love and General Manigat are the most honest and brave men of Hayti, and that President Hyppolite is everything that is bad'.[50] All this gives us a new perspective on the statement in the petition that 'the subjects of her Majesty, generally law-abiding everywhere, are no less so in this country, where they demonstrate, in at least as great degree as any other foreign colony, respect for the law and authority of the Government'. Not surprisingly Love was deported by Hyppolite. Others flirted with high politics in Haiti. Solomon N. Crosswell and his brother Arthur also operated in these dangerous waters. Arthur Crosswell and Frederick Coles had been involved in the complicated bank affair of the mid-1880s and Arthur, who died in 1892, claimed that the government owed him substantial sums for negotiating a loan. His brother alleged that he had been fired at in 1891 when both brothers were summoned again by the Haitians and warned to be careful by the British consul. Solomon Crosswell who had lived in Haiti since 1876 was an ally of the fugitive Minister of War, Anselme Prophete, at the time of Legitime's fall in 1889 and four years later was suspected of engaging in a propaganda campaign against the Hyppolite government. Not surprisingly he was imprisoned on 1 October 1893 and expelled from Haiti in 1894. He later returned to Haiti and engaged in an extensive correspondence with the Foreign Office in an attempt to obtain 27,000 gourdes owed him by the Haitian Government for three 'ordonnances de defense' dated 1888–89. These were probably issued by Legitime's government during his struggle with Hyppolite and were consequently not honoured by the successful Hyppolite after 1890.[51] By 1901 Crosswell was once more a resident in Haiti and a pillar of the British colony for he transmitted a loyal address to Edward VII signed by, among others, his brother's old comrade in misfortune, Coles.[52] The records provide no evidence of this sort of involvement in the even more dangerous political events in the years leading up to the American intervention. Other British West Indians suffered more than the Crosswell brothers, Coles and Love through their usually involuntary entanglement in Haitian politics. The fires in Port-au-Prince on 4 and 7 July 1888 which destroyed the property of so many poorer West Indians were alleged to have been started in the home of M. Artaud, the Minister of Finance.[53] These fires involved 80 claims. From 1888 to 1891 the disturbed political situation gave rise to another 34.[54] One man claimed for wounds suffered in Haitian government service; some were by sailors serving on Haitian vessels; one by a gunner in the armed forces; several were for houses burnt in disturbances. Clearly Samuel Burnet of the *Dessalines* was also a victim in 1898 of politics. Voluntary or involuntary engagement in Haitian politics could prove to have serious effects but the poor, through their involuntary engagement, could suffer relatively greater losses.

With the Haitian people, rather than with the police or the politicians, relations appear to have been better. The number of claims arising from the 1888 fires is unusual – on the whole we have only single complaints which suggest that fairly untroubled relations were the norm. In part this must be due to the small size of the community and the concentration in towns. The antagonism against foreigners appears to be political and directed at those who dabbled in politics. More personal relations appear to have been better. Vansittart in his customary style commented in 1905

> As regards the Br. West Indians, they are all either coal black negroes, or dark chocolate coloured mulattoes. When they marry Haytian coloured women (and they nearly all do, or live in open concubinage) the offspring is certainly a pronounced Haytian African Negro speciem. These children (with few, if any exceptions) can only speak French Creole, and do not know the colour of the British flag, and still less any thing of our habits and ways .... Every now and again though one meets with a worthy coloured Jamaican, who in spite of his being married with a Haytian woman endeavours to bring up his children as Britishers ... they are very few and far between.[55]

The 1905 petitioners emphasized their own Britishness but the main grounds of their complaint was the denial to the children of Haytian mothers of the protection of British nationality. Amidst the uncertainties of the early twentieth century, such protection was too valuable to surrender but we may deduce from this objection that for the respectable, as for the poor, unions with Haitian women were common. In 1908 Vansittart's more balanced successor, Murray, confirmed at least part of the former's description, writing of 'the local patois ... the language spoken by all the lower classes and the majority of British subjects resident here'.[56] Most would have learnt *Kreyol* in Haiti; others from islands like St. Lucia and Dominica would have

brought their own versions. In 1913 another consul, Pyke, provided
evidence which confirmed the view that many, especially the poorer
West Indians, had been assimilated into Haitian society when he wrote
of the small community at Gonaives 'as they normally intermarry
with the Haytians, a considerable proportion of those who consider
themselves British, being of the third generation, have lost their
nationality'.[57] This retention of a national identity when social integration had taken place had two causes: one was its utility in troubled
times, the other lay with the Haitian authorities. Though the children,
born in Haiti of British West Indian parents of African origin, could
expect in the period 1867 to 1889 to be Haitian citizens, the Foreign
Office remarked that prior to 1904 the Haitian government had always
refused them the privileges of citizenship, one of which was the
right to own property.[58] There was therefore a constitutionally based
pressure on British West Indians choosing to settle in Haiti and
wishing to own property to marry Haitian women, who would then be
the legal holders of the property. This undoubtedly helped to quicken
the pace of their integration into Haitian society: J.B. Coles' wife for
instance was Haitian and his business as a merchant was registered in
her name.[59]

British West Indians were undoubtedly attracted to Haiti, as they
were to other destinations, by economic opportunities.[60] While the
optimistic hopes for Haitian development of mid-century observers
like Bishop Holly and Dennis Harris were not fulfilled, the frag-
mentary figures available suggest that the last four decades of the
nineteenth century were not entirely bleak. Coffee exports held their
levels from the 1860s to 1914; logwood exports increased from the
1860s to the 1870s and reached a plateau lasting to 1914; cotton
expanded during the American Civil War, declined to the mid-1900s
and recovered in the decade to 1914. Smuggling was a constant
problem, so that the figures for coffee exports are almost certainly
underestimates, though even so it constituted between two-thirds and
four-fifths by value of Haitian exports to France in the years 1867 to
1896. Despite the political instability of the late nineteenth century and
the grave crisis of the early twentieth century, Haiti in that period
offered more economic opportunities than it had previously. Rotberg
described the 1890s as representing 'a high point in the economic
fortunes of nineteenth century Haiti'. British West Indians were also
pushed by the deteriorating economic conditions of their own countries
from the 1850s and especially from the 1870s onwards. It was not by
chance therefore that in 1873 Mrs Maunder should choose to recruit
them for her concession where under her direction they 'constructed a
large number of roads, established plantations, built houses, and in fact
organized the whole working of the estate on an extensive and solid
footing'. But the opportunities in Haiti for British West Indians to work
on the land were rare. There was no lack of indigenous labourers
in Haiti and the traditional export crop coffee was not worked by

imported labour on modern plantations and the Haitian sugar industry, which did not entirely disappear in the nineteenth century was not, like others, modernized during this period. Hence West Indians moved to urban centres to fill the occupational niches which we have described. Even there, of course, the almost complete dominance of agriculture in the Haitian economy left them subject to the uncertainties of price movements for coffee mainly and the other exports. In 1903 the acting consul reported to the Foreign Office on his mission to the Government of Jamaica:

> Jamaicans are being warned that unskilled labourers intending to proceed to Hayti incur a considerable risk at the present time of suffering great hardship; that there is much destitution among British subjects in Port-au-Prince and other Haytian towns.[61]

Coffee prices had fallen to below ten US cents a pound in 1898 and did not rise above that figure until 1912.[62] Economic depression also affected the occupational opportunities for women in a most unsavoury fashion and instructions had been given confidentially to the police to supervise emigration to Haiti 'more especially young females, who almost without exception are brought here for immoral purposes and join the already large contingent of disreputable and criminal women who inhabit a certain quarter of the city'.[63] In the 1880s there was only one reference to prostitution among West Indian women and the context of the reference makes it slightly suspect.[64]

By 1911 the Foreign Office had decided that 'British interests in Hayti are no longer of sufficient importance to justify the maintenance of an official of the rank of His Majesty's Consul-General at Port-au-Prince'.[65] Protesting against that decision, the Wesleyan minister Turnbull argued that 'at this time ... the country is being opened up by Railways and Banana cultivation chiefly through the labour of British workmen from neighbouring British possessions'.[66] That the recovery was illusory is suggested by the fate of two Indian immigrants from Trinidad who had read a newspaper advertisement for labourers to build a railway from Port-au-Prince to Cap Haitien, only to discover that this was not true and 'by being unacquainted with the language of the country' they had been unable to find work.[67] The majority of British West Indians were finding Haiti a disappointing destination in the period before the American occupation and the development of the Dominican sugar industry was proving more attractive. In the early 1880s there were only about 500 West Indians there; by 1910 it was estimated that there were about 8,000 'more or less permanently settled' there (the Domincan Republic was proving too attractive: two years later a law was passed excluding British West Indian immigrants, though the law was never enforced).[68] Some Haitians had been concerned in the early 1880s about the growth of the Domincan economy and the stagnation of the Haitian.[69] At the end of the period the gap was wide and the economic and political problems of Haiti provided little attraction to British West Indians.

Despite the weak performance of the Haitian economy in this period, compared to other similar countries, it could still prove attractive to better-off West Indians. Using Gunnar Myrdal's concept of the 'soft state', that is one in which corruption rules and the state is exploited for personal gain by the powerful, Lundahl has analysed the disastrous effects of the development of such a state on the economy and people of Haiti.[70] Love and the Crosswells were plainly during the 1880s and 1890s players in the game where the wielders of state power benefitted themselves greatly and the country very little. But this was a dangerous game and became more so in the early twentieth century. One group that consistently did well were the merchants: the Crosswells and Coles and the others, who described themselves thus in the 1905 petition, were rather better cushioned against economic fluctuations than the Haitian and West indian poor. Either political or commercial success provided protection but by the beginning of the twentieth century the lack of economic development and the chaotic state of public finances, which resulted from the economic and political activities of the elite, had created the conditions and the excuses for American intervention.

Yet it would be wrong to conclude that British West Indians went to Haiti for purely economic reasons. Haiti provided them with opportunities not available, either at home or abroad. Though there were some well-to-do coloured and black families in the British West Indies during the nineteenth century and Barbados, of all places, could have a black man as attorney general, the difficulties placed in the way of the upward social mobility and political participation of black and coloured West Indians were enormous within their own societies. Outside of the Empire barriers were no lower. For example, the Jamaicans resident in Costa Rica, during the 1880s building railways were working for banana companies in the 1890s and West Indians working on the Panama Canal were paid in silver, not gold, to differentiate them from white American employees.[71] The story of limited marginalization can be repeated for any of the other migrations. Interestingly the migration to Haiti most resembles that to the United States where by the 1920s and 1930s British West Indians were as a group better off, better educated, and significantly different in occupational structure and residence to the native black Americans.[72] Despite the barriers erected by racism in American society, the economy was expanding sufficiently fast and the black population large enough to allow West Indians to find a niche in American society. The migration to Haiti was in some ways a preview in miniature of that later, much larger and better-known one. It was, however, a preview with some important differences. West Indians' education, superior to that of the host communities, gave them an advantage over nearly all black Americans and Haitians but was inferior to that of the Haitian elite. In Haiti, however, they had access to the elite, an opportunity denied to them in the United States. In the United States on the other hand material rewards, even in the depression of the 1930s, had a more solid foundation than those of the earlier immigrants to Haiti. Haiti had one great attraction that all the other places lacked. Many like Love, who had lived in the United States and Haiti, must have found living in the Black Republic more satisfying than the more certain material rewards of even the United States. Vansittart put his finger on this attraction of Haiti to British West Indians when he wrote angrily that the West Indians in Haiti 'are of a most insolent demeanour. This being the Black Man's paradise, the few whites (myself included) have to take a back seat, and eat humble pie'.[73] This reference to the attitudes of poorer immigrants and the rejection of discriminatory treatment by the better off provide clear evidence that even in the darkest days of 'scientific racism' a number of British West Indians repudiated that particular fallacy. They were, however, well aware that Haiti was not paradise but a place where for people of African descent their supposed racial characteristics did not determine their opportunities in life.

PETER D. FRASER
Goldsmiths' College, London

NOTES

1. James G. Leyburn, *The Haitian People* (New Haven, CT, 1941), p.266.
2. Benoit Joachim, *Les Racines du Sous-developpment en Haiti* (Port-au-Prince, 1980), pp.100–101.
3. CO 318/388/2; CO 318/394/3; CO 318/423/9.
4. Mats Lundahl, *Peasants and Poverty: A Study of Haiti* (London, 1979), p.190; Joachim, op. cit., pp.101–2.
5. Stuart to FO, 23 March 1881, FO 35/114.
6. Joachim, op. cit., pp.101–2 and Robert I. Rotberg with Christopher K. Clague, *Haiti: The Politics of Squalor* (Boston, MA, 1971), p.97, footnote 50.
7. FO 86611 Register of British subjects in Haiti; for a reference to repatriation see FO 35/79; St. John to FO, 2 April 1872, FO 35/87.
8. 'Statement relating to the Island of Tortuge, or La Tortue, in Hayti, in lease to Mrs. Maunder', FO 35/141.
9. Stuart to FO, 23 Sept. 1875, FO 35/98.
10. Stuart to FO, 23 March 1881, FO 35/114.
11. FO 35/126.
12. Dutton to FO, 17 June 1885, FO 35/126.
13. Petition of 21 July, 1887, FO 35/135.
14. Letter of proceedings H.M.S. *Proserpine*, 22 Sept. 1889, FO 35/174.
15. Vansittart to FO, 11 Jan. 1907, FO 369/84.
16. Petition of 22 Oct. 1913 and Pyke to FO, 5 Sept. 1913, FO 369/587.
17. Murray to FO, 15 July 1909, FO 369/222.
18. Pyke to FO, 5 Sept. 1913, FO 369/587.
19. FO 35/141.
20. FO 35/184.
21. Robert A. Hill (ed.), *The Marcus Garvey and Universal Negro Improvement Association Papers* (Berkeley; Los Angeles; London, 1983), I, pp.532–6.

22. FO 35/147.
23. S.N. Crosswell to FO, 22 April 1901, FO 35/176; Duncombe to FO 27 Oct. 1902, FO 35/178; FO to Duncombe, 31 Dec. 1903, FO 35/179; Vansittart to Murray, 8 Dec. 1907, FO 369–151.
24. Petition from Samuel Burnet, 10 Jan. 1899, FO 35/174; letter from Elijah Daniel, 12 Jan. 1898, FO 35/173.
25. Petition from British West Indian residents of Les Cayes (undated), FO 369/587.
26. Vansittart to Maycock (private), 5 Jan. 1905, FO 35/184.
27. See Rowley to FO, 22 Oct. 1907, FO 369/84; for Lyons, Murray to FO, 29 Dec. 1910, FO 369/385 for Louisy.
28. See letter from Nathaniel McGhie, 27 Jan. 1886, FO 35/147.
29. Velma Newton, *The Silver Men: West Indian Labour Migration to Panama, 1850–1914* (Kingston, 1984), p.95.
30. Bonham C. Richardson, *Panama Money in Barbados, 1900–1920* (Knoxville, 1985).
31. Franklin W. Knight, 'Jamaican Migrants and the Cuban Sugar Industry, 1900–1934', in Manuel Moreno Fraginals, Frank Moya Pons and Stanley L. Engerman (eds.), *Between Slavery and Free Labour: The Spanish-Speaking Caribbean in the Nineteenth Century* (Baltimore, MD; London, 1985), pp.95, 105–6.
32. Bonham C. Richardson, *Caribbean Migrants: Environment and Human Survival in St. Kitts and Nevis* (Knoxville, 1983), p.173.
33. Spencer St. John, *Hayti or the Black Republic* (reprint of 2nd edition, 1889, London, 1971), p.287.
34. For Love's career see Hill (ed.), op. cit., pp.532–6; St. John, op. cit., p.287 for Wesleyan numbers; Leslie Griffiths 'The Black Man, or Haitian Independence; The Wesleyan Mission in Haiti, 1816–1915', African History seminar paper, School of Oriental and African Studies, University of London, Dec. 1982, p.9 for 1915 figures. Griffiths has been writing a history of the Wesleyans in Haiti.
35. Letter of 30 March 1885, FO 35/126.
36. Letter of 5 Jan. 1905, FO 35/184.
37. McGuffie to FO, 23 June 1887, FO 35/135; Cohen to FO, 23 March 1901, FO 35/176, transmitting loyal address; for petition see FO 35/184.
38. Murray to FO, 20 Sept. 1910, FO 369/304.
39. Wyndham to FO, 7 July 1885, FO 35/126.
40. For the petitions in these cases see FO 35/147.
41. St. John, op. cit., p.320.
42. McGuffie to FO, 28 June 1887, FO 35/135.
43. F.F. Stines to FO, 23 Sept. 1901, FO 35/176; Mathurin to Jamaican Government, 4 July 1898, FO 35/173; Petition from Burnet, FO 335/174.
44. For position of foreigners see Vansittart to FO, 22 Nov. 1904, FO 35/184; for Vansittart's views on the differences in character see Vansittart to FO, 7 June 1906, FO 369/23.
45. Vansittart to FO, 24 Oct. 1906, FO 369/23.
46. Murray to FO, 15 July 1909, FO 369/222.
47. Lewison to FO, 19 July 1911, FO 369/385. For reestablishment of vice-consulates see minute by Nightingale, FO 369/587.
48. Hunt to FO, 3 Nov. 1885, FO 35/126.
49. Zohrab to FO, 24 July 1999, FO 35/152.
50. Tweedy to FO, 24 June 1891, FO 35/159.
51. The affairs of the Crosswells can be followed at length in the consular despatches. Cohen to FO, 24 Sept. 1896, FO 35/170 refers to A. Crosswell's affairs and FO 35/173 contains extensive correspondence from S. Crosswell.
52. For loyal address see Cohen to FO, 23 March 1901, FO 35/176.
53. For claims see FO 35/141 and for allegation see Zohrab to FO, 1 Oct. 1888, FO 35/141.
54. Tweedy to FO, 5 March 1891, enclosing claims, FO 35/159.
55. Vansittart to FO, 5 Jan. 1905, FO 35/184.

56. Murray to FO, 31 Jan. 1908, FO 369/151.
57. Pyke to FO, 5 Sept. 1913, FO 369/587.
58. FO to Vansittart, 8 Oct. 1904, FO 35/184.
59. For details about Coles and his wife see FO 35/159.
60. The comments on the late nineteenth and early twentieth century Haitian economy are based on Joachim's and Rotberg's discussion. See, especially, Rotberg, op. cit., pp.384–94. The quotation is from p.96.
61. See Wardrop to FO, 16 April 1903, FO 35/179 for request to visit Jamaica. For extracts from Wardrop's report see FO to Colonial Office, 15 July 1903, CO 137/638. For correspondence about warning to migrants in early 1910s, see FO 369/587.
62. Rotberg, op. cit., p.390.
63. FO to Colonial Office, 15 July 1903. CO 137/638.
64. See Zohrab to FO, 24 July 1888, FO 35/152 in which he attacked Love by making allegations about his daughter. Zohrab to FO, 3 Oct. 1888, FO 35/152, describes Love as 'a man of such vile antecedents'.
65. FO to Treasury, 25 Aug. 1911, FO 369/385.
66. A.F. Pakinson Turnbull to FO, 22 Dept. 1911, FO 369/385.
67. Pyke to FO, 12 Aug. 1912, FO 369/479.
68. For reference to this see FO 369/479. See also, Patrick E. Bryan, 'The Question of Labor in the Sugar Industry of the Domincan Republic in the Late Nineteenth and Early Twentieth Centuries', in Fraginals et al. (eds.), op. cit., pp.242–3.
69. Le Commerce (Port-au-Prince), 12 Aug. 1882 in FO 35/116.
70. Lundahl, op. cit., pp.326 et seq.
71. See Newton, op. cit. and Richardson, Panama Money for Panama; Jeffrey Casey Gaspar, Limon 1880–1940: Un Estudio de la Industria Bananera en Costa Rica (San Jose, Costa Rica, 1979).
72. See the classic work by Ira de A. Reid, The Negro Immigrant: His Background, Characteristics and Social Adjustment, 1899–1937 (New York, 1939).
73. Vansittart to FO, 5 June 1905, FO 35/184.

Indians and Blacks in Jamaica in the Nineteenth and Early Twentieth Centuries: A Micro-Study of the Foundation of Race Antagonisms

The immigration and settlement of East Indians in Jamaica had important consequences for the pattern of race relations in that island. More specifically, the presence of Indians created hostility between Indians and blacks, two subordinate groups in Jamaica's plural colonial society. Economic competition, particularly in the twentieth century, combined with the mutual display of feelings of racial and cultural superiority which led to stereotypical behaviour on the part of both racial groups, destroyed whatever semblance of amicability may have initially existed between Indians and blacks in Jamaica for part of the nineteenth century.

I

Race relations studies in Jamaica show an overwhelming concern with black–white relations,[1] with only a few dealing in any detail with the interaction of other race groups in a situation of multiple-ethnic contact.[2] Indeed, though the subject of race relations in multi- and bi-racial societies has for long engaged the attention of historians and sociologists, most of the studies which have emerged have tended to focus on the relations between dominants and subordinates, ignoring, for the most part, the subject of subordinate group relations. By locating this micro-study of Jamaican race relations within the context of Indian–black relations in a plural colonial society, two things will be achieved. In the first place, it will serve to highlight the historical foundations of racial antagonisms between Indians and blacks in Jamaica. Second, it will serve as a contribution to the field of subordinate group relations.

For the purposes of this analysis, a tripartite sequential model will be adopted. The three historical periods to be covered are 1845 to the 1870s, 1880 to about 1930, and from 1930 to 1945. In the first historical time-frame, there was much opposition to the importation of Indian labourers on what were termed 'moral', and economic grounds. It was feared that Indian immigration would intensify racial antagonisms, particularly between Indians and blacks, and reverse the 'civilizing' influence of Christian missionaries on the black population. Such fears were not generally realized in this period, however.

The second period witnessed an increase in the rate of settlement of ex-indentured Indians in Jamaica. This made greater contact between blacks and Indians inevitable. Racial prejudice and mutual stereotyping also increased.

In the third period, competitive race relations caused a deterioration in Indian–black relations and witnessed an increase in racial conflicts. The economic depression of the 1930s forced both groups to compete for scarce jobs and resources and led to a relationship increasingly marked by hostility.

II

It should be noted that even before the arrival of Indian indentured labourers, a race-relations situation had existed in Jamaica. Indeed, Indian–black relations must, of necessity, be analysed against the background of Jamaica's colonial social structure; for it has been argued that the nature of race relations depends on the degree to which social structures are embedded in a colonial past, and, further, that it is the characteristics of social structures that determine and define relations between groups defined as racially distinct.[3] Following Kinloch's formulation of the colonial model, Headley in his structural analysis of the evolution of black–white relations in Jamaica noted that in a colonial setting,

> 'race relations' involve a particular elite which defines certain physical differences as socially significant (e.g. the importance of 'whiteness' over 'blackness'). This negative social definition is translated into political policy through the subordination and exploitation of certain groups defined as 'races'. In this manner, a racist social system is developed on an ongoing basis by a colonial elite – i.e., an external group that migrates to another society, conquers the local population and imports other race groups for economic labour purposes, and develops a racist economic and social structure to ensure its superordinate position.[4]

Such a racist social system, though developed under slavery, continued into the post emancipation period and was supported by racist ideologies which promoted the notion of white superiority. These ideologies provided the dominant elite with the moral and intellectual justification for the exploitation of non-white groups.[5] Jamaica's social structure, in fact, reflected this notion; in this structure, the white social section was placed at the apex of the social triangle, followed by varying shades of browns with the blacks placed at the base. Class position in this society invariably coincided with skin colour.[6]

It was, therefore, into such a virulently racist colonial regime that East Indians were imported into Jamaica. Even before their arrival they were accorded inferior status within Jamaica's racio-social structure. By the guidelines of religion and European culture, they were regarded as 'uncivilized'. This is reflected in the anti-immigration and 'anti-slavery' correspondence.[7] One of the foremost opponents of Indian immigration into Jamaica was the Baptist Union. The Baptists opposed Indian immigration on what they termed 'moral' grounds. In giving such justification they used negative and racist terms to describe the Indians. According to the Baptists,

> the introduction of a number of heathen and pagan foreigners with their religious superstitions, idolatory and wickedness, will act most injuriously on the morals of the [black] population and hinder ... the efforts that are now in operation for their moral and religious improvement.[8]

Continuing in a similar vein two years later, a writer who signed his name as 'Publicola', in a letter to the editor of the *Morning Journal* lamented thus: '... better for Jamaica, if her soil had never been pressed by the foot of a Coolie – it appears to be of little advantage to them – [for] they show little disposition to imitate us and will never make a material progress in our customs ...'.[9] Given these factors, one can understand how race and culture later came to influence how blacks and Indians viewed each other.

III

One of the hopes of the planters in Jamaica was that the presence of indentured Indian immigrants would create competition for estate jobs, thereby depressing wage rates and forcing black labourers back to the estates in 'reliable' numbers. For this reason they agitated successfully for Indian immigration schemes, which commenced in 1845 with the arrival of 216 Indians on the Barque *Blundell*.[10] Indians continued to be imported, though with intermittent breaks in the shipments, down to 1916.[11] Had all the planters' hopes materialized, economic competition would have early laid the foundations for racial antagonisms between Indians and blacks; for, according to van den Berghe's typology of competitive race relations, economic competition determines race relations in capitalist societies where equal subordinates compete for scarce resources. Such competition usually manifested itself in racial prejudice, expressed in such ways as aggression and avoidance behaviour.[12]

However, the fear that the importation of Indian indentured labourers would create competition for jobs and that the overstocked labour market which would develop would serve to depress existing wage rates failed to materialize in the nineteenth century. As a result this century was not characterized by widespread open conflict between Indians and blacks over economic issues.

Indeed, only one case of violent confrontation between Indians and blacks in Jamaica in the nineteenth century has, so far, come to light, and stemmed from a petty quarrel among Indian and black labourers on Danks Sugar Estate in Clarendon. According to the report of the incident carried in the *Falmouth Post* of 20 May 1845, an Indian labourer on Danks accused a black labourer working in the mill-yard of deliberately allowing a horse to step on his foot. The Indian, offended by the incident, retaliated by hitting the black labourer. A fracas developed as a result as other Indian and black workers immediately joined in the fight on the sides of their respective countrymen. Several workers were wounded in the ensuing fight. The headman, who came to investigate the source of the fracas, found his path blocked by blacks who also tried to hide the black labourer involved at the start of the fight. The indentured Indian labourers consequently surrounded this hiding place calling for justice to be done. The case had to be referred to the Court of Assizes for settlement. Unfortunately, I have been unable to trace the outcome of this case in Court. It is possible that similar local, petty incidents occurred where Indians and blacks worked together on the same estates; but this does not seem to have been the norm.

One possible reason for the low level of open conflict between Indians and blacks in this period over economic issues could be that the volume of Indian immigration was comparatively small and, further, was not as sustained as in Trinidad and Guyana. In Trinidad, for example, Indian immigration continued even when the sugar market was depressed.[13] In Jamaica, this was not the case. Furthermore, the great political opposition to Indian immigration being financed out of the public purse, and planter preference for black labourers limited Indian immigration to times when black labourers could not be obtained in adequate numbers. In his evidence before the Sanderson Committee on Indian immigration in 1909, Governor Olivier expressed such planter preference. He stated that '... Jamaican planters exhibit a preference for Creole labourers. When they can be obtained, employers will not employ one more coolie labourer than is necessary.'[14] Consequently, Jamaica received only seven per cent of the approximately 543,914 Indians imported into the Caribbean between 1838 and 1917.[15] Afro-Jamaicans were, therefore, not displaced from this 'favoured' position by the importation of Indians.

Far from fearing their importation in the nineteenth century, blacks came to anticipate and welcome Indians. Several contemporary sources attest to this fact. After the arrival of the first batch of Indians in 1845, for example, the *Falmouth Post* reported that '... the few negroes who were present at the first landing of the East Indians seemed rather pleased than otherwise and mingled with them readily'.[16] A somewhat similar report was contained in the *Morning Journal* after the *Athenian* landed. In its editorial of 15 April 1847, it stated: 'Indians who arrived on the Athenian were cordially welcomed by their black brethren who generously offered them oranges, sugar-cane, and various description of fruit, as well as bread cakes [sic] and trifling articles of clothing for the children ...'.[17] The *Morning Journal* further reported that '... the immigrants have been well treated by the peasantry in the country, [who have] promised to do all in their power for the "strangers who have come to a strange land"'.[18]

Continuing on this note of amicability was the Indian government official, Surgeon-Major Comins' comment on Indian–black relations in Jamaica in the nineteenth century. According to Comins, '... as a rule, Coolies and Negroes get on well together and live amicably on the estates'.[19] Sohal notes that blacks welcomed Indians as potential consumers for their provision crops. Apparently, on one occasion when blacks on an estate were told that 'lots of Coolies are coming', they jokingly replied, '... make them come now massa, they will buy our provisions fro' we'.[20] The blacks clearly perceived the economic benefits which would accrue to them, as an established peasantry, from the presence of labourers who did not have the advantage of provision plots from which they could meet their food needs.

Another possible explanation for the comparatively low level of Indian–black conflict in this period lies in the fact that blacks did not view Indians as settlers. They saw them as transient 'slave coolies' who would return to India at the expiration of their ten-year compulsory residence in Jamaica. Indeed, repatriation commenced in 1853 as Indians, making use of the provisions in the immigration law for their repatriation, returned to India from Jamaica.[21] Furthermore, Indian–black contact during the period of indentureship was limited. Blacks generally lived off the estates in their free villages, while Indians lived on the estates in barracks spatially separated from those of the few blacks who still resided on the estates. Even where they worked on the same estates Indians and blacks were usually separated into different gangs under their respective headmen – though in a few cases black headmen were placed in charge of Indian gangs. One is forced to agree with Gillion's conclusion in his analysis of a comparable social situation – Fijian–Indian relations in the period of indentureship – that such separation precluded conflict.[22]

The absence of widespread open conflict was not an indication that Indians and blacks necessarily liked each other. The blacks may initially have tolerated Indians because they were 'strangers in a strange land' and were no threat to their immediate economic interests; but they still derided them as 'slave coolies' as they had accepted contract labour – shunned by blacks – on the estates, in conditions little removed from slavery.[23] Using the yardstick of European culture, blacks also felt that Indians were culturally inferior to them.

The Indians, for their part, brought with them to the Caribbean the characteristic northern Indian contempt for darker-skinned people, coming as they did from a country with an entrenched caste system. According to 'Publicola' '... they [the Indians] fancy they are a superior race, and openly avow their dislike of them [the Blacks]'.[24] Brereton further suggests that, by the guidelines of caste, Indians decided that blacks were 'hopelessly polluted', and so assumed a superior attitude to them.[25] A similar view was expressed by van den Berghe who, in his analysis of Indian–black relations in East Africa, observed that the Indians themselves were caught in the racist dynamics of colonial society, for they assumed their cultural superiority over Africans. Their intense pride in their cultural heritage, according to him, '... led them to ... accept as axiomatic their ethnocentric belief in their cultural superiority over Africans'.[26] Phenotypical characteristics, such as hair texture, were also used by Indians to claim superiority over blacks.[27] Such attitudes encouraged stereotyping and laid the foundations for mutual prejudice and antipathy between the two races. As in other colonies, the mutual contempt held by blacks and Indians for each other, reinforced the existing network of prejudice surrounding race and colour in Jamaican society.[28]

These feelings on the part of Indians and blacks caused them to avoid close social interaction. For those working on the same estates, contact was not extended beyond working hours. Such behaviour has been described by Blalock as one of the subtle manifestations of racial prejudice in situations involving potential intimacy.[29] An indication that limited social interaction took place among Indians and blacks on the estates is Comins' report on sexual relations between them. According to Comins, Indian–black relations '... do not go so far as sexual intercourse'.[30] What seems certain is that creole women in this period exhibited an aversion to sexual relations with Indian men. This is clearly demonstrated in a letter from Governor J.P. Grant to the Earl of Kimberley in 1871. Grant, basing his comments on the attitude of creole women to Indian men, on the report of the Agent-General of Immigration, informed Kimberley that '... the indisposition of creole women to form connections with [male] Indian immigrants appears to remain unchanged'.[31] This attitude on the part of creole women in Jamaica seems to have been a reflection of the general attitude in other East Indian importing countries which had a black population. Henry Taylor of the Colonial Office had requested information on Indian– black relations from British Guiana, Trinidad, St. Lucia, St. Vincent, Grenada and Mauritius. From the replies he received he concluded that '... connections between creole and Indians are not increasing or likely to increase ...'.[32]

The aversion to sexual relations with creoles was equally evident on the part of the Indians, according to Jamaica's Agent-General of Immigration. In a letter to the Colonial Secretary he explained:

> This indisposition seems to me to be equally strong on the part of the Coolies, as they appear rarely to forget the family and race associations of their own country. I have found many who have been in this colony upwards of twenty years still only mixing with their own people ....[33]

The male-dominated nature of Indian immigration (by itself) does not even seem to have forced Indian men to find sexual partners among black women. Indeed, when towards the end of the nineteenth century limited sexual interaction took place between Indians and blacks, they were more usual between Indian women and black men rather than between Indian men and black women. According to Comins, writing in 1893, '... in very rare cases cooly women cohabit with negroes, but I have never seen any case of a man being married or living in concubinage with a negro woman'.[34]

Rather than develop relationships with black women in this period, the Indian men competed for the favours of the few Indian women. This inevitably led to the development of polyandry in the colonies and also caused an increase in uxoricide as jealous Indian men took revenge on unfaithful wives and paramours.[35]

While both Indians and blacks frowned on the development of sexual relations, however, other levels of interaction on the estate seem to have been tolerated. During the period of indentureship, for example, blacks were active participants in the Muslim Hussay Festival.[36]

IV

The original intention of Indian immigration was to provide transient labourers for the estates. For this reason repatriation for 'time-expired' Indians was an integral part of the immigration law. Despite its original intention, however, Indian immigration by 1920 had developed into permanent settler migration, with close to 62 per cent of the imported Indians eventually remaining in Jamaica at the expiration of their indentured contract.[37] The 1881 Census revealed that in that year there were 11,016 Indian settlers in Jamaica compared with 14,432 whites, 109,946 coloureds, 99 Chinese and 444,186 blacks.[38] Indian settlers were distributed across the island as shown in the following table (Table 1).

The expansion of the banana industry in St. Mary in the 1890s and the increasing use of Indian labourers in that industry, combined with the migration of rural Indians to the urban sector of the plantation economy, made St. Mary and Kingston the densest areas of Indian settlement by 1911 (see Figure 1).

In this second period with which we are concerned, the Indian community was transformed from an essentially transient to a pre-dominatly settled one. This change had implications for Indian–black relations, especially as the Indians began the trek from the estates. In the first place, whereas spatial separation on the estates helped to facilitate Indian ethnic exclusivism, increased contact with blacks as the Indians settled off the estates militated against such behaviour. Unlike in Trinidad, Guyana, Fiji and Mauritius, exclusive Indian enclaves failed to develop in Jamaica. Rather, as Indians in Jamaica gradually moved off the estates, they were forced to disperse among blacks in existing villages.[39] Only those villages which were in close proximity to estates on which Indian labourers worked in large

TABLE 1

INDIAN SETTLERS IN JAMAICA, BY PARISH, 1881

Parish	Blacks	Indians
Kingston	19,160	205
St. Andrew	27,988	473
St. Thomas	29,382	596
Portland	23,588	560
St. Catherine	46,626	2,115
St. Mary	30,890	1,698
St. Ann	36,113	60
Clarendon	38,932	2,075
Manchester	39,776	106
St. Elizabeth	40,174	408
Westmoreland	37,106	2,024
Hanover	22,775	310
St. James	26,232	193
Trelawny	25,444	193

Source: Blue Book of Jamaica, 1884, p.3

numbers developed the reputation of 'coolie towns',[40] and allowed a certain degree of racial separation. Although there is no empirical evidence that such increasing contact led to greater overt conflict, there is evidence that on the group level, racial prejudice and stereotyping intensified. Greater exposure to aspects of Indian religious and cultural practices as the Indians settled among the black population led to the development of a whole range of stereotypes about them. Brereton's observations on these stereotypes in Trinidad are equally applicable to Jamaica. According to her,

> ... Indians were considered to be deceitful, prone to perjury and fond of litigation. Their thrift was considered to be almost a vice and their traditional dress was subject to ridicule. They were said to be too mean to dress properly – too uncivilized to dress themselves in a christian fashion.[41]

The Indian manner of speech was also a subject for ridicule not only by blacks but by other members of the host society. The Presbyterian missionaries, for example, described the result of the Indian attempt to speak the English language as 'bad' English, '... the badness of which is a different badness from that spoken by Jamaicans of the same class'.[42]

In this period too, Indians resisted integrative agents such as education and religion. Their avoidance of creole schools was based primarily on the prejudices they held against the blacks. This is borne out by the fact that, initially, Indians refused to send their children to schools attended by black children.[43] Their main reason is summed up by the Protector of Immigrants' Report of 1909. According to Charles Doorly, the Protector, 'East Indians will not allow their children to attend the native school owing to deep-rooted prejudice which they

FIGURE 1

THE AVERAGE DENSITY OF EAST INDIANS IN JAMAICA IN 1911

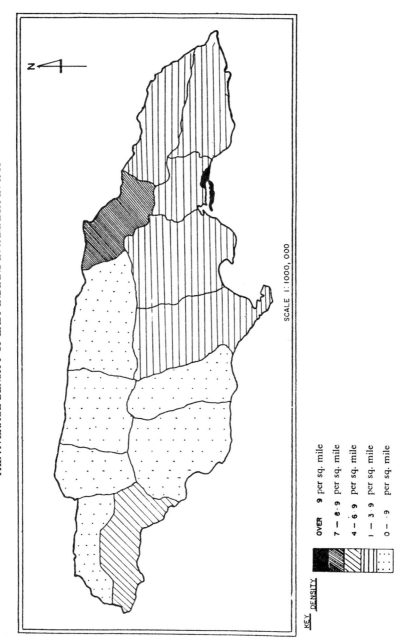

SCALE 1 : 1000, 000

KEY DENSITY

OVER 9 per sq. mile

7 — 8·9 per sq. mile

4 — 6·9 per sq. mile

1 — 3·9 per sq. mile

0 — ·9 per sq. mile

entertain against Negroes, and their objection to any intercourse with them .... They use the word 'Kafari', meaning 'infidel' to describe Negroes.'[44] Between 1879 and 1910, Indians consistently agitated for separate Indian schools. These were allowed for a brief period in the first quarter of the twentieth century but were soon disallowed by the government which increasingly urged the Indians to become part of Jamaican society.[45]

Indians also generally avoided Christian churches, though the relentless proselytizing effort of the Euro-Christian missionaries who visited the estates resulted in the conversion of a considerable number to Christianity by 1943.[46]

One of the problems in dealing with race relations is that one needs to address the subject of cross-cultural transmission which takes place wherever several ethnic groups are juxtaposed and confront each other in what is more than casual relationships. In addition, there is usually a difference in relations at the group and individual levels. Whereas at the group level Indian–black prejudices and hostilities kept the groups apart, on the individual level, cross-cultural transmission took place as Indians and blacks in the same districts bridged the cultural gap. This did not, however, result in complete integration or assimilation which, according to sociologists (like Park), who hold to the cyclical theory of race relations, is the final stage in a 'natural' cycle of competition, conflict, accommodation and assimilation.[47] Although there may have been greater participation in Indian festivals and although Indian cuisine began to be adopted by some blacks, the fact that there was still not in this period any significant level of miscegenation, meant that the Indians still remained an unassimilated ethnic group.

V

In the third period, 1930–45, there was a general deterioration in race relations in Jamaica. In the riots of 1938, for example, the property and persons of Jews, 'Syrians' and Chinese – ethnic minorities whose members constituted an integral part of the middle stratum and of the distributive sector – were attacked.[48] Indian–black hostility also increased. As with the hostility among other racial groups, there was a direct causal relationship between economic competition and such Indian–black hostility which was evident. Unlike the anti-Chinese feeling attributed by some to creole jealousy of the commercial success of the Chinese community,[49] anti-Indian feeling was based on their potential threat to employment in a situation of scarce jobs among primarily agricultural labourers. The fortunes of these workers were tied to the fluctuating fortunes of the two main agricultural industries in the island – sugar and banana – which experienced retrenchment in the 1930s. The result, according to Ken Post, was that as many as three people would have been competing for each available job at peak periods.[50] In such a situation wages could be kept at an average low of

from 9d. to 1/7d. as there was a large army of reserve labourers just '...
breathing down the necks of those lucky enough to have jobs'.[51]
The level of unemployment was further increased as a result of the
return of migrants. From the 1880s, blacks had been leaving the island
at a considerable rate for Cuba and Central America to seek better
jobs. Fifty thousand are estimated to have emigrated between 1891 and
1916, for example.[52] Indeed, the Jamaican labouring population had
become an active labour reserve between 1850 and 1920 as developments in Jamaica after emancipation had gradually brought that island
into the category of a peripheral supplier of surplus labour.[53] Suddenly,
the slowing down of global capital accumulation reduced the need for
labour supplies everywhere. By the mid-1930s, for example, Panama,
Cuba and Costa Rica had all passed state legislation which effectively
closed their boundaries to further labour migration from Jamaica
and other West Indian islands. Having served as a regional pool of
reserve labour, these workers were also subject to being denied further
employment. They were then forced to face the prospect of becoming
part of the labour reserve of their own national territory.[54]
The cessation of state-regulated repatriation of time-expired
Indians, in 1930, further served to increase the number of jobless
agricultural labourers in Jamaica. The labour front was, therefore, a
volatile one as the stage was set for increasing inter-racial confrontation
and discrimination. In the case of the blacks, particularly those who
had returned to the island with new agricultural skills, the age-old
planter preference for their services guaranteed some of them jobs.
Unemployment was consequently greater among East Indians who
often lost their jobs to blacks. While acknowledging that both racial
groups suffered from the wave of unemployment in Jamaica in the
1930s, a visiting Indian government official, J.D. Tyson, reported
that, '... to this is added in the case of the East Indians, a growing
competition ... in fields hitherto regarded as their own, from West
Indian labour returning from Cuba and elsewhere, with some training
and experience in estate work'.[55] He observed that '... headmen on the
estates are mainly drawn from other races and tend to favour their own
people in the distribution of piecework, especially when there is not
enough to go around'.[56] Tyson further complained that on many estates
– both sugar and banana – '... East Indians are getting not more than
two days' work a week, out of crop season: many complained to me that
they were not getting so much'.[57]
Tyson's views were supported by the East Indian Progressive Society
(hereafter EIPS), which explained that before and immediately after
the abolition of indentureship, the labour market had not been a keen
one and consequently, there had been no great difficulty among East
Indians seeking estate jobs.[58] East Indians who migrated to the urban
sector of the plantation economy had similarly experienced very few
conflicts with blacks in the city. This was in spite of the fear which
had been expressed by the Protector of Immigrants, who constantly

opposed the migration of rural Indians to the city. His opposition was based on two factors. In the first place, he deplored the loss of potential estate workers created by such migration, and, secondly, he feared that Indians might compete with blacks in the city for jobs they considered their preserve.[59] The latter fear did not materialize, however, as the main income-generating activity of Indians in Kingston and St. Andrew became market gardening. The economic crisis of the 1930s, nevertheless, changed this relatively conflict-free relationship between Indians and blacks in the city, as will be later demonstrated.

In the riots of 1938–39 in Jamaica, Indians and blacks in Jamaica also came into direct conflict, especially as the greater part of the Indian population was, as Figure 2 shows, located in Westmoreland, St. Mary and Kingston – the areas of great labour unrest during 1938–39. During the months of May and June, Jamaica was the scene of island-wide demonstrations involving strikes, looting, damage to property and person and loss of life. During this period, according to St. Pierre, 'both employed and unemployed came out in protest against the precarious economic position of the mass of Jamaicans and engaged in pitched confrontations with the forces of law and order'.[60] Despite the depressed economic condition of Indians, however, they generally stayed aloof from the riots and demonstrations in rural and urban Jamaica.[61] Except for St. Mary, where Indians are reported to have joined in hunger marches,[62] neither oral history nor documented sources has revealed other cases of Indian participation. This non-participation in the urban areas led to physical attacks on Indians by blacks. Such attacks occurred, for example, on the Kingston wharves, where the few East Indian employees allegedly tried to break the strike.[63]

In the rural parishes, particularly in the towns, conflicts also developed over the allocation of jobs under the relief employment scheme. This scheme was set up after the riots to reduce the level of unemployment. In the rural areas, the scheme was administered by the Parochial Boards, and in Kingston by the Labour Bureau. Indians complained, however, that a discrimination similar to that occurring among agricultural labourers applied to those living in the towns of each parish and applying for such jobs. Sumdath Maharaj of Port Antonio in Portland, complained, for example, that of 520 who were given relief work in Prospect, only two were Indians even though Portland had a large Indian population, a significant portion of which was unemployed.[65] Tyson endorsed these statements claiming that '... in the course of some 700 miles' touring in the island, I saw scarcely an Indian in the very large number of gangs engaged in road repairs'.[66]

Similar complaints were made in the urban areas of Jamaica. It is true that, formerly, Indians and blacks in Kingston engaged in different occupations in the city and seldom came into conflict over economic matters. However, several developments among the Indian population in Kingston and St. Andrew in the 1930s and 1940s had increased

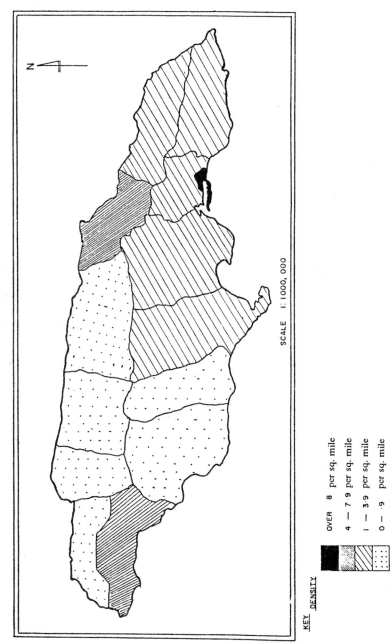

FIGURE 2

MAP OF JAMAICA SHOWING AVERAGE DENSITY OF EAST INDIANS IN JAMAICA IN 1943

SCALE 1: 1000, 000

KEY DENSITY

OVER   8   per sq. mile

4 — 7 . 9   per sq. mile

1 — 3.9   per sq. mile

0 — .9   per sq. mile

the economic hardships of the Indians and thrown them into the ranks of the unemployed in the city. They therefore had to apply for relief work in the same way that Afro-Jamaicans did.

These developments were, in the first place, the increase in the rent rates for market garden plots, which forced many Indians out of production. Secondly, the general slum clearance undertaken by the government on the recommendation of the Moyne Commission after 1938 resulted in the destruction of East Indian vegetable plots. Though compensation was offered in some cases, this was said to have been inadequate. Indeed, where slum clearance was effected in order to construct roads no compensation was paid. Thirdly, the ban on the house to house sale of vegetables effected by the Kingston and St. Andrew Corporation (KSAC) Law Chapter II, Section 31 of 1931, deprived Indian market gardeners of their primary income-generating activity. These developments caused Indians to swell the ranks of the urban unemployed and forced them to apply for poor relief and relief employment.[67]

These were not obtained without some difficulty, however, for to be eligible for jobs under the government relief work scheme, persons seeking such jobs in Kingston, for example, were required to register in person at the Kingston Employment Bureau where they would obtain tickets and be given jobs whenever these became available.[68] Whenever Indians joined the queues in order to register and obtain their tickets, however, it is alleged that they were frequently 'elbowed' out of such queues, by blacks.[69] Those who managed to remain in the lines to have their names registered, claimed that they were not always issued with tickets as ticket distributors tended to favour blacks. Indians charged that '... even ex-criminals and people of desperate character are given relief work over the heads of honest, hardworking East Indians'.[70]

The reason for such acts of aggression against Indians on the part of blacks in the twentieth century may be found in Blalock's explanation that aggression serves the purpose of reducing competition with the minority or of handicapping potential competitors. His general theory is that in times of crises, minorities are especially likely to be selected as targets for aggression.[71]

Another reason, however, might be found in certain actions of the Indians in this period which aroused the anger of blacks. One such action was their formation of communal associations in keeping with their expressed intention of maintaining, as much as possible, ethnic exclusivism in Jamaica. This sentiment was expressed in the evidence of a member of the East Indian National Union (EINU) before the Moyne Commission of 1938. According to Mr Emanuel Raout, '... Indians have their own customs and culture. They do not like to mix. They are against adopting western principles of socialism ....'[72] Mr Coy, the EINU's solicitor, added in his evidence, that '... the majority of Indians regard themselves as a separate community ....

(Only a very minor proportion … feel that they are Jamaicans).'[73] In addition, the Indians, through their communal associations, namely the EIPS, EINU and East Indian Association of Jamaica (EIAJ), lobbied for special economic benefits such as special consideration for land and poor relief benefits. Their rationale was that the Jamaican government was responsible for their economic plight and should compensate them in some way.

The blacks, who indeed regarded East Indians (whether or not they had been born in Jamaica) as aliens, resented the Indians for the special considerations they claimed. Indeed, between 1940 and 1950, the 'alien debate' took place in Jamaica. People competed with each other in order to give what would be considered to be the 'correct' definition of a 'true Jamaican'. From the numerous letters to the editors of the major newspapers of that time it became clear that not all subscribed to the view that being born in Jamaica made a person a Jamaican. The Organizer-General of the Afro-West Indian League, for example, advanced the analogy that simply being born in Jamaica did not make one a Jamaican '… in the same way that a chicken hatched in an oven cannot be called a bread'.[74] Thus the society was divided into aliens and Jamaicans. The general feeling was that aliens should neither dominate, nor benefit from, Jamaica's economic resources, particularly since even as settlers, their adaptation to the Jamaican environment did not extend to a complete assimilation or identification with creole society. Whenever and wherever Indians and blacks competed for scarce resources, therefore, the issue of 'alienism' was applied.

VI

In conclusion, the failure of the Indian presence in Jamaica to have the expected result of depressing wages by creating a reservoir of cheap surplus labour defused a potentially volatile situation among the labouring population in the nineteenth century and in the first quarter of the twentieth century. Economic problems in Jamaica in the post-First World War years, however, created massive unemployment among both black and Indian labourers and brought them into confrontation where previously a certain degree of separation and the lack of economic competition had tended to preclude violent conflict. Indians, increasingly regarded by Afro-Jamaicans as aliens who were not entitled to any benefits in the island, were often passed over in the allocation of jobs. One is forced to conclude, therefore, that one of the most important variables which determine the presence or absence of conflict between Indians and blacks, is the economic variable. As long as Indians did not threaten the economic (and therefore, social) status of Afro-Jamaicans, conflicts were low-level, except where triggered off by petty incidents or group stereotypes. Where both groups competed in the same job market, conflicts increased.

VERENE A. SHEPHERD
Lucy Cavendish College, Cambridge

NOTES

This article is a revised version of an earlier draft presented as a paper at the 18th Annual Conference of the Association of Caribbean Historians held in Nassau, Bahamas in April 1986. That paper was later published by *Caribbean Quarterly*, 32 (Dec. 1985). I should like to thank the following people who offered constructive criticisms of that earlier draft: Dr Betty Wood, Faculty of History, University of Cambridge; Dr Brian Moore, Department of History, University of the West Indies, Mona, Jamaica, and Glen Richards, Pembroke College, University of Cambridge.

1. See, for example, G. Knox, 'Race Relations in Jamaica' (unpublished Ph.D. dissertation, University of Florida, 1962); R. Nettleford, *Identity, Race and Protest in Jamaica* (London, 1970); B. Headley, 'Toward a Cyclical Theory of Race Relations in Jamaica', *Journal of Black Studies*, 15 (1984), pp.207–22; L. Broom, 'The Social Differentiation of Jamaica', in P. van den Berghe (ed.), *Inter-Group Relations: Sociological Perspectives* (New York: London, 1972); F. Henriques, *Family and Colour in Jamaica* (London, 1968).
2. These exceptions include H. Johnson, 'The Anti-Chinese Riots of 1918 in Jamaica', *Immigrants and Minorities*, 2 (1983), pp.50–63, and A.S. Erlich, 'Race and Ethnic Identity in Rural Jamaica: The East Indian Case', *Caribbean Quarterly*, 22 (1976), pp.19–27.
3. See Headley, op. cit., p.212.
4. Ibid., p.210. See also G. Kinloch, *The Dynamics of Race Relations* (New York, 1974), p.6.
5. For a detailed discussion of such ideologies, see G.K. Lewis, *Main Currents in Caribbean Thought: The Historical Evolution of Caribbean Society in its Ideological Aspects 1492–1900* (Kingston: Port-of-Spain, 1984), pp.307–320; Headley, p.214; Sandra Wallman, 'The Boundaries of Race', *Man* 13 (1978); Erika Vora, 'The Evolution of Race', *Journal of Black Studies*, 12 (1981) and P. van den Berghe, *Race and Racism: A Comparative Perspective* (New york; London; Sydney, 1967).
6. M.G. Smith, *The Plural Society in the British West Indies* (Los Angeles; London, 1965), pp.92–115; D. Lowenthal, *West Indian Societies* (London, 1972), pp.81–2 and Knox, op. cit., pp.23–4 and 271–2.
7. Anti-Slavery Correspondence, 1847. CO 318/173.
8. Gt. Britain Parliament, *Papers Relating to the West Indian Colonies and Mauritius*. Enclosure signed by J.E. Henderson in Darling to Stanley, 29 March 1858.
9. *Morning Journal*, 14 and 15 April 1847, p.3. 'Publicola' to the Editor, CO 142/7.
10. Central Government File (hereafter CGF) 1B/9/1, Papers of the *Blundell*, Jamaica Archives.
11. For detailed information on Indian Immigration and Indentureship in Jamaica, see H.S. Sohal, 'The East Indian Indentureship System in Jamaica, 1845–1917' (unpublished Ph.D. dissertation University of Waterloo, Canada, 1979) and V.A. Shepherd, 'Separation vs. Integration: The Experiences of the Indian Group in the Creole Society of Jamaica, 1879–1945' (unpubished M.Phil thesis, University of the West Indies, Mona, Jamaica, 1984).
12. P. van den Berghe, *Race and Ethnicity: Essays in Comparative Sociology* (New York: London, 1976), pp.20–41.
13. B. Brereton, *Race Relations in Colonial Trinidad, 1870–1900* (Cambridge, 1979), p.190.
14. Sanderson Committee Report. Evidence of Governor Sydney Olivier, 1 July 1909. It should be noted that the importation of Indians was greatest during the years of black emigration to Cuba and Central America where they went to seek better paid jobs.
15. G.W. Roberts and J. Byrne, 'Summary Statistics on Indenture and Associated Migration Affecting the West Indies, 1834–1918', *Population Studies* 20 (1966), p.129.
16. *Falmouth Post*, 20 March 1945.

17. *Morning Journal*, 15 April 1847, p.3, CO 142/7.
18. Ibid.
19. Indian Office Records (hereafter IOR) V: (30) 1991, No. 4, D.W.D. Comins, *Note on Emigration from India*, 1893, Sec. 49, p.26.
20. Sohal, op. cit., p.38.
21. V. Shepherd, 'Transients to Citizens', *Jamaica Journal*, 18 (1985), pp.17–26.
22. K.L. Gillion, *The Fiji Indians: Challenge to European Dominance, 1920–1940* (Canberra, 1977), p.14.
23. Henriques, op. cit., p.48; Knox, op. cit., p.226.
24. *Morning Journal*, 14 and 15 April 1847, p.3. 'Publicola' to the Editor, CO 142/7.
25. Brereton, op. cit., pp.188–9.
26. P. van den Berghe, *Race and Ethnicity*, p.294.
27. Erlich, 'Race and Ethnic Identity', p.21.
28. Brereton, op. cit., p.89.
29. H.M. Blalock, Jr., *Toward a Theory of Minority Group Relations* (New York; London; Sydney, 1967), p.51.
30. Comins, *Note on Emigration*, p.26.
31. Governor J.P. Grant to the Earl of Kimberley, 8 Nov. 1871, No. 161, CO 137/459.
32. Ibid., Minute by Henry Taylor.
33. Agent General of Immigration to the Colonial Secretary, 19 Oct. 1871. Enclosed in Grant to Kimberley, 8 Nov. 1871, No. 161, CO 137/459.
34. Comins, *Note on Emigration*, p.26. This numerical disparity was a matter of concern throughout the period of Indian immigration and led to the stipulation by law of a minimum ratio of 40 females to every 100 males. This ratio was not always maintained, however, CO 571/3, Immigration correspondence.
35. For an elaboration of this point see V.A. Shepherd, 'The Emigration of East Indian Women to Jamaica and Their Experiences in the Plantation Society, 1845–1945: A Working Paper', Social History Workshop, UWI, Mona, Jamaica, 8–9 Nov. 1985.
36. Shepherd, 'Separation vs. Integration', p.229.
37. Shepherd, 'Transients to Citizens', pp.17–26.
38. *Blue Book of Jamaica*, 1884, p.3.
39. A. Erlich, 'History, Ecology and Demography in the British Caribbean', *South-Western Journal of Anthropology*, 27 (1971), pp.169–78.
40. Personal interviews with 'Jattan', Westmoreland, Dec. 1982 and 'Baburam', Portland, Aug. 1983.
41. Brereton, op. cit., pp.186–9 and Erlich, 'Race and Ethnic Identity', pp.21–24.
42. *The Presbyterian* (Jamaica), 27 (1935) and V. Shepherd, 'The Presbyterian Mission to the East Indians in Jamaica, 1894–1936: A Note on Cultural Integration in a Multi-Racial Society', paper presented at a Symposium on the Cultural Heritage of Jamaica, UWI, Mona, 10–14 Oct. 1983.
43. Shepherd, 'Separatism vs. Integration', p.165.
44. CGF, 1B/9/28, Doorly to the Colonial Secretary, 31 Dec. 1909.
45. See V. Shepherd, 'The Education of East Indian Children in Jamaica, 1879–1949', postgraduate seminar paper, UWI, Mona, Dec. 1983.
46. Shepherd, 'The Presbyterian Mission', p.15. The census of 1943 indicated that 80 per cent of the East Indians in Jamaica were Christians.
47. Cited by E.F. Frazier, 'Sociological Theory and Race Relations', in van den Berghe (ed.), *Inter-Group Relations*, p.20.
48. Johnson, op. cit., and Knox, op. cit., p.233.
49. Sir Leslie Probyn Governor of Jamaica in 1918, made this observation in a despatch to the Secretary of State for the Colonies, in that year. See Johnson, op. cit., p.53.
50. Ken Post, *Arise Ye Starvelings* (The Hague, 1938), p.119.
51. Ibid.
52. Governor Manning to the Secretary of State for the Colonies, 3 Jan. 1916, CO 571.
53. See Elizabeth Petras, 'Black Labour and White Capital: The Formation of Jamaica as a Global Labor Reserve, 1830–1930' (unpublished Ph.D. dissertation, State University of New York, 1981), pp.362–422.

54. Ibid., pp.421–2.
55. J.D. Tyson, *Report on the Conditions of Indians in Jamaica, British Guiana and Trinidad* (Simla, 1939), p.33.
56. Ibid.
57. Ibid.
58. CGF, 1B/9/111/31, Report of a meeting between the EIPS and F.A. Stockdale, Government Comptroller, 11 Oct. 1941.
59. Protector of Immigrants Report, 1914–1915.
60. M. St. Pierre, 'The 1938 Jamaica Disturbances: A Portrait of Mass Reaction against Colonialism', *Social and Economic Studies*, 27 (1978), p.171.
61. IOR L/P and J/8/108/17. C.C. Woolley to Malcolm McDonald, June 1938.
62. Personal interview with Jaghai, St. Mary, 14 Dec. 1982.
63. *Daily Gleaner*, 2 Dec. 1983. The EINU before the Moyne Commission.
64. CGF, 1B/9/108/29A, James Hassan to the Protector of Immigrants, 7 Aug. 1941.
65. CGF, 1B/9/88, 'Interviews and Statements'.
66. Tyson Report, p.33.
67. See V. Shepherd, 'Depression in the "Tin Roof Towns" ', paper presented at the Third Conference on East Indians in the Caribbean, St. Augustine, Trinidad, 28 Aug.–4 Sept. 1984, and 'From Rural Plantations to Urban Slums', *Immigrants and Minorities*, 5 (1986), pp.129–44.
68. CGF, 1B/9/156, The Labour Advisor to the Protector of Immigrants, 15 Feb. 1941.
69. CGF, 1B/9/111/29, P. Arms' report of a meeting between F.A. Stockdale and the Protector of Immigrants, 20 Feb. 1941.
70. CGF, 1B/9/156, Fred Payne, Managing Director, Kingston Employment Bureau, to the Protector of Immigrants, 24 Jan. 1941.
71. Blalock, op. cit., p.49.
72. *Daily Gleaner*, 1 Dec. 1938.
73. ibid.
74. See, for example, *Jamaica Times*, 3 Feb. 1950. Letter from the Organizer-General of the Afro-West Indian League.

Structure, Process and Indian Culture in Trinidad

This article deals with the internal process of adjustment within the Indian community of Trinidad, a subject which has not been a significant area of interest since the overall preference is usually for a discussion located within the context of the larger national framework. It argues that the Indian population – indentured labour in origin – was more diverse than has been supposed but, in the collapsed space of Trinidad, people who would not normally have met each other in the ancestral land engaged in a jostling for status and dominance. Instead of a levelling, the result was a leavening process in which points of reference associated with various localities and communities in India were submerged in favour of more Pan-Indian considerations.

Several factors combine to make the Indian population of Trinidad fairly unique among overseas Indian communities. While the Trinidad Indians do not represent the largest such group outside of India, they do constitute one of the largest outside the Indian Ocean area. The slightly more numerous communities in the United States, Canada and the United Kingdom (no one knows the real figures) are the product of recent immigration, both legal and illegal, unlike the Trinidad Indians who are part of the nineteenth-century movement of Indians overseas. Nowhere in the western hemisphere, except in neighbouring Guyana and Suriname, is the proportion of Indians in the national population as high as in Trinidad, and nowhere except in Mauritius (and for a breathless few days in Fiji) is their presence in national decision-making as significant as it is in Trinidad. If a composite score were derived based on numbers, ratio to total population, length of settlement, population density, distance from India and participation in national life, the Indian community of Trinidad would certainly lead all others. Arguably, then, the Trinidad experience, which this article seeks to explore, has ramifications that spread beyond the island itself.

I start with a curious document, unearthed a few months ago by one of my research students. It was contained within the pages of an old copy book, such as elementary school children use; it was dog-eared and slightly soiled, but evidently lovingly kept, and written partly in pencil and partly in ink. It belonged to a man who claimed to be almost a hundred years old, and it purported to be his life story. On examination it seemed to consist really of fragments of his life enmeshed in a collection of folk songs and poems some apparently of his own composition. Many features of this document were puzzling. To begin with, the script was a curious amalgam of Urdu and Hindi styles and there was no clear reason for the transition from one to the other. The grammar and vocabulary too were mixed – mainly Hindi and Urdu words, but liberally sprinkled with Bengali and some Garhwali terms, with Assamese suffixes. It took more than one person to decipher it, and in the event only incompletely and with some difficulty. The old man was a Muslim but many of his poems were in praise of Hindu divinities. Many of his ideas were pure *bhakti*.[1] The document was, in a word, a startling cultural pronouncement.

I did not interview the man but surmised that he was probably born in the Garhwal tracts in the foothills of the Himalayas; that he had come down to the Gangetic plains to look for work; that, in a not unusual story, he had been lured first to the tea plantations of Assam and subsequently to the emigration depot at Garden Reach in the city of Calcutta, and that he had finally found his way to Trinidad. His cultural baggage bore the marks of his experiences and in this he was not unique.

This man represents an internal process of adjustment within the Indian community on which it is the aim of this article to focus. This is quite deliberate, for it is part of the argument that it is the unwillingness or hesitation to consider this crucial first step in preference to the equally important but nevertheless secondary stage of locating the dynamic of Indian culture within the mainstream of national and regional life, which has had the result of framing a picture which is potentially misleading. Both academic theorists and administrators and politicians have looked to this second stage as a matter of primary concern which explains why so much of the literature is grounded in the impulses of a plural society or in an inconclusive expression of perceived trends in assimilation and integration. In a way, this is understandable, for in an era of political independence and nation-building – now reconstruction[2] it made sense to emphasize the wider claims of nation and region, to look for what was common or could be made common, to forge – as the patriotic songs would urge – a common melody in the same cradle.[3] Of course Indians have for long felt uncomfortable about this partly because they seemed powerless in the exercise of definition. Trinidad culture – whatever that was – came to have a special meaning which seemed not to incorporate but to be a counterpoint to Indian culture. A good example of a situation which points to this conclusion is the National Music Festival where Indian instruments or vocal performances have yet to find a place in the programme. As for Caribbean culture, that was considered even more insidious – a device by which the national community could leap-frog the Indian presence in Trinidad in the name of some greater entity. In a word, if a calaloo was cooking Indians seemed neither chefs nor even kitchen assistants.

The predominance of the claims of nation and of region indicated to some that in cultural terms a jigsaw puzzle could be put together without any examination of the pieces that made it up. Those who were perverse enough to eye the individual pieces were to be castigated if the result of their exertions were to reveal that the general picture would not come out quite as it had been projected. Thus Morton Klass, in one of the pioneering studies of Indian culture in Trinidad, centred on the fictional village of 'Amity'[4] would attract the scholarly and political ire of no less than the then Prime Minister who seemed as much incensed by the subtitle of the book – 'A Study of Cultural Persistence' – as by anything which it actually contained. The simple reason was that persistence did not exactly fit the general picture. Moreover, it raised troublesome questions which integration and assimilation could not handle. For there was always a lurking suspicion that the passage of time might not after all – however fondly it was hoped – prove equal to the task of suitably reducing Indian culture. It was always possible to discern a vague warning – however earnestly it might be denied – that what it was popularly (though somewhat erroneously) felt had happened to the culture of the slaves might not after all happen to the culture of indentured Indians. So resilience was misunderstood as the preserve of those who knew no better but to cling to old ways. And so too was versatility: thus even a Chief Justice-to-be felt that he could take judicial notice of the practice of Indian *betis* [young girls] dancing to calypso music as if that portended that a different view must then be taken of the place of Indian culture in the national life.[5]

In retrospect confusion was difficult to avoid. Since the first step – an examination of processes internal to the Indian community – was to be skipped over it was easy to make the wish father of the deed. Why waste time exploring what was destined to disappear, or, even more of a put-down, why look backwards when we should all be looking forward? After all, the comparisons showed that Trinidad Indians were not the same as India Indians. Therefore, it was argued, change had started, both irresistible and irreversible. Nobody stopped to consider that the bases of comparison which resulted in the prophecy of disappearance were misguided; that it was rather like sampling one dish in a buffet and pronouncing on the fare as a whole. Such an exercise was at the very least statistical nonsense. And, in any event, in empirical terms, the comparator either with respect to time or space could not be identified. Yet, somewhat like Christian missionaries who when faced with the puzzling obduracy of their potential converts concluded that it was all a test of the devil to try their mettle and that the proper response was therefore a redoubling of effort, so too those who emphasized the claims of nation or region could and did strive to compartmentalize into oblivion this enigma called Indian culture. But this domestic tactic could not be taken too far, for it did not square with the requirements of external diplomacy or touristic imperatives. It was nice, even profitable, to be able to say that this was a cosmopolitan country. Consequently, somewhat imperceptibly and virtually without fanfare a new tactic was introduced, the watchword of which was selectivity.

Under this policy, 'cooking-night' songs[6] which were as inexplicable, indeed less inexplicable to performers or audience than Parang,[7] would not be incorporated into the mosaic. Tassa[8] drumming, however, was a different story. Yet whose were the invisible hands, if hands there were, behind this process and who or what determined the criteria of selection were questions hardly posed, let alone answered.

Oblivion and selectivity were the parameters of adaptation, defined *exparte*, from the outside; but resilience and versatility were the internal side of the story. This is best illuminated by an appreciation first of the structure of the Indian community in Trinidad, and then of the processes through which it has journeyed. The dividing line is not as rigid as it might be imagined for changing structure is itself a process. Thus, to take one example, flow or the yearly renewal of the community by fresh batches of indentured Indians, and in modern times by the peripatetic visits of religious and other cultural ambassadors, was always an important feature of the structure of the population as well as part of the process in which the community was involved. To take another example, naming or designation was a technique to describe structure but it was also a process. For the purposes of this analysis the elements of structure to be explored include physical aspects – composition, numbers – and conceptual ones – ideas, definitions. In terms of process, certain key concepts are introduced and discussed – collapsing space, leavening as opposed to levelling, resilience and versatility. Put together, it is hoped that this framework will serve to illuminate both the prospects as well as the way through the maze of contemporary challenges facing Indian culture.

The most important corrective with respect to the structure of the Indian population in Trinidad is that it was, after the initial decades of the Indian presence here, much more entire or whole than has been popularly conceived. On the face of it one could be forgiven for believing that indentured immigrants, as a group, must have represented a skewed segment of the population of the homeland. One could reasonably hold the notion that the structure of the immigrants was bound to be characterized, for example, by a predominance of lower-caste members, or in whatever other social terms one might prefer, by the marked presence of those low down on the scale. But these views were always more impressionistic than substantial. Modern research has demonstrated, to take the caste example, that the composition of the immigrants as a group was a fair reflection of that of the homeland population, or, to put it in other words, that the caste make-up of the Indians who came to Trinidad was roughly parallel to that of the areas from which they came.[9] With a moment's reflection it becomes puzzling why this fact did not surface earlier; surely, with hindsight, it was not difficult to imagine that the forces set loose in the Indian country-side which prompted emigration would be fairly indiscriminating in their general effect. In particular years, certain types might be more common, for example, disbanded soldiers in the wake of the Great

Mutiny, or more district specific, following perhaps a local famine, but in the long run the recruiter's net caught a representative sample.

The point has been made so far in relation to caste, but that is making it in relation to a great deal where Indian society – both Hindu and Muslim – is concerned; (by the nineteenth century in India the Muslims too had come to develop caste-like structures). It is making it in relation to a range of occupations especially involving skills normally associated with artisan or performing groups – potters, weavers, jewellers, musicians, folk performers, all with their own inherited traditions. It is making it in relation to differing world views, expectations, prospects – all characteristic of a special place in the social system. True, there were two areas of distortion: one to do with age and the other to do with sex, for the preference of the recruiters, as might be expected, was for males in the prime of their life. But these were neutralized before long by local births in the population, especially as female infant mortality consistently lagged behind that of male siblings, and as young men after indentured service opted to stay in Trinidad instead of returning to India. The implication of this is that what we are dealing with was a 'whole' population, a vehicle and a receptacle for cultural ferment and effort.

The second important corrective has to do with flow, both in the grand sweep of history as well as in the more immediate local context. Immigration was a long process, spanning – in the case of Trinidad – nearly three-quarters of a century. It would be rash to expect, therefore, that the cultural baggage of the first immigrants would be exactly the same as that of those who came much later. To believe that would be uncritically to accept the now academically (but by no means popularly) discredited view that Indian culture was static and unyielding, and that Indians themselves were ultra-conservative and impervious to change. Any reading of the development of Indian civilization would quickly dispel that view; if anything, it would persuade one in the opposite direction, of India as the land of the proverbial melting-pot, and of continuous but harmonious change as the one key variable of Indian culture.

To follow this point: we may discern, at the risk of oversimplification, three far-reaching cultural clashes in the broad panorama of Indian civilization. First, in ancient times between the Indus Valley people, and the invading pastoral Aryans, producing after centuries of interaction a classical Hindu culture. Next, in the Middle Ages, between this new construct and the in-coming Islamic peoples, resulting in an unashamedly synthetic Indo-Islamic culture. And finally in the modern period, a third clash with Western impulses, producing modern Indian civilization. At each stage a new synthesis was produced. At each stage, also, two complementary processes were at work: an impetus to substitute from the outsider; as well as a tendency to replicate from one's own past. Put together, they explain why continuity and change are the keynotes of Indian culture. They also explain the antiquity and longevity of the Indian tradition, for in common sense terms, it is clear that nothing could have lasted so long unless it was responsive to change.

To revert to the local context, the flow of Indian immigrants to Trinidad was important for the constant sense of renewal which it engendered, though it must be admitted that the response could be somewhat two-faced: on the one hand, veneration of the man born in India, but, on the other, a jaundiced view of the latest batch of bound coolies.[10] Flow was also important for continued emphasis of the point of reference, for notions of authenticity and the stamp of approval, for finding out if that was the way things were done in the ancestral land. These attitudes are in contemporary times only slightly less pronounced.

To turn to ideas, here again the significant point is variety. The 1891 census of Trinidad reveals in the Indian population a preponderance of Hindus and Muslims much smaller in number, but also that there were Parsis and Buddhists! Any District Gazetteer relevant to the geographical sources of immigrants would show the widely differing ways of naming and doing things, from dress to the work of the field, from village beliefs to perceptions both of the outside world and of each other. As a matter of fact, for many Indians, their fellows would have been the outside world had they all remained in India. But in Trinidad adjustments were necessary, beginning with the process of self-definition. The tangible result – old ladies in the villages called after the days of the week and the corrupt variations in the spelling of personal names. It is difficult with precision to draw a causal connection between this and cultural development, to say what the psychology of the one did to the reality of the other. But it is clear that important processes were in train and to these we must now turn.

The preceding section has sought to establish the initial variety which characterized the Indian population of Trinidad. It seems relatively clear, if we may extrapolate from that, that in leaving India the indentured Indian had not really stepped out of his society but had simply carried a slice of it abroad with him. Thus, notwithstanding the physical separation, severance would be an inappropriate description of his relationship to the ancestral land. Many did in fact return, and many kept it for long as a goal. But it was a slice of life which had crossed the seas, and in Trinidad it was subject to the press of collapsing space. Those who came from the epicentre of emigration – the Bhojpuri cultural area – had less of an adjustment to make but even within that tradition there was an appreciable degree of variation which would not have troubled the immigrants had they remained in India. In their new situation, however, with the slice of life collapsed in spatial terms, with the variety of some two dozen districts (old British administration units) squeezed into what, in terms of space, amounted to no more than a single district (and this is for the moment discounting the contribution of outlying areas in the Punjab, Eastern Bengal and perhaps more significantly the Madras districts) uncertainty and bewilderment must have been a pervasive mood. The telescoping of a range of cultural practices and their juxtaposition in close proximity led to a jostling for status and pre-eminence. When the dust settled, a new construct had emerged.[11]

The powers in Trinidad society at that time – British in politics, French in culture – were engaged in their own struggle, over language, education, religious practices and law; in fact, over the same issues which the Indians in their turn would have to take up with the larger community. The British and the French were busily settling the grand question of whether Trinidad was to be in culture one or the other. They scarcely had the time or the inclination to note what was happening within the Indian community, and if they paid it any attention, the temptation was strong to see developments as a kind of reduction to the irreducible minimum, or as a levelling off to a common code. But the new creation did not occupy a flat surface on the landscape. It had to rise above the sum of its parts. This is why the leavening image is more appropriate, carrying as it does the implication of a new and fresh product and inviting, with more accuracy than we may on the face of it suppose, the designation 'real Indian culture'. For the squeezing together of various Indian cultural forms which we have described has taken place nowhere else except in similarly situated overseas Indian communities, and in the large urban conglomerations of India where the impact of regional points of reference is less decisive, and where to some extent Pan-Indian considerations can prevail.

The drift from estate barracks to village communities provided a space for the embellishment of this local and therefore Trinidadian Indian culture, but given the atavistic penchant for harmony and reconciliation, the task still remained to find a place for this product within the Great Tradition framework. In this regard the experiences of the 1930s were crucial. These have recently been described by V. S. Naipaul himself in the now more and more frequent references to his father's time and career.[12] They include the Arya Samaj and Islamic missionaries of the 1930s and the debates and disputations which enlivened the Indian community, and introduced at once a sense of pride and polemic. It was a time when Indians felt they were on the march. The national movement in India itself had something to do with this; one-fifth of humanity was caught up in a struggle unprecedented in the history of the modern world. Trinidad Indians followed the news with concern and expectation, and that was why it was such a great let-down when after independence Prime Minister Nehru sought to advise overseas Indians to throw in their lot with their country of domicile. This advice was not really needed, though to be fair, it was not intended for Indians in Trinidad: it had been prompted more by the require-ments of India's African diplomacy. However, it did provide an excuse for dismissing Indian aspirations in the local context.

It was no more than a fleeting hiccup, though, for the gigantic contribution of Indian culture during the previous hundred years had put it on an ineradicable footing. Cultural resilience was indeed the main form of worker resistance during indenture and after. It permitted a definition of otherness which amounted to defiance, both in the insulation and consequent feelings of solidarity which that promoted, as well as in the divergent concepts of status and rank which were implied. Culture defined an area to which Indians, after the trials of the work-place, could retreat to heal and bind the wounds, before sallying forth again. If there was derision and degradation on the outside, the safety of the cultural boundaries did allow scope for refreshment and for the infusion of self-esteem.

Trinidad Indian culture was, as we have seen, a mix of various local practices and beliefs brought from India, but before long the Bhojpuri tradition became dominant. This was characterized in language by Bhojpuri and in religion by the great epics, the *Mahabharata* and the *Ramayana*. These two religious works, but more especially the latter, provided the basis for folk songs and stories and defined ideals and values. Without instigating an attitude of dogmatism, they nevertheless allowed Indians to feel that those who did not share their ideals were the poorer for having yet to discover what life was all about. The performance of life-cycle rites and ceremonies of a private kind set the seal on all of this. The public celebrations and festivals which could also become undisguised demonstrations against the established order, as during the Hosea [*Muharram*] of 1884, served to reinforce the point.

By the 1950s, then, a community which had only been partially dislocated had reassembled itself, not as little India – which did not exist, and was in any case unachievable – and had settled its connection to the Great Tradition. Now, it was to undergo another process: it was about to be 'cinematized'. The Indian community was always more amenable to oral and visual reception than to the written record: it was thus admirably suited to the stimuli of the cinema, especially the Indian social cinema of the 1950s and early 1960s. In many rural areas the cinema was a prime form of entertainment, with female patrons at half price on Wednesday nights, and the whole family, or as much of it as one could afford, in attendance on Saturday. Role models, personal names, developing conventions could all be traced to this; nor must the connection with radio be forgotten, and the ubiquity of the 'playback singer' without whom no-one was born, married or – increasingly these days, it seems – cremated. The full ramifications of this process have yet to be explored but it is certain that they were of a significance for the Indian community which it would be difficult to exaggerate.

In every decade in this century it is possible to point to periods of heightened concern within the Indian community about its traditions and culture. It is almost as if there is some internal engine which predictably slips into gear at measured intervals. In retrospect this is why, for example, the 1950s and 1960s are still in some circles remembered as the good old days especially in terms of song and music.

Black Power in the 1970s brought in its wake a kind of Indian revival, and there is now in the 1980s a contemporary surge of interest. In all these stages the debates seem to have a timeless quality; the same issues seem to crop up time and again. But for a resolution of the issues it is important to recognize the presence in all periods of the twin forces of replication and substitution, of seeking sustenance from the past while responding to the challenges of the present. Repeated exposure to these forces has produced a degree of versatility within the Indian community, traceable to the very origins of the Indian presence here, when, for example, the enduring ties of *jahaji bhai* or brotherhood of the boat, transcending as it did ordinary divisions of caste and religion, indicated how prepared the community was to devise new approaches to suit new circumstances. These examples can be multiplied, like the *betis* dancing calypso music; the problem is to identify them as a strength, not a weakness, of the culture.

This article has identified the twin processes of substitution and replication and their central place in the development of Indian culture.[13] The picture would be incomplete unless one notices in addition a pulverizing force at work which allows facets of the outside world to be selected, tested, ingested and to emerge, after a suitable time has elapsed, in a form that is recognizably Indian. It should be obvious that the presence of these mechanisms make it nonsensical to view the persistence of Indian culture in Trinidad as a matter of permission, or of historically being allowed – as it is usually put, in contrast to the experience of African slaves – to keep one's culture. What is perhaps needed is an attitude that is more intensely self-conscious about these mechanisms, and a shifting of discussion away from the mathematical computation of radio and television time for Indian culture and the fairly sterile debates which that prompts, to issues that go more to the root of the matter. For example, what balance or mix between substitution and replication is necessary to preserve the integrity of Indian culture? How far is it possible, if at all desirable, to secularize the culture, that is, to separate it not in content but analytically from its religious overtones? Or how far should the operation of these forces aid the process of definition so that not only what is transportable on radio, television or the stage is recognized as culture? What about instruction, and to what extent is the model of obedience in the guru relationship compatible with the critical inquisitiveness of student and audience alike? Even more mundane matters need to be addressed: for example, what is the place of new technology in the rustic arts, or how do we relate the demands of time to outdoor epic theatre, bearing in mind that time has a different meaning in the ancestral land?

Obviously, these issues are not going to be resolved overnight, and there is the persistent temptation to postpone their examination and to accord priority to concerns that seem more national or which appear to involve more than one community. The real difficulty is to identify the stage at which an 'Indian' issue becomes a national one. Perhaps therein lies the true enigma of arrival.

KUSHA R. HARAKSINGH
*University of the West Indies,
St. Augustine, Trinidad*

NOTES

1. Devotion, one of the accepted Hindu pathways to salvation.
2. A motto taken from the name of the party currently in power in Trinidad and Tobago – the National Alliance for Reconstruction – formed out of a unification of parties and commanding widespread Indian political support.
3. The Reference is to 'folk' songs deliberately composed on the eve of political Independence in 1962. Twenty-five years later their words are scarcely remembered.
4. M. Klass, *East Indians in Trinidad: A Study of Cultural Persistence* (New York, 1961).
5. 'Beti' is Hindi for daughter, used in an intimate way to connote parental love. The reference is to a 1985 bar licensing case in which the pundit of an adjacent temple complained that noise from the juke-box as well as the behaviour of the bar's patrons constituted a nuisance. The judge took the standard approach in the matter of law between neighbours – live and let live – but his remarks about *betis*, using the word in Trinidadian slang to mean young girls, a usage which has found its way into local calypso, offended many Indians.
6. Cooking-night refers to the evening before a wedding. Some of the songs, like the 'challenge' songs among Indians in Fiji, are sung in 'broken' Hindi. See J. Wilson, 'Text and Context in Fijian Hinduism', *Religion* 5 (1975), pp.54–68, 101–16.
7. Parang is part of Trinidad's Spanish heritage; it refers to music as well as songs performed originally in serenade fashion in the Christmas season.
8. A type of Indian drum.
9. B.V. Lal, *Girmitiyas: The Origin of the Fiji Indians* (Canberra, 1984).
10. The local term for indentured Indians used to distinguish them from Indians who had completed their indentured service. Sometimes used perjoratively to refer to all Indians.
11. A recent article, following Edward Braithwaite's work on creolization in Jamaica, sees a certain amount of 'interculturation' in the development of this new construct. See R. Jain, 'East Indian Culture in a Caribbean Context: Crisis and Creativity', *India International Centre Quarterly* 13 (1986), pp.153–64.
12. See, in particular, V.S. Naipaul, *Finding the Centre: Two Narratives* (New York, 1984) and *The Enigma of Arrival: A Novel in Five Sections* (London, 1987).
13. Processes obviously not confined to the Trinidad situation. See, for example, R.M. Lee and R. Rajoo, 'Sanskritization and Indian Ethnicity in Malaysia', *Modern Asian Studies* 21 (1987).

Overseas Indians in Malaysia and the Caribbean: Comparative Notes

This article compares the experiences of overseas Indians in two settings: in Trinidad from the late nineteenth century and in Malaysia from the 1960s. It focuses on the differential impact of the plantation experience on caste and social stratification in both contexts. It concludes that the East Indian population in Trinidad, unlike that in Malaysia, is marked by the importance of race and religion (rather than caste) in a society where they have long been settled.

To provide a dependent, cheap and reliable labour-force on European-owned plantations in Malaysia and the Caribbean, among other parts of the colonial world, rural immigrants from India, both north and south, were imported in large numbers between c.1840 and 1940. Indian labour in the Caribbean was almost wholly introduced under indentureship (for example, in Trinidad between 1845 and 1917) and in Malaysia, initially under indenture (1840–1910) and subsequently (1910–38) under 'kangany recruitment' (to be discussed later). Much scholarly work has appeared on the beginnings, vicissitudes and consequences of this colonial system, of semi-enforced immigration and settlement of Indians overseas. The dominant tendency in the social anthropological literature on this topic has been to take note of the initiating historical conditions and also to attempt to integrate the findings about the social structure and culture of the overseas Indian 'communities' in a 'plural society' framework as the macro-setting of conditions under which data were collected through intensive participant observation or 'fieldwork'. The emphasis in these studies, inevitably, has been on the middle-ground – not so much the initiating conditions and consequences in a historical framework – but on social structure and culture as recorded at the time of fieldwork. Generalizations, if any, are cast in the usual anthropological mode of conceptualizing time in society and culture, namely, 'the ethnographic present'. The main casualty in this approach has been what I termed earlier the 'vicissitudes' experienced by Indians overseas.

The aim of the present exercise is to try and remedy this lacuna in a preliminary manner by comparing two samples of overseas Indian populations of which I have first-hand experience. I believe that the conventional scholarly barriers in the theoretical understanding and explanation of society between sociology on the one hand and history and geography on the other, are a hindrance.[1] In this same task (the theoretical understanding and explanation of society) the distinction between macro-perspective and micro-studies does not have the relevance and importance usually accorded to it. The macro–micro dichotomy has plagued 'the plural society' framework for locating the import and significance of geographically and historically specific anthropological community studies of overseas Indians. 'The plantation mode of production' and 'plantation economies of the third world' theses by Beckford,[2] for example, valorize the macro-structure of political economy to such an extent that the 'experience' of people in specific lived-in structures and systems remain in danger of escaping the net of theoretical understanding and explanation. This is not to say that 'plural society' and 'the plantation mode of production' are irrelevant as historical orientating devices – but the experiences of populations involved in processes of adaptation and change require ancillary tools of analysis.

I

One may begin with a socio-historical conundrum regarding the mainly labouring Indian populations, descendants of original immigrants, to Malaysia and the Caribbean.[3] My text for Malaysia is a report published in the *Straits Times* of 28 May 1962:

> The development of the rubber industry's 'wonder clones' will soon lead to the emergence of the tappers as Malaya's new middle class, said Mr. P.P. Narayanan, general secretary of the N.U.P.W. (National Union of Plantation Workers) in an interview here last night. ... Mr Narayanan, who is optimistic about the future of natural rubber thinks that the day will not be distant when rubber tappers will cease to be labourers and become the new middle class of the country, the new 'scooter-owning class', who can afford the luxury of an evening out with a girl friend.[4]

In 1960 the Indians comprised an overwhelming majority of unionized rubber tappers in Malaya. In 1957, 69.4 per cent of the Indian population in Malaya was returned as 'rural'. Furthermore, in 1960 there were 2,306 rubber estates in Malaya, employing 285,300 persons, of whom 60,740 were Malays, 85,540 were Chinese, and 138,200 were Indians.[5] Since the estates mentioned included those owned by Asians as well as Europeans, these figures do not give an accurate estimate of the still larger proportion of Indians among employees, mostly labourers, on rubber estates owned by Europeans. Mr Narayanan's remarks can therefore be legitimately construed as reflecting his future vision of the socio-economic mobility of a large majority of Indians in Malaya.

My text for the Caribbean is extracted from Howard Johnson's paper, 'The Origins and Early Development of Cane Farming in Trinidad, 1882–1906.[6] It refers specifically to the response of the sugar estate sector in Trinidad to the post-1884 depression:

Depression in the sugar industry had resulted in large scale unemployment as well as in the emergence of concomitant social evils such as pauperism among the labouring class and the consequent overloading of the inadequate welfare services. To the respectable classes mass unemployment emphasized the existence of a property-less rural proletariat, in an age when only persons with property were regarded as having a vested interest in social stability. Thus we find expressed at this time the hope that cane farming would create a middle class which would soften any possible conflict between the colony's ruling class and its large labouring population. As Lewis points out, this re-appraisal of the plantation system, previously unquestioningly accepted, was one which took place in most British West Indian Colonies during the depression years.

The ideas discussed above were clearly articulated by L. A. A. de Verteuil in 1884. He foresaw with the erection of central factories the emergence of a middle class of peasant factories [sic] who would ensure social stability:

I have always been convinced that the existence of such a body [a middle class] is a necessary element in the welfare of all communities, but particularly of those which are chiefly or solely addicted to agricultural pursuits. Wherever such a class does not exist there is an immense gap left open, which the lower classes will invariably attempt to fill up, either by forcing themselves through or dragging the higher classes in the same, thus creating permanent danger to the social institutions. The danger is greatly mitigated, if not entirely obviated, when there is a gradation established from the lowest up to the highest. Those who start from below to meet midway must interchange ideas in their progress upwards and downwards, and form as an intermediate link between the two extremes of the social scale.

These ideas were reiterated, if not so explicitly, in the leading Trinidadian newspapers. They took the view that not only would the cane farmer be prosperous, but he would also increasingly appreciate the virtues of hard work, thrift and sobriety – the social imperatives of Victorian Trinidad.

The two texts are comparable in that both express a sanguine hope for the emergence of a middle class out of the plantation system, but at first sight they are comparable within fairly narrow limits. To begin with the differences: the time-period referred to is the turn of the nineteenth century for Trinidad and the early 1960s for Malaysia. Naturally enough, P.P. Narayanan speaks of the 'new' middle class while Johnson's reference is to a Victorian middle class. More importantly, the text for Trinidad, in contradistinction to that for Malaya, does not envisage the emergence of the 'middle class' from among ranks of Indian estate labourers. Johnson has cited statistics to show convincingly that the alternative of cane farming to estate production resorted to by the planter following the 1884 crisis was geared initially to meet the needs of the unemployed creoles (officially designated 'West Indians' in opposition to 'East Indians'. These creoles were largely Negro factory-hands and supervisors on estates and white settler-farmers. Interestingly enough, however (and notwithstanding the time gap of more than 50 years between the Malayan case and the Trinidad one), the actual basis of comparability of the two examples is closer than it might seem at first sight. For in Trinidad, within a matter of a few years, East Indians decisively outnumbered West Indians as cane farmers and by the end of the indenture (1917) there were 12,055 Indian farmers and only 8,948 creoles.[7] There is also evidence of the growing diversification of Indian activity. Unfortunately, there are no detailed statistics indicating the occupations pursued by Indians before the 1890s but one trend is clear: the shift to cane farming and diversification of agriculture at the turn of the century shows progressive decline in the proportion of Indians residing on estates as agricultural labourers; from 68.4 per cent in 1871 to 33.45 per cent in 1891 and 19.9 per cent in 1900.[8] That only a small minority had yet escaped agricultural labour is another story, to be taken up later.

In reproducing the above two texts I have spoken of a socio-historical conundrum. There are two ways of conceiving the particular riddle; a pragmatic one and a theoretical one. The first approach involves the question: did a 'middle class' actually emerge from the ranks of Indian estate labourers in Malaya and Trinidad? The second approach – a more difficult one – leads to the question of the meaning, validity and effectiveness of conceptualizing the socio-economic mobility of Indian estate labour in the two contexts within the framework of an emerging middle class. It raises the question, ultimately, of understanding and explaining the overseas Indian experience in 'class' terms, however defined. The two approaches are, of course, inextricably bound up with each other as we shall see. Heuristically, however, we may try to grapple with each in turn.

II

In the case of Malaysia there is overwhelming evidence that P.P. Narayanan's optimism has proved unfounded. I am not competent to say what happened, technically, to the 'wonder clones' of the rubber industry, but the following developments have affected the Indian rubber tappers, on Malaysian estates adversely.[9] In the late 1950s and 1960 many rubber estates were sold by Europeans to local syndicates that subdivided the plantations into small plots and sold to individuals. This practice consequently led to the termination of the services of thousands of workers, of whom a majority were Indians. The switch from rubber to oil palm on several estates in the 1960s also led to the retrenchment of thousands of rubber tappers as the oil palm estates requires a smaller labour-force. Following the May 1969 racial riots in Malaysia, work permits were introduced for non-citizen workers. Self-employed workers were, however, exempted from having work permits. This move affected many Indians working on plantations, compelling many to migrate to urban areas 'where they took to petty trading'.

As a result of these and other factors, despite the overall increase in Indian population in Malaysia (from 707,000 in 1957 to 936,000 in 1970 and 1,171,000 in 1980), their share of the total population showed a decline (from 11.3 per cent in 1957 to 10.7 per cent in 1970 and 10.2 per cent in 1980). Urbanization increased. In 1957 the proportion of Indians living in urban centres was 30.6 per cent in 1970, 34.3 per cent and in 1980, 41 per cent. The overwhelming majority of these urban migrants are squatters on the outskirts of cities and large towns displaying all the socio-economic characteristics of slum-dwellers.[10] And, despite accelerated urbanization and consequent occupational diversification two-fifths of the Indians in peninsular Malaysia in 1970 were employed in a single industry – 'agricultural products requiring substantial processing' (another name for the plantation sector). Finally, unemployment rate amongst Indians is high, being 8.8 per cent of the total working population aged ten years and above. This pro-portion was not only high when compared with the national unemploy-ment level of 5.6 per cent in 1970, but also showed a sharp increase when compared with the 1957 unemployment figures of 1.8 per cent for Indians. Figures for a progressive increase in real wages in the Malaysian rubber plantation sector are not available but the glut in the labour market rules out any possibility for realizing the rosy picture painted by Narayanan in 1962. If, at all, they may be characterized as a 'labour elite'. So much for the socio-economic mobility of rubber tappers and their emergence as the new 'middle class' in Malaysia.

It should be mentioned that the Indian participants in the 'middle class' stratum of Malaysian society show a high degree of correlation with subethnicity and caste. Whereas the majority of the estate labourers are Tamil, even their union leader and spokesman (P.P. Narayanan) is a Malayalee who rose to union leadership from the ranks of the estate clerical staff. The microcosm of a microcosm – an actual rubber estate settlement in Malaysia – reflects this correlation. What has happened in such a Malaysian setting is that caste has passed into subethnicity tellingly expressed in the linguistic trick often of using the same term *jati* to designate both these phenomena. At the level of the region and the nation – and transnationally – in relation to the Indian 'homeland' (notice the large number of non-citizens denied work permits) the same correlation of occupational mobility and this augmented subethnicity holds. This is an aspect of 'involution' set off by the particular plantation experience and constraints for the Indian population in Malaysia.[11]

III

The situation of overseas Indians in Trinidad is, in many crucial respects, different from that of Indians in Malaysia. The obvious difference of geographical distance in the case of the former and of proximity to India in the case of the latter may be noted at the outset. Second, whereas Indians in Malaysia constitute a mere ten per cent of the population, they are as much as half of the total population of Trinidad and Tobago. Third, whereas the majority of recruits for Trinidad came from north India, the Malayan recruits were largely south Indians, mainly Tamils. Fourth, immigrant Indians were introduced in Trinidad to work on the seasonal crop of sugar cane as indentured labourers, whereas in Malaysia after initial experimentation with large-scale sugar cane and coffee planting with indentured Indian labour (1840–1910), the bulk of Indian labourers were recruited to work for the perennial crop of rubber under the 'kangany system' from 1910 to 1938. The latter was opposed to the former system in many respects: indenture implied an *individual contract* for a period of three to five years but the kangany system was essentially geared to indefinite employment in the rubber estate sector on the basis of a *gang member's* loyalty to and supervision under a recruiter-foreman (kangany) usually from the same village or region in India as the labourer himself. Family, kin and caste ties were preserved and respected much more in the kangany system than under indenture. Similarly, patron–client ties between the kangany and his recruits – even when they left one estate and took up employment on another under pressure of 'crimping' during periods of high demand for labour – were an enduring feature of the latter system. In broad terms, therefore, the system of recruitment and settlement of immigrant Indian labour as it obtained in Trinidad and as was eventually established in Malaya could be distinguished as 'individualistic' in the former and 'communal' in the latter. Paradoxical as it may seem, in socio-cultural rather than politico-economic terms, the indentured recruit in Trinidad had greater occupational freedom than his kangany-recruited counterpart in Malaya. Combined with the facts that in Malaya there was an indigenous peasantry (the rural Malays), while the remaining crown lands were progressively cornered by the large European-owned plantations under the highly profitable perennial crop of rubber, Indians in Malaya did not become peasants.[12] In Trinidad, on the other hand, the lack of an indigenous peasantry in a 'settlement society',[13] the exigencies of a seasonal, rather than a perennial, crop of sugar cane, and the imperative to cut costs following the depression in sugar prices after 1884 – all combined to create favourable conditions for the contract-expired or 'free' Indian recruits to take up peasant activities.

To return to the question of a 'middle class' emerging in the agricultural sector in Trinidad at the turn of the century as hoped for by de

Verteuil and others, as already indicated, the precise expected process was 'subverted', in the first place, by the increasing preponderance of East Indians labourers rather than creole elements into the ranks of cane farmers. It should be noted that the established planter interests, with the connivance and blessings of the colonial government saw to it that indentured labour continued to flow and the unemployed 'free' Indian labourer shared the uneconomic costs of planting and harvesting cane (so far exclusively grown on plantations) by gravitating in increasing numbers to the cane-farming sector. From the point of view of East Indians in Trinidad, however, certain socio-economic characteristics of this shift are noteworthy as they bear on the hypothetical question of a 'middle class' emerging from the ranks largely of Indian labourers–turned–farmers if not creoles.

By the 1880s there already was a tradition of farming among East Indian labourers, especially the ex-indentured ones. Between 1869 and 1880 free Indians were granted ten or, later, five acres of crown lands if they did not take up the free return passage. And Indians increasingly from about 1870 also bought Crown lands. It is true, none the less, that only a small number were willing or able to take advantage of these opportunities. Indians themselves were suspicious of the commutation scheme as 'nothing more than a trick to defraud them of their return passage'. More importantly, planter interest dictated that immigrants should work on estates for wages, not on their own lands for an independent subsistence. To them the success of commutation and settlement schemes for Indians was to be measured by the extent to which the settlements' inhabitants continued to work on estates, especially during the crop season. As early as 1874 the planters began to complain that the inhabitants of the settlements were doing too little work on the neighbouring estates, although the evidence suggests that the planters greatly exaggerated the withdrawal of labour. It was this planter opposition that ultimately saw the abandonment of the commutation scheme at the end of 1890. In the absence of occupational breakdown figures for Indian immigrants prior to the 1890s, it is difficult to say what proportion went into farming at the end of their indenture contracts, but there is enough evidence that large numbers drifted into labouring work on the roads and railways, petty contracting for the government, such as clearing bush, and services such as gardeners, grooms, watchmen and domestics in businesses and private homes. Other non-agricultural activities included work as porters and scavengers and the field of transport. They bought carts and hackney carriages which they drove or hired out.

The increasing number of Indian immigrants in farming after 1884 was a reflection, firstly, of unemployment and retrenchment of free labourers from sugar estates. This factor was closely related to the planter policy of renting out or contracting abandoned estate land to 'free' labourers with the stipulation that they plant cane in a certain manner (frequently under estate supervision), grow subsidiary crops only in certain years, and assume responsibility for tax-payment if a house was built. Indeed, when one takes into account the continued employment of indentured labour for estate work, the widespread practice of renting and contracting rather than owning property among ex-labourers, the preponderance of extremely small holdings of Indian 'farmers' contrasted with the large and medium-size properties of creole farmers with whom they competed (unfavourably) for the cultivation and sale of cane. With the resultant necessity of these largely tenant-farmers to supplement their earnings by regular or irregular work as agricultural labourers on estates, the rise of an Indian peasantry and their possible rise as a vanguard 'middle class' turned out to be an absolute chimera. The figures, cited earlier, both for the large number of cane farmers among Indians and the labourers' progressive abandonment of residence on estates have to be placed in this perspective. Table 1 (Occupations of Indian Immigrants, 1891) tells its own story, with 38,889 agricultural labourers and 720 peasant proprietors in a gainfully employed population of 49,401. K.O. Laurence[14] cites cases of two labourers who became big property-owners but describes them as 'most exceptional'. As the *Mirror* of 13 April 1901 remarked: 'Comparison is often made between our cane farmers and the peasantry in other countries, but there is not the slightest similarity. The cane farmer is simply a labourer the exigencies of the sugar industry has placed in his present position. As a rule he has no means and lives from hand to mouth'.[15]

To complete the picture for Indians in Trinidad, let me briefly note the social character of Indians at the turn of the century who could be said to belong to a 'middle class'. Unlike in Malaya, there was no overall correlation between subethnicity and social class among Indian immigrants to Trinidad. There were among Indian immigrants to Trinidad, from the same regions and range of castes, members of what John Rex calls, 'the pariah and commercial groups'.[16] These included shopkeepers, sirdars, and pandits (priests) and they seem to have had a headstart for mobility in the relatively open (as compared to Malaya) socio-cultural 'Indian' environment of Trinidad. However, to ascribe their actual or potential mobility to their caste or subethnicity, is a highly dubious proposition. This can only be understood in the context of what was happening to caste in Trinidad. And, of course, there is no question here of caste (*jati*) passing into subethnicity.

IV

In a recent paper[17] I have argued, with the overseas Indian communities as my main focus, that contemporary theories of social stratification need to be augmented and renewed by fresh thinking on and analytical integration of the dimension of culture. At a more general level, rethinking the notion of 'class' and exemplifying it with reference to French society, Pierre Bourdieu has resuscitated the Weberian

TABLE 1

OCCUPATIONS OF INDIAN IMMIGRANTS, 1891

Agricultural labourers	38,889
General labourers	5,585
Railway and municipal workers	253
Priests and teachers	150
Domestic servants, gardeners	1,242
Drivers, overseas	250
Estate owners, managers	25
Merchants, agents, dealers	30
Shopkeepers	665
Carters	202
Bakers	24
Barbers	64
Tailors	65
Chemists, druggists	4
Hucksters	320
Goldsmiths, silversmiths	125
Peasant proprietors	720
Midwives	13
Seamstresses	99
Stockmen	--
Watchmen	--
Charcoal burners	65
Grass sellers	110
Milk sellers	68
Shopmen, clerks	231
Fishermen	22

Source: K.O. Laurence, 'Indians as Permanent Settlers in Trinidad Before 1900', in J. LaGuerre (ed.), *Calcultta to Caroni* (second revised edition, Trinidad, 1985), pp.110–11.

concept of *stand* or status-group and rehabilitated it as an intrinsic 'cultural' dimension in a theory of class distinctions.[18] What I have to say about caste, ethnicity, race and class among the two populations of overseas Indians partakes of this new thinking; as shall become progressively clearer, a cultural analysis is germane not only to traditional modes of social stratification, for example, caste but also to the characterizations of these populations located in 'a plantation mode of production' as a plantation proletariat or a rural proletariat. These considerations also impinge centrally on the understanding and interpretation of social mobility among overseas Indians whether as a 'middle class' or not.

I begin with the vicissitudes experienced by these two populations regarding the traditional institution of social distinction and inequality in India – the caste system. To be able to appreciate the Indian caste system in dynamic terms it is useful to view it as a segmentary structure[19], that is, its potential for fission and fusion in ascribing identities and positions to individuals, categories and groups according to context. Among south Indian labourers resident on rubber plantations in Malaysia *jati* exists as a framework for ascribed identity and distinction on various levels of the segmentary scale. For carrying out traditionally ascribed functions – those of priests, drummers, washermen, for example – a distinction and hierarchy is maintained between the non-Brahman and Adi-Dravida (roughly, ritually 'clean' and 'unclean' castes, respectively). It is a fact, for Malaysia as a whole, that Brahmans did not migrate to work as estate labourers and are, therefore, conspicuous by their absence in labour lines. Marital ties, increasingly but yet thinly, are formed right across the board of the caste structure (for example, there are reported cases of marriages between Adi-Dravida men and Non-Brahman women),[20] but there are two especially dense points of distribution: the Vanniar as a subcategory of the non-Brahman but in itself a 'fusion' of several endogamous non-Brahman *jati* of Tamilnadu and the 'kindred-around-kangany' or 'micro-caste' given the traditional preference for cross-cousin marriage among south Indians. The Vanniar level is located in the middle ranges of the segmentary caste structure and the 'micro-caste' at the lower end. This system of caste stratification is cut across by the common status of labour-line residents as wage labourers on the plantation, but only imperfectly. The system of kangany recruitment and supervision and the formation of 'kindreds-around-kanganies' among both the non-Brahman and the Adi-Dravida had led to the marginal retention of caste, by and large, in marriage, in the distribution of informal power and social control and even in the settlement pattern of a typical large European-owned rubber estate in Malaysia.[21]

It is significant to note that the particular articulation of the labour-line residents' caste identities and their common identity as a 'plantation proletariat' found cultural expression in the 1950s and 1960s in and through collective mobilization as 'Tamilians', that is, a subethnic categorization. I am not here concerned with the historical origins, manifestations and organizational vehicles in south India and Malaysia of this populist ideology but its salient features included the fact that it cut across castes without being specifically anti-caste but by being anti-Brahman. Thus its target of attack, conveniently, were the Brahmans who were not usually estate workers. It was also derived from India, and hearkened back to another mythical target for Malaysian Indians, the southern Indians' rebellion against the dominant north Indians. Moreover, it marginally reflected the knowledge and the overall structural significance of subethnicity in this population of Malaysian Indians. It was a 'false consciousness' (that is, opposed to their potential 'class' consciousness as a plantation proletariat) which functioned to legitimize symbolically their particular station in life as an *Indian* plantation proletariat in Malaysia. For these Malaysian Indians, India is more than a myth, it is a reality.[22]

In Malaysia plantation Indians live in a situation of closed resources and due to a variety of factors[23] have experienced virtually no mobility from the ranks of estate workers. However, wherever possible these workers have invested their savings either in buying land in India or in such minor non-estate ancillary occupations as running a pirate-taxi. In the absence of recent economic data on plantation Indians in Malaysia it is hard to determine the extent to which land buying in India has persisted despite the post-1969 legislation requiring them to secure work-permits because they have taken up Malaysian citizenship. But geographical proximity to south India and the spread of their kinship and marriage ties straddling India and Malaysia must provide a basis for comparing their economic fortunes in Malaysia more favourably with their previous circumstances in the Indian villages. This is one aspect of the Malaysian Indian estate workers' status as a 'rural proletariat' which should be remembered. Second, notwithstanding a common 'Tamilian' style of life in the labour lines, there exist economic strata among the labourers. Because of differential skill in 'line' entrepreneurship among labourers on the estates – through participation of the same families in various petty-capitalistic operations like the rotating credit association with constant differential advantage – there grew up a novel mode of stratification in the labour lines. A distinction has to be made in these conditions between these labourers who do not only work for money but also know how to make money work for them. The latter group can aptly be termed a 'labour elite'.

I earlier noted the drift, under the current economic and political circumstances in Malaysia, of large numbers of former plantation labourers and their progeny to urban areas. Their ethnically segregated residential pattern and socio-economic structure in suburban squatter settlements has been the subject of a recent study.[24] When seen in conjunction with the demographic picture for Indians in Malaysia as a whole, the appearance of such settlements can be taken as representative not only of the plantation workers' 'movement without mobility' but – in economic terms – of downward mobility. Secure permanent jobs on plantations are cherished but scarce; a much large proportion of women work as wage-labourers on estates than their urban and suburban counterparts. When comparing the plantation Indians with those in squatter settlements it is useful to bear in mind Bourdieu's distinction between 'economic capital' and 'cultural capital'. Compared to the squatter Indians the plantation Indians rate higher on the former scale but lower on the latter scale. The differential in cultural capital is nowhere more clearly seen than in the religious life of the two populations. I shall compare only the majority population of Tamil Hindus in these two settings. The residents of Pal Malayu (the rubber estate community studied by me in the early 1960s) and those of Kampong Kasturi (the squatter settlement studied by Rajoo in the early 1980s) differ in that the former continue to worship the non-Brahman and Adi-Dravida deities Mariamman, Muniandy, and Munnadayan, whereas the latter have no Mariamman temple (a *sine qua non* of a rubber estate community) and are increasingly worshipping the 'sanskritized' deities Shiva and Subramaniam. Indeed Rajoo describes 'sanskritization' – the well-known process of caste-mobility in India – as a significant movement of religious mobility in Kampong Kasturi. It is important to note that this is not a movement of castes (caste has to that extent detached itself from Hinduism – a phenomenon we shall encounter more clearly in Trinidad) but of religious upgrading – a move towards the 'great tradition' of Hinduism. The mechanism is a 'sponsored mobility'[25] with the legitimization of demands for a higher cultural status resting in the hands of Brahman priests, who have always held the monopoly of priesthood in the Hindu temples of urban Malaysia in contrast to the 'Tamilian' temples on estates which have always operated with non-Brahman priests. This is an appropriate point at which to turn to social stratification and mobility among Indians in Trinidad.

In discussing the Indian population in Trinidad, an adjustment of perspective is called for. In contrast to Malaysia where, as late as 1970, a full two-fifths of the Indian population resided on plantations, Indians in Trinidad from the turn of the nineteenth century had begun drifting away from barrack settlements of sugar estates to independent locations. As early as 1918 (one year after the end of the indenture system) there were 129,251 Indians in Trinidad – only 690 of them were indentured on the estates; 12,451 were free labourers on the estates and 116,615 were living free outside the sugar estates.[26] However, quite apart from the fact that a large number of Indian rural settlements in Trinidad were in close proximity to sugar estates to enable these 'farmers' to supplement their independent income by wage labour on estates during crop season, the large number of cane farmers among the settlers were dependent for the sale and processing of their product on factories in the plantation sector. The dependence of the East Indian farmer on the estate sector in Trinidad persists to this day, as a study conducted in 1972–73 clearly shows.[27] However, starting from a largely tenant farmer or agricultural labourer base, most Indian peasants through the cultivation of cocoa, coconuts and vegetables – and in several moves – acquired their own land and houses. Another distinguishing feature of the Indian economic experience in Trinidad is the diversification of occupations, with farming as the core. Within the scope of the present article, it is not possible to present a statistical profile of the changing occupational structure of Indians from 1901 to 1980, but for the period up to the 1930s decennial figures are available even in secondary sources.[28] For the post-1930 period, there is a general lack of such processed information, but there are useful analyses of income levels of the Indian population during 1960–80.[29] Generally, the years surrounding the Second World War caused considerable economic change in Trinidad. Industrialization became a prominent force, and oil achieved even greater importance in the economy of the island. With the rise of industrialization, participation in the wider cash economy became essential for all, including the basically 'farmer' Indians. Indeed a split has appeared within the East Indian community between the 'sugar people' and the 'oil people'[30] though the former are still in the majority. Following from Beckford's conclusion that 'the dominance of the plantation mode of production is the single most limiting factor inhibiting peasant development and the associated necessary economic and social transformation in the Caribbean',[31] it is obvious that in Trinidad the Indian population mainly involved in this 'mode of production' must be adversely affected by the hindrances to peasant development.

It is clear, though, from comparative figures provided by Beckford[32] that in 1961 compared to any other Caribbean territory (with the sole exception of British Virgin Islands) where small-sized farms (less than five acres) constitute above 75 per cent of the total number of farms, in Trinidad and Tobago, middle-sized farms (five to 25 acres) are as numerous as the small-sized ones (46.8 per cent respectively). Yet the combined percentage of small- and medium-sized farms even in Trinidad and Tobago is 93.3 per cent. The area in farms under these categories, on the other hand, is only 37.6 per cent of the total, indicating the hegemony of the plantation sector. This hegemony cautions us against indiscriminate use of the blanket-category 'middle class' to designate – except a small number of professionals, established businessmen and large contractor-farmers – the upwardly mobile and multiple-occupation-pursuing East Indian families. Finally, to clarify further a neat micro–macro distinction in delineating the 'fall-out' of Indian plantation experience in Trinidad is Rubin's perceptive observation on the sociological character of 'rural' communities in that country: 'schools, cinemas, radio, roads and buses, improved public health and welfare services bring urban culture within the rural orbit and impinge on folk practices characteristic of isolated cultures. Thus ... the countryside appears more semi-urban than rural.'[33] Stated more than 20 years ago, this impression is doubly reinforced in contemporary Trinidad (though the shock of 'downturn' in the oil economy of the mid-1980s leads to weird imaginings about 'back to *dal* and *baji*' in the Indian group) and stands in stark contrast to the isolated and insulated existence of the typical rubber estate community in Malaysia. At the same time, however, all these differences do not invalidate a comparison of differently modulated plantation experience in Malaysia and the Caribbean.

Unlike in Malaysia, the recruitment and settlement of Indian immigrants to Trinidad from 1845 to 1917 as individual labourers struck a death-blow to caste as the traditional functional system of social stratification in the new setting. Neither the recruitment procedures, nor the long journey and, least of all, the patterns of life and labour on the sugar estates, were favourable to the recreation of mutually interdependent and clearly hierarchized functioning groups to which the immigrants belonged in rural north India. The historical delineation of this change has been done *ad nauseam* in Caribbean scholarship; the anthropological contributors to this topic also usually sketch in the historical background before reporting their field-data of the 1950s and 1960s.[34] By comparing various anthropological reports on caste among overseas Indian communities (including those from the Caribbean area mentioned above) and placing them in relation to research on caste in South Asia, Adrian Mayer draws out an empirical generalization:

> ... within the pan-Indian sphere, there is a continuum of situations: at one end may be placed the Pathan pattern, in which the ideological elements of Hindu caste are at a minimum; and at the other end are overseas Indian communities, in which caste's structural characteristics are of less importance than is a caste ideology which is then applied to relations within the new society.[35]

With some theoretical reservations about being able to distinguish sharply between 'structural characteristics' (for which better read 'structural-functional') and 'ideology', I take this view to be a succinct statement of the nature of significance of Hindu caste in the Caribbean. It can serve as a point of departure for our exploration of the culture of caste in shaping the experiences of stratification and mobility for the East Indian population in Trinidad. It should be noted that the 'disintegration' thesis for caste in overseas Indian communities to which I subscribe for Trinidad is sometimes associated with an effort to mark out historically specific phases of 'deinstitutionalization' and 'reinstitutionalization'.[36] I believe such a view to be theoretically mistaken since destructuration and restructuration are coeval social processes. Mayer's conclusion about the endurance of a caste ideology in overseas Indian populations provides a corrective. In following up the implications of caste ideology in the case at hand we shall also explore a phenomenon to which the Malaysian case has already alerted us, namely, that this ideology and its fragmented structured manifestations can bear an altogether different practical relationship with Hinduism than reported for India.

In a situation like that of Indians in Trinidad, what obtains of caste as a segmentary structure? It is worth emphasizing that a conceptualiza-

tion of caste in segmentary terms does not predispose us to a sociology of groups but is geared more to a relational perspective among
individual, categorical and also, potentially, group or quasi-group
identities, as well as coalitions, of agents.[37]

Where, as in the case of Trinidad Indians, the functions of caste
groups – internal cohesion (for example, largely through endogamy),
interdependence (for example, through *jajmani* relationships) and
hierarchy (through a precise attribution of ritual purity and pollution)
– are largely removed, caste ideology of inclusion and exclusion
operates at a high level of segmentation, incorporating the similarly-
circumstanced non-Indian population, namely, the creole. In contrast
to Malaysia, immigrant Indians after completing their contracted
indenture terms were free to take up residence and mingle with the non-
Indian population. There were no legal barriers as, for example, in Fiji
or Malaysia to this free mingling. The possibility of this intercourse
between the Indian and non-Indian populations in Guyana, as contrasted to Fiji, has been commented upon by Jayawardena[38] and I have
described in some detail the nature of 'interculturation' in the East
Indian community of Trinidad.[39] In the latter context it is interesting
that there is an East Indian term '*Kirwal*' to designate the creole
population and, individually, to denote a person of Negro or Negro-
mixed descent. The clearest manifestation of this articulation between
caste and race by the medium of the segmentary structure is the almost
total lack of East Indian–creole marriage in Trinidad. Such marriages
as do occur are severely looked down upon by the East Indians, and
their progeny are called 'dougla' (literally 'bastard'). Research is badly
needed on the 'dougla' population in Trinidad; there is some indication
that from the Indian point of view interracial hypergamous marriages
(an Indian male marrying a creole female) do not arouse as much social
obloquy as hypogamous ones. Although reports of mutually pejorative
stereotypes between the East Indian and creole populations are
numerous in Caribbean scholarship, I met a Negro gentleman recently
who grew up in an East Indian neighbourhood of Trinidad and recalled
with great puzzlement the fact that as a child he would be especially
invited to Hindu *pujas* and weddings and before any of the guests
arrived would be fed and given gifts by the hosts after being seated in a
room all by himself! Could this be similar to the north Indian cultural
practice of 'using' menial caste person (a barber or washerman) ritually
to avert the evil eye at auspicious occasions?[40] In the present state
of our knowledge we are not in a position to answer such questions
precisely but in the 'open' interracial and inter-caste environment of
the Caribbean there are interesting possibilities of discovering not only
non-Brahmans who have 'passed' as Brahmans (it is widely held among
Trinidad Indians that there are two kinds of Brahmans: the 'real
Brahmans' and the 'boat Brahmans') but also – at a different onto-
logical level – of caste having 'passed' into race.

Following on the implications of the segmentary caste model for the *internal* structure of the East Indian population in Trinidad it may fairly accurately be said that there are no distinct levels above the *jati* of the individual. The north Indian hierarchical classification between the *dwija* (the twice-born) and the rest is not operational, nor for that matter, the fourfold *varna* scheme. Although attempts have been made by scholars to provide statistical models of endogamous and exogamous marriages in East Indian communities (using the criteria of *jati* and *varna* which identities, with varying frequencies, the investigators claim are known to individual agents), none of these are anywhere near being mechanical models.[41] There remains a 'bonus of esteem' for members of the highest caste, that is, the Brahman and a corresponding heritage of social obloquy for those of the lowest caste, that is, the Chamar. The former is centrally associated with the Brahmans' continuing role as high priests of Hinduism in Trinidad representing a structural transformation over their corresponding status in north India. As to the latter, when a person is abused as being 'Chamar', the reference is to his or her 'nation', a Caribbean designation more ethnic and racist than caste, and certainly not translatable directly as *jati*. There is a lingering folk form of earth-worship among the Chamar (personal communication from Steven Vertovec), but that seems to me related to a particular sectarian symbolization of land possession by families who call themselves Chamar (of which more later) rather than a symbolic representation of *jati* identity. That hierarchical distinctions of relative purity and impurity between the Chamar and the higher castes – including the Brahman – are completely obliterated is more than amply borne out by free exchange of labour and of food and drinks among members of teams for agricultural operations (*guayap* groups) reported on for rural Trinidad as early as 1890s[42] and, again, as recently as the 1960s (Klass[43] gives the name *hur* for this arrangement and Schwartz[44] provides details). It is noteworthy that such mutual co-operation in manual labour tasks – especially for house construction – still takes place irrespective of caste even among largely urban and suburban East Indians.

The disintegration of caste as a functional system and the attempted transformation and incorporation of race at the higher margins of its segmentary structure were two conditions – internal and external respectively – for the East Indian population in Trinidad delimiting the social space for positions defining stratification and mobility in the new setting. In the initial stages, the repository of symbolic capital for this population was Indian culture. The bases for economic and social capital presented themselves in the material or embodied forms of owning land and house and the diversification of occupations, on the one hand, and opportunities for education on the other. Profits in the form of institutionalized relative socio-economic positions were to be derived through symbolic struggles.

A telling manifestation of this process, banal as it may seem, is a practice – commented upon by many investigators – of Indians in

Trinidad raising flags (*jhandi*) of different colours outside their houses and temples after ceremonial worship (*puja*). The practice is so uniform and widespread among the Indians of Trinidad (and Guyana) that a fair estimate of the population of East Indian homes in a settlement can be formed on this basis. Interestingly enough, this practice is not found in the Indian villages from which the immigrants came. Among explanations offered for this phenomenon are the religious ones. Local pundits will tell you which colour stands for which deity and what is the astrological significance − ensuring auspiciousness and prosperity − of these flags. There is also a social explanation: in a multiracial society, flags on Indian houses and temples distinguish the Indians (sometimes, 'Hindus') from the rest. This is not an especially sociological explanation but the local pandits offer it freely. It may sometimes be couched in mythical-functional terms as in the instance where a visitor from India was told that a flag would denote to a thirsty Indian passer-by a house at which he may safely accept a drink of water, that is, without being polluted! These explanations − and others besides − make sense, given the multivalent significance of symbolic practices. I wish to add another, converging with the phenomenology of Mr Biswas's quest in Naipaul's justly famous novel about Trinidad Indians.[45] The raising and periodic renewal of the flags is the visible mark of 'distinction' (as Bourdieu would have it), a sign of the Indian in Trinidad having arrived, the symbolic embodiment of his position in the social space. A house on land owned by the individual or family and the temple on land owned by the community signals that the economic capital has been acquired and the installation of the flag through proper ritual means, signifies 'for all time to come' that the economic capital has been converted into symbolic capital.

The implications of this analysis are far-reaching. The Indian process of 'sanskritization' though sometimes loosely applied to the Indian population of Trinidad[46] does not operate in this setting. If, at all, there is a process of 'desanskritization', the Brahman priests ministering to the symbolic aspirations of their clients in exchange for material rewards and in the process willingly compromising their ritual sanctity (accepting cooked food, drinks and other forms of intercourse with anybody and everybody). The raising of flags is done, moreover, in all Hindu homes, irrespective of caste or sect, and also in those non-Hindu homes where at least one member or a relative may be Hindu. It is therefore a symbolic representation of, more than anything else (in its inclusiveness), *the propertied Indian status* in Trinidad. And this immediately brings to the fore the doubt − already expressed − as to the applicabiity of the designation 'rural proletariat' even for the mainly farmer-Indian whose position in the social space is so trenchantly defined, symbolically, in terms of property. The proposition often offered that 'family' and 'community' ties among East Indians have 'replaced' caste is not particularly illuminating unless the social agents' struggles for symbolic profit are located in the social space

constructed on the basis of principles of differentiation or distinction constituted by the set of properties active within the social
universe in question, i.e., capable of conferring strength, power
within that universe on their holder .... The active properties that
are selected as principles of construction of the social space are the
different kinds of power or capital that are current in different
fields .... The position of a given agent within the social space can
be defined by the positions he occupies in the different fields, that
is, in the distribution of the powers that are active within each of
them. These are, principally, economic capital (in its different
kinds), cultural capital and social capital, as well as symbolic
capital, commonly called prestige, reputation, renown etc. which
is the form in which different forms of capital are perceived and
recognized as legitimate.[47]

To be able to draw to a satisfactory conclusion this discussion of
social stratification and mobility of the East Indian population in
Trinidad, something should have been said of the symbolic struggles
for profit in the field of social capital, namely, education. Religion –
largely set free from caste – in the form of a homogenized Hinduism and
conversions to Christianity has been the main vehicle for mobility in
this field. This is in sharp contrast to Malaysia: there are no upwardly
mobile Indians in Malaysia who have converted to Christianity for the
sake of gaining admissions and securing employment as teachers
to denominational schools. The upwardly mobile Indian plantation
labourers in Malaysia aspire to become school-teachers in Tamil
schools none of which have a significant nexus with Hindu religious
organizations or instruction. This is a manifestation among Malaysian
Indians on rubber plantations of the salience of subethnicity rather
than religion though 'high' Hinduism seems to be emerging as a
potential force in squatter settlements.

V

In presenting this comparative picture of the vicissitudes experienced
by the two populations of overseas indians, I have, intentionally, not
discussed the data on exploitation and conflict normally viewed in the
framework of colonialism and dependency. I have attempted instead to
reveal dimensions of ethnicity, race, caste and class – active principles
of social differentiation in the universe of plantations societies east
and west – through the culturally regulated 'lived in' experience of
immigrant Indian groups in two settings. The salience of subethnicity in
the Malaysian case is a product of this population's 'enclave' status in a
double sense – as a relatively insulated and isolated sector of the
Malaysian society and as an appendage, existentially and cognitively –
of the south Indian rural society. The East Indian population in the
Caribbean, on the other hand, is marked by the salience of race

and religion, itself a product of a long historical 'settlement society' syndrome.[48] The 'enclave' structure of the Malaysian Indian population and the ongoing structuration process in the Caribbean counterpart should warn us against hasty type-casting of these populations as proletarians or middle class. Finally, an approach to social stratification where culture is shown to be a constitutive dimension of social stratification also counters the view recently expressed[49] that culture and ethnicity in overseas Indian communities be seen as variables *dependent* upon the overall mode of social stratification.

RAVINDRA K. JAIN
Jawaharlal Nehru University

NOTES

1. See, for example, A. Giddens, *The Constitution of Society* (Cambridge, 1984), pp.355–68.
2. See George L. Beckford, *Persistent Poverty* (London, 1972) and 'Caribbean Peasantry in the Confines of the Plantation Mode of Production', *International Social Science Journal (Food Systems)*, No. 105 (1985), pp.401–14.
3. Unless otherwise specified, my illustrations from the Caribbean will refer to the East Indian population in Trinidad where I have conducted my researches from September 1984 onwards.
4. Cited in R.K. Jain, *South Indians on the Plantation Frontier in Malaya* (New Haven, CT, 1970), p.430.
5. See *Annual Report of the Ministry of Labour for the Year 1960* (Kuala Lumpur, 1962).
6. See Howard Johnson, 'The Origins and Early Development of Cane Farming in Trinidad: 1882–1906', *Journal of Caribbean History*, 5 (Nov. 1972), pp.46–74. The references in this excerpt are to W.A. Lewis, 'The Evolution of the Peasantry in the British West Indies', Foreign and Colonial Office Library, *West Indies & South American Pamphlets*, Vol. 15, No. 656 (1936) and L.A.A. de Verteuil, *Trinidad: Its Geography, Natural Resources, Administration, Present Condition and Prospects* (2nd edition, London, 1884).
7. See B. Brereton, 'The Experience of Indentureship: 1845–1917', in John LaGuerre (ed.), *Calcutta to Caroni* (second revised edition, Trinidad, 1985), pp.21–32.
8. See K.O. Laurence, 'Indians as Permanent Settlers in Trinidad Before 1900', in John LaGuerre (ed.), op. cit., pp.95–116.
9. See Manjit S. Sidhu, 'Some Aspects of the Population Geography in Peninsular Malaysia', paper presented at the Third Conference on East Indians in the Caribbean, St. Augustine, Trinidad, 1984.
10. See Rengasamy Rajoo, 'Politics, Ethnicity, and Strategies of Adaptation in an Urban Indian Squatter Settlement in Peninsular Malaysia' (unpublished Ph.D. thesis, University of Malaya, Kuala Lumpur, 1985).
11. For concepts of 'labour elite' among plantation workers and 'involution' of Tamil culture in Malaysia, see R.K. Jain, 'South Indian labour in Malaya, 1840–1920: Asylum, Stability and Involution', in K. Saunders (ed.), *Indentured Labour in the British Empire 1840–1920* (London and Canberra, 1984), pp.158–82.
12. For exceptions, see R.K. Jain, *Ramnathpuram Experiment: Paradigm of an Estate-Farm-Factory Community in Malaya* (Maitland, Australia, 1966) and 'Kampong Padre: A Tamil Settlement near Bagan Serai, Perak', *Journal of the Malayan Branch Royal Asiatic Society*, 36, Part I, May 1963 (1969), pp.153–81.

13. See R.K. Jain, 'The East Indian Culture in a Caribbean Context', *India International Centre Quarterly*, 13 (1986), pp.153–64.
14. Laurence, op. cit., pp.111–12.
15. Cited in Johnson, op. cit., pp.73–4.
16. John Rex, 'Introduction', in UNESCO, *Race and Class in Post-Colonial Societies* (Paris, 1978), pp.11–52.
17. R.K. Jain, 'Social Stratification, Culture and Ethnicity: A Note', *Journal of Sociological Studies*, 3 (Jan. 1984), pp.13–18.
18. See Pierre Bourdieu, *Distinction* (Cambridge, 1984) and 'The Social Space and the genesis of Groups', *Theory and Society*, 14 (Nov. 1985), pp.723–44. See, also, R. Brubaker, 'Rethinking Classical Theory: The Sociological Vision of Pierre Bourdieu', *Theory and Society*, 14 (Nov. 1985), pp.745–76.
19. See, for example, Andre Beteille, 'A Note on the Referents of Caste', *European Journal of Sociology*, 5 (1964), pp.130–34.
20. Rajoo, op. cit.
21. For details, see Jain, *South Indians*, pp.345–53.
22. Cf. the contrast between Guyana and Fiji; Chandra Jayawardena, 'Culture and Ethnicity in Guyana and Fiji', *Man* (n.s.), 15 (1980), pp.430–50.
23. Jain, *South Indians*, Ch. 9.
24. Rajoo, op. cit.
25. Ralph H. Turner, *The Social Context of Ambition* (San Francisco, CA, 1964).
26. Trinidad & Tobago Council Paper No. 56 of 1920.
27. J. Nevadomsky, 'Economic Organization, Social Mobility and Changing Social Status among East Indians in Rural Trinidad', *Ethnology*, 22 (1983), pp.63–79.
28. See Laurence, op. cit., pp.110–11 for 1901; LaGuerre, 'Afro-Indian Relations in Trinidad & Tobago: An Assessment', *Social and Economic Studies*, 25 (1976), pp.291–306 for 1921; Y. Malik, *East Indians in Trinidad* (London and New York, 1971), p.13 for the late 1930s.
29. See, for example, Winston Dookeran, 'East Indians and the Economy of Trinidad and Tobago', in John LaGuerre (ed.), op. cit., pp.63–76.
30. Michael V. Angrosino, 'Sexual Politics in the East Indian family in Trinidad', *Caribbean Studies*, 16 (1976), pp.44–66.
31. Beckford, 'Caribbean Peasantry', p.413.
32. Ibid., p.409.
33. Vera Rubin, 'Culture, Politics and Race Relations', *Social & Economic Studies*, 11 (1962), pp.433–55.
34. See essays by Schwartz, Smith and Jayawardena, Niehoff, Singer and Speckman in B.M. Schwartz (ed.), *Caste in Overseas Indian Communities* (San Francisco, CA, 1967).
35. Adrian C. Mayer, 'Introduction', in B.M. Schwartz (ed.), *Caste in Overseas Indian Communities* (San Francisco, CA, 1967), p.18.
36. K.N. Sharma, 'Changing Forms of East Indian Marriage and Family in the Caribbean', mimeo (n.d.), 64 pages.
37. Note the yet unrealized possibility of a theoretical cross-fertilization between the 'sociology of non-groups' perspective offered by anthropologists; see, for example, J. Boissevain, 'The Place of Non-groups in the Social Sciences', *Man* (n.s.), 3 (1968), pp.542–556) and the critique of Marxian 'class as social group' formulation by Bourdieu (op. cit., *Theory and Society*).
38. Jayawardena, op. cit.
39. Jain, 'The East Indian Culture'.
40. More precisely this practice is not an aspect of *caste* ideology as such but of hierarchy as a relation between high and low or, specifically, between the encompassing and the encompassed (Louis Dumont, *Homo Hierarchicus*, London, 1970). The inauspicious in opposition to the auspicious in Hindu culture [T.N. Madan, 'Concerning the Categories *Shubha* and *Shuddha* in the Hindu Culture', paper prepared for Conference on Religion in South Asia, Washington, DC, 1980)] include not only the menial castes mentioned above but also those Brahmans, called

Maha Brahmans, who receive gifts on behalf of the spirit of the dead thus accepting, in exchange, the sins of the deceased [J. Parry, 'Ghosts, Greed and Sin: The Occupational identity of the Benares Funeral Priests', *Man* (n.s.), 15 (1980), pp.88–111]. In the Trinidad case the role and function assigned to the Negro boy in Hindu ceremonies may be seen as a symbolic representation of encompassing the marginal reality by incorporating it into the segmentary structure.

41. The distinction between these two types of models closely follows Levi-Strauss, including the proposition that models of frequency-distribution in class societies practising homogamy and hypergamy remain statistical rather than mechanical ones. C. Levi-Strauss, *Structural Anthropology* (New York and London, 1963), pp.277–345.

42. Johnson, op. cit., p.57.

43. Morton Klass, *East Indians in Trinidad* (New York, 1961).

44. Schwartz, op. cit., pp.130–37.

45. V.S. Naipaul, *A House for Mr. Biswas* (London, 1961).

46. Rhoda Reddock, 'Freedom Denied: Indian Women and Indentureship in Trinidad and Tobago, 1845–1917', *Economic and Political Weekly*, Vol. 20, No. 43 (1985). See also, R.K. Jain, 'Freedom Denied? Indian Women and Indentureship', *Economic and Political Weekly*, Vol. 21, No. 7 (1986).

47. Bourdieu, op. cit., *Theory and Society*, pp.723–24.

48. Jain, 'The East Indian Culture'.

49. Jayawardena, op. cit.

Index